"SALVATION IS FROM THE JEWS"

ROY H. SCHOEMAN

"SALVATION IS FROM THE JEWS"

(John 4:22)

*The Role of Judaism in Salvation History
from Abraham to the Second Coming*

IGNATIUS PRESS   SAN FRANCISCO

Cover art: *Sacrifice of Isaac* (detail)
Byzantine mosaic
Duomo, Monreale, Italy
copyright Scala/Art Resource, New York

Cover design by Roxanne Mei Lum

© 2003 Roy Schoeman
All rights reserved
ISBN 978–0–89870–975–9
Library of Congress Control Number 2003105176
Printed in the United States of America ∞

Contents

Preface

If there is one theological issue that both Jews and Christians should be able to agree on, it is that "salvation is from the Jews". It has been a constant teaching of Judaism from the days of Abraham onward that the salvation of all mankind is to come from the Jews. That is the primary sense in which the Jews are "the Chosen People". And Christians, or at least Christians who believe in the accuracy of the New Testament, have no choice but to believe that "salvation is from the Jews", since those are the very words that Jesus spoke to the Samaritan woman at the well (John 4:22). This book is an attempt to examine the meaning of those words, from a Jewish perspective within the Catholic faith.

As a Jew who has entered the Catholic Church, I might be accused by some of being singularly unqualified to speak for Judaism—that I am the worst of all possible Jews, an apostate, a traitor, a turncoat, a Jew who has "switched allegiances" and become Catholic. Yet on the contrary, I would claim that a Jew who has become Catholic is the best person to explore the true meaning of Judaism. To understand salvation history, one must be a Christian, since the Incarnation, death, and Resurrection of Christ are at the center of salvation history, and the fullness of the relevant doctrine is contained in the teaching of the Catholic Church. A Catholic who is not from a Jewish background would necessarily have a more abstract and incomplete understanding of Judaism than someone who grew up within Judaism. This problem is compounded by the variety and inconsistency of beliefs within the Jewish community, sometimes making it difficult to ascertain "what Jews believe" or "what Judaism says" about a certain topic.

Although Jews might question the right that an "apostate" Jew has to represent Judaism, that characterization in itself points to the heart of the underlying problem. Is the issue who "we" are, or who Jesus was? If Jesus was the Jewish Messiah—the Messiah long prophesied, expected, and prayed for by the Jews—then a Jew can either be right and accept that He was the Messiah or be wrong and maintain that He was not. If Jesus was the Messiah, then Jews who reject Christianity (or Messianic Judaism) are wrong; if Jesus was not the Messiah, then Christians, however well meaning, are wrong. There is not necessarily any moral shame or culpability in being wrong, but it is nonsense to maintain that somehow Judaism is right for Jews, and Christianity is right for Christians, and that the truth is dependent on what group one belongs to. If Jesus was the Jewish Messiah, then of course the entire meaning and purpose of the Jewish religion revolve around its role in bringing about the Incarnation of God as man, and any Jew who does not accept Jesus is necessarily in the dark about the true role of Judaism in salvation history. So the issue is not whether one is an "apostate" or "real" Jew, but whether one recognizes or does not recognize that Jesus was the Messiah. Obviously, one who does is in a better position to understand the unfolding of salvation history.

In no way does this book intend to offend or criticize Jews who remain loyal to Judaism and reject the claims of Christianity. I certainly know from my own experience that it is only grace that can bring the truths of faith to anyone. The grace that brought about my conversion was entirely unmerited, and I can only pray for a similar outpouring of grace on as many of my coreligionists as possible, that they too might come to an awareness of the fullness of the beauty, of the truth, of the glory of Judaism, of the nobility and incomprehensible honor of being members of the race that was chosen to bring about the Redemption of all mankind, by bringing about the Incarnation of God Himself as a man of flesh and blood, of *their* flesh and *their* blood.

Acknowledgments

My first and greatest debt of gratitude is owed to my parents, who brought me into this world and imbued me with my first love for Judaism. Their love and supportiveness throughout this process, including the writing of this book, given its inevitably painful aspects, were far greater than I had dared hope.

I would also like to thank the three Rabbis to whom God entrusted my formation in Judaism. These happen to also be three of the most distinguished Rabbis in contemporary American Jewish life[1]—my hometown Rabbi, Rabbi Arthur Hertzberg, who was my Rabbi for the first seventeen years of my life; Rabbi Arthur Green, who was my religious education teacher and spiritual mentor during my high school and early college years; and the late Rabbi Shlomo Carlebach, with whom I studied and traveled and who introduced me to Hasidic Judaism and, more importantly, to the direct experience of ecstatic worship and love of God. May his soul rest in peace.

[1] Rabbi Arthur Hertzberg has served as president of the American Jewish Policy Foundation, president of the American Jewish Congress, and vice president of the World Jewish Congress; he has taught at Princeton, Rutgers, Columbia, Dartmouth, and New York University; and he has authored a number of widely read books on Judaism. Rabbi Arthur Green has been president of the Reconstructionist Rabbinical College, and he taught there, at the University of Pennsylvania, and at Brandeis, and has authored several books on Jewish spirituality. Rabbi Shlomo Carlebach developed a following of many thousands worldwide, which still continues strong despite his death in 1994.

God was no less generous in my Christian formation. I would like to thank Father Marcellin Theeuwes, the Carthusian monk and priest who took me under his wing even before my baptism and whose prayers, love, guidance, and wise spiritual direction have sustained me ever since; Father Greg Staab, O.M.V., who catechized me as a new entrant into the Church, gave me my foundation in dogmatic theology, and was unstintingly generous of his time, love, and direction; and Father Pierre Marie Joly, O.S.B., whose love and friendship have made his monastery a second home for me. Lastly, I wish to thank Father Charles Higgins of the diocese of Boston. The initial idea for this book sprang from a conversation we had on a pilgrimage to Auschwitz, and from that point on his encouragement, enthusiasm, and suggestions have been a constant source of consolation and inspiration. Without him, writing this book would have been, if not impossible, certainly far less enjoyable.

Of course, in the long run all the gifts in our lives come from God. This book is dedicated, with love and gratitude, to the greatest gift that God has ever given mankind (besides Himself), to the young Jewish girl who was the very first to recognize and welcome Jesus as the ever-so-Jewish Messiah, to the Jewish mother who brought me to her Son, to the *Blessed Virgin Mary*.

CHAPTER ONE

The Jews and the Coming of the Messiah

Since the purpose of this investigation is to explore the real meaning of Judaism—that is, the role of the Jews[1] and Judaism in the salvation of mankind—the first step is to examine the meaning of Judaism prior to the coming of the Messiah.

God's ultimate revelation of Himself to man was in the coming of Jesus Christ—that is, in God Himself taking on human flesh and revealing Himself to man in His own person and then providing a continuing revelation of Himself through the Holy Spirit's guidance and protection of the teaching office of the Catholic Church. Yet prior to the Incarnation, it was Judaism that represented the fullness of God's self-revelation to man, and the faith of the Jews was the fullest possible expression of man's allegiance and loyalty to God.

Perhaps the easiest way to start is to consider the situation from God's point of view. What preparations would have to be made to make the world ready for the Incarnation? Since He would be born to a particular woman who was a member

---

[1] Technically, the precise meaning of the term "Jew" raises some complex issues. In this book, unless otherwise noted, the term will be used in its general sense, i.e., "Jew: Orig., one of the tribe of Judah; hence, any person of the Hebrew people or anyone whose religion is Judaism", *Webster's New Collegiate Dictionary* (Springfield, Mass.: Merriam Co. 1961), p. 453, s.v. Jew.

of a particular people, this people would have to already know enough of God and His ways to be able to make sense of the Incarnation. In order to make sense of the Incarnation, they would have had to be prepared for it beforehand through prophecy, so that they would be able to recognize, acknowledge, and understand it, at least to some extent, when it happened. Thus they already would have had to have learned a good deal of theology, of how God works, of the relation between God and man, of the state of the soul, of the fall of man, of the meaning of life on earth, and of eternal life, and so forth, in order to understand the Incarnation and its meaning at all. They would have to have been purified from the influence of false "gods", from false or demonic religions, from idols, from practices that linked them to the influences of the fallen angels, in order not to hopelessly pollute the revelation. There would have to be a family and, more specifically, a mother to whom the God-man would be born; she would have to be of sufficient purity and virtue not to make the Incarnation itself a sacrilege. Since God relies on man's prayer to bring about His plans, this people would have had to have been taught for generations to pray and beseech God to send the Messiah. Finally, they would have to provide a society and an infrastructure that could serve as a platform from which the news of the Incarnation, the propagation of the religion established by the God-man, could go out to all the world.

The entire history of the Jews shows how they were chosen and groomed to fulfill these roles.

Beginnings of the Jewish People

The history of the Jews began with Abraham. God chose him to leave his people, go to a distant land, and found a new and great people. God's call of Abraham—at the time still named Abram[2]—came in Genesis 12:1–3:

> Now the LORD said to Abram, "Go from your country and your kindred and your father's house to the land that I will show you. And I will make of you a great nation, and I will bless you, and make your name great, so that you will be a blessing. I will bless those who bless you, and him who curses you I will curse; and by you all the families of the earth shall be blessed." [3]

Note that already here there is a foreshadowing of the role that the Jewish people were to play—for it was through the Messiah that "all the families of the earth shall be blessed."

Much of the story of Abraham in Genesis points up his noble character and virtues, including his boundless trust in God, his generosity, his loyalty, his reverence, and worship and fidelity to God. The ultimate "test" of Abraham, the incident which epitomizes his loyalty to and faith in God, occurs in Genesis 22:1–18:

> After these things God tested Abraham, and said to him, "Abraham!" And he said, "Here am I." He said, "Take your son, your only son Isaac, whom you love, and go to the land of Moriah, and offer him there as a burnt offering upon one of the mountains of which I shall tell you." So Abraham rose early in the morning, saddled his ass, and took two of his young men with him, and his son Isaac; and he cut the wood for the burnt offering, and

---

[2] God changed Abram's name to Abraham in Genesis 17:5.

[3] The translation throughout is the Revised Standard Version (RSV) except as noted. Here the RSV has been slightly modified. The RSV uses "bless themselves" here, but the underlying Hebrew word is the *Niphal* conjugational form of the verb "*barach*", "to bless", which carries either a passive or reflexive sense; "be blessed", as used in the Douay-Rheims, is more probable.

arose and went to the place of which God had told him. On the third day Abraham lifted up his eyes and saw the place afar off. Then Abraham said to his young men, "Stay here with the ass; I and the lad will go yonder and worship, and come again to you." And Abraham took the wood of the burnt offering, and laid it on Isaac his son; and he took in his hand the fire and the knife. So they went both of them together. And Isaac said to his father Abraham, "My father!" And he said, "Here am I, my son." He said, "Behold, the fire and the wood; but where is the lamb for a burnt offering?" Abraham said, "God will provide himself the lamb for a burnt offering, my son." So they went both of them together. When they came to the place of which God had told him, Abraham built an altar there, and laid the wood in order, and bound Isaac his son, and laid him on the altar, upon the wood. Then Abraham put forth his hand, and took the knife to slay his son. But the angel of the LORD called to him from heaven, and said, "Abraham, Abraham!" And he said, "Here am I." He said, "Do not lay your hand on the lad or do anything to him; for now I know that you fear God, seeing you have not withheld your son, your only son, from me."

And Abraham lifted up his eyes and looked, and behold, behind him was a ram, caught in a thicket by his horns; and Abraham went and took the ram, and offered it up as a burnt offering instead of his son. So Abraham called the name of that place the LORD will provide; as it is said to this day, "On the mount of the LORD it shall be provided."

And the angel of the LORD called to Abraham a second time from heaven, and said, "By myself I have sworn, says the LORD, because you have done this, and have not withheld your son, your only son, I will indeed bless you, and I will multiply your descendants as the stars of heaven and as the sand which is on the seashore. And your seed shall possess the gate of their enemies, and in your seed shall all the nations of the earth be blessed,[4] because you have obeyed my voice."

This story illustrates the quality for which Abraham was chosen to start the Jewish race—his total dedication to God. This quality was also to be the central characteristic of the entire race, the quality that would enable it to undertake all that was necessary to prepare the world for the coming of the Messiah. Abraham had to wait until he was over ninety before having his first child with his wife, Sarah, a child through whom God had promised to make him a great nation. Yet without a moment's hesitation or a single question Abraham was willing to sacrifice him to God. The Scripture makes it clear that it was Abraham's behavior during this test that would earn for him, and hence for the Jewish race, the honor of bringing forth the Messiah—"and in your seed shall all the nations of the earth be blessed, because you have obeyed my voice" (Genesis 22:18).

This same passage illustrates very powerfully another aspect of the relationship between the Jews and the coming of Christ. Abraham's willingness to sacrifice Isaac was intimately linked to, one could even say reciprocated by, God's willingness, two thousand years later, to sacrifice *His* only begotten Son on the very same mountain, just a few hundred yards away, at the spot known as "Calvary". The very circumstances of Abraham's act foreshadowed, reflected in

[4] As before, the RSV has been slightly modified here. The underlying Hebrew form is the *Hithpael* conjugation of the verb "*barach*", "to bless". The RSV renders it "bless themselves", but "be blessed", as used by the Douay-Rheims both here and in the other occurrences of the same form in Isaiah 65:16 and in Psalm 72:17, is more probable.

advance, the ultimate fulfillment two thousand years later. "Take your son, your only son, whom you love" (Genesis 22:2) was echoed two thousand years later in "For God so loved the world that he gave his only Son . . . [His] beloved Son" (John 3:16; Matthew 3:17). As the son of Abraham climbed the mount with the wood on his shoulders for his own execution, so too did the Son of God. So we see that Abraham's utterance "God himself will provide the lamb for a burnt offering" (Genesis 22:8) was prophetic far beyond anything he knew, referring not only to the provision of the ram "provided" by the Lord, but also referring far more profoundly to the only truly acceptable sacrifice, that of God's Son Himself on the altar of Calvary.

Roles Played by the Jewish People

In this we see three of the roles that the Jewish people were called upon to play in salvation history—first, to give themselves completely to God, resulting in a uniquely intimate covenant between them and God; second, by their loyalty and virtue to bring blessing, and eventually the ultimate blessing of the Redeemer, to all of mankind; and third, to foreshadow prophetically later salvation history in their own history.

Yet this does not exhaust the role that the Jews were to play. The Jews were also to host the Incarnation itself, to be the people among whom God would become man. If God was to be on a uniquely intimate basis with the Jews and eventually to incarnate among them, they would have to be free from all involvement with other deities, free from all spiritual pollution. Hence the severity of the restrictions in the Old Testament against any form of idolatry or sorcery, both of which establish ties between the practitioners and fallen spirits. This purity, and the development of virtue and piety among at least some of the Jews, would have to reach its ultimate fruition later in producing an individual of such devotion and virtue that she could give her flesh to be the flesh of the God-man, that she could be His human mother. This individual was, of course, the Blessed Virgin Mary.

If redemption through the Messiah, when He came, would require a high level of moral behavior, then mankind would have to be prepared for this higher moral standard, too. Judaism performed this function when it introduced God's morality to man through the revelation of the Torah[5] to Moses on Mount Sinai.

If mankind were to be able to recognize the Messiah for who He was when He came, it would have to be prepared by being taught beforehand to expect His coming. Judaism performed this role, too. At the time of Jesus, not only was the Messianic expectation at the very heart of Judaism, but the Jews lived in eager anticipation of the imminent arrival of the Messiah, in part because it was the time given by the Messianic prophecy in the book of Daniel.[6] This expectation is evident in Luke 3:15: "[T]he people were in expectation, and all men questioned in their hearts concerning John, whether perhaps he were the Christ". Even independently of the veracity of the Gospels, this must have been an accurate representation of the Messianic expectations of the Jews at the time, since they themselves were part of the original intended audience for the Gospels. The authors could not have misrepresented their beliefs without entirely discrediting

---

[5] "Torah" is the Jewish name for the Scriptures revealed to Moses on Mount Sinai, i.e., the first five books of the Old Testament.

[6] This prophecy is discussed at length in Chapter 4, "The Messianic Idea in Judaism".

themselves. The Messianic expectation remained the heart of
Judaism until the end of the Middle Ages.[7]

Next, since God brings His plans into being through the
mediation of man's prayer, and because man's highest purpose is to worship and praise God, God wished there to be
a people on earth who would worship and adore the Messiah even before He came and who would fervently pray for
His coming. This role, too, was fulfilled by the Jews; consider, as a single example, the love that permeates David's
prophetic depiction of the crucified Christ in Psalm 22:14–18:

> I am poured out like water, and all my bones are out of
> joint; my heart is like wax, it is melted within my breast;
> my strength is dried up like a potsherd, and my tongue
> cleaves to my jaws; thou dost lay me in the dust of death.
> Yea, dogs are round about me; a company of evildoers
> encircle me; they have pierced my hands and feet—I can
> count all my bones—they stare and gloat over me; they
> divide my garments among them, and for my raiment they
> cast lots.

Finally, God would need a people to provide a temporal home
for the Messiah when He came and to announce His arrival
to the world. This role, too, was entrusted to the Jews.

Thus the roles entrusted to the Jews included:

1. exhibiting a faithfulness and devotion to God that
    would support a unique intimacy and covenant with
    Him, through which the Messiah could eventually
    come;
2. in this loyalty and covenant being the primary chan-
    nel of grace for all of mankind;

---

[7] This too is further discussed in Chapter 4, "The Messianic Idea in Judaism".

3. prophetically, typologically foreshadowing salvation history in their own history;

4. providing a people of sufficient spiritual purity, virtue and morality to be able to be the people among whom God became man;

5. making God's laws known to mankind;

6. preparing the Mother of the Redeemer;

7. praying for the coming of the Messiah;

8. adoring and worshiping the Messiah before He came;

9. providing a temporal home for the Messiah and announcing the "good news" when He came.

Consider how beautifully some of these are reflected in the Marian hymn "O Mary of All Women", used in the Liturgy of the Hours for the Common of the Blessed Virgin Mary:

O Mary of all women, you are the chosen one,
Who, ancient prophets promised, would bear God's only Son;
All Hebrew generations prepared the way to thee,
That in your womb the God-man might come
   to set man free.

O Mary, you embody all God taught to our race,
For you are first and foremost in fullness of his grace;
We praise this wondrous honor that you gave birth to him
Who from you took his manhood and saved us from our sin.

CHAPTER TWO

How Well Did the Jews Do?

Having considered the role of Jews and Judaism in the period leading up to the coming of the Messiah, let us now consider their role when He did, in fact, come.

"Faithful Remnants" in the Scriptures

The story of the Jews' behavior when the Messiah did come is not, of course, a happy one, and it is easy to jump to the conclusion that the Jews failed in the task for which they were chosen. Yet such is not, in fact, the case.

Throughout Sacred Scriptures we see the same pattern repeating itself—God works through small numbers, "faithful remnants" almost invisible within a larger sea of largely unfaithful humanity.

The first time we see this is in the story of Noah. God was disgusted with mankind and determined to make an end to the experiment and blot them off the face of the earth. But the presence of a single man, Noah, who was pleasing in God's sight, was enough to cause Him to relent and to spare the race through his descendents (Genesis 6:5—7:7):

> The LORD saw that the wickedness of man was great in the earth, and that every imagination of the thoughts of his heart was only evil continually. And the LORD was

sorry that he had made man on the earth, and it grieved
him to his heart. So the LORD said, "I will blot out man
whom I have created from the face of the ground, man
and beast and creeping things and birds of the air, for I am
sorry that I have made them." But Noah found favor in
the eyes of the LORD. . . . And God said to Noah, "I have
determined to make an end of all flesh; for the earth is
filled with violence through them; behold, I will destroy
them with the earth. Make yourself an ark. . . . For behold, I will bring a flood of waters upon the earth, to
destroy all flesh in which is the breath of life from under
heaven; everything that is on the earth shall die. But I will
establish my covenant with you; and you shall come into
the ark, you, your sons, your wife, and your sons' wives
with you." . . . Noah did this; he did all that God commanded him. Then the LORD said to Noah, "Go into the
ark, you and all your household, for I have seen that you
are righteous before me in this generation." . . . And Noah
and his sons and his wife and his sons' wives with him
went into the ark, to escape the waters of the flood.

Here we see the human race itself preserved because one
man was pleasing in the sight of God.

The pattern is repeated a bit later in human history, with
the story of Sodom and Gomorrah. The wickedness of those
cities was so great that God determined that, in justice, He
was compelled to destroy them; yet, through the pleading of
Abraham, He agreed that the cities would be spared if just
ten just men could be found in them (Genesis 18:20–29):

Then the LORD said, "Because the outcry against Sodom
and Gomorrah is great and their sin is very grave, I will
go down to see whether they have done altogether according to the outcry which has come to me. . . ." Then
Abraham drew near, and said, "Wilt thou indeed destroy

the righteous with the wicked? Suppose there are fifty righteous within the city; wilt thou then destroy the place and not spare it for the fifty righteous who are in it? . . . And the LORD said, "If I find at Sodom fifty righteous in the city, I will spare the whole place for their sake." Abraham answered, "Behold, I have taken upon myself to speak to the Lord, I who am but dust and ashes. Suppose five of the fifty righteous are lacking? Wilt thou destroy the whole city for lack of five?" And he said, "I will not destroy it if I find forty-five there." Again he spoke to him, and said, "Suppose forty are found there." He answered, "For the sake of forty I will not do it."

In like manner, Abraham gradually negotiates God down to the point where He concedes: "For the sake of ten I will not destroy it" (Genesis 18:32).

This basic pattern—of an entire people being saved for the sake of a tiny "faithful remnant"—is a constantly recurring theme throughout the Old Testament. Another instance was when the entire population of grumbling and idolatrous Jews in the desert, during the exodus from Egypt, was spared for the sake of Moses (Exodus 32:7–14):

And the LORD said to Moses, ". . . your people, whom you brought up out of the land of Egypt, have corrupted themselves; they have turned aside quickly out of the way which I commanded them; they have made for themselves a molten calf, and have worshiped it and sacrificed to it, . . . I have seen this people, and behold, it is a stiff-necked people; now therefore let me alone, that my wrath may burn hot against them and I may consume them; but of you I will make a great nation." But Moses besought the LORD his God, and said, "O LORD, why does thy wrath burn hot against thy people, whom thou hast brought forth out of the land of Egypt with great power and with a mighty hand? Why should the Egyptians say, 'With evil intent did he bring them forth, to slay them in the mountains, and to consume them from the face of the earth'? Turn from thy fierce wrath, and repent of this evil against thy people. . . ." And the LORD repented of the evil which he thought to do to his people.

The same pattern was again repeated when a drought over the entire land of Israel was lifted for the sake of Elijah, recounted in 1 Kings 18.

This is the context in which we must see the betrayal of Jesus by the Jews. Yes, the crowd shouted, "Crucify Him!" (Mark 15:13–14; Luke 23:21). Yes, the crowd uttered that horrible self-imprecation "His blood be on us and on our children!" [1] (Matthew 27:25). The masses betrayed Jesus; the masses were fickle and evil-hearted. However, there was a faithful remnant. A faithful remnant of Jews who were worthy of the calling for which they were chosen—a remnant that included, first and foremost, the Blessed Virgin Mary, and Joseph and Elizabeth and Zechariah and John the Baptist, and the apostles (with one unfortunate exception), and the first martyr, Stephen, and the other disciples. This seems to be the way that God works, and, in fact, all that God, in the long run, realistically expects from any people—even, unfortunately, the Church. Even the Church, made up of Catholics who have the inconceivable graces that come from the sacraments, who have the fullness of the Truth taught through the Magisterium, who have the example, inspiration, and intercession of all the Saints—even among them, unfortunately, there may be only a "faithful remnant" that

[1] "Of old, they [the Jews] called down upon themselves the Blood of the Savior, may it now descend upon them a laver of redemption and life", Prayer of Pope Pius XI for the Feast of Christ the King.

remains pleasing to God. For did not our Lord say, "Enter by the narrow gate; for the gate is wide and the way is easy, that leads to destruction, and those who enter by it are many. For the gate is narrow and the way is hard, that leads to life, and those who find it are few" (Matthew 7:13–14).

The final proof, of course, that the Jews did in fact succeed in their mission—although one could say "despite themselves"—is the fact that the Incarnation and subsequent evangelization through them did succeed. So one could conclude that the Jews, as a people, are twice blessed—blessed once through their election as the seed of Abraham, and blessed a second time by the God-man taking on their flesh and their blood in His Incarnation. The continuing blessing on the Jewish people, even after the horror of the rejection, betrayal, and crucifixion of Christ, is explicitly discussed—with the full authority of scriptural inerrancy—in St. Paul's Letter to the Romans (from Romans 9 and 11):[2]

> They are Israelites, and to them belong the sonship, the glory, the covenants, the giving of the law, the worship, and the promises; to them belong the patriarchs, and of their race, according to the flesh, is the Christ. . . . I ask, then, has God rejected his people? By no means! . . . God has not rejected his people whom he foreknew. Do you not know what the scripture says of Elijah, how he pleads with God against Israel? "Lord, they have killed thy prophets, they have demolished thy altars, and I alone am left, and they seek my life." But what is God's reply to him? "I have kept for myself seven thousand men who have not bowed the knee to Baal." So too at the present time there is a remnant, chosen by grace.

---

[2] This passage is discussed at greater length in Chapter 9, "The Return of the Jews".

Where does this leave us? The Jews succeeded in their mission of bringing the Messiah to the world. This success was effected through a small fraction of the Jews, a "faithful remnant", but this should not surprise us because throughout salvation history God has always worked through just such small "faithful remnants". The infidelity of many of the Jews brought down an imprecation on the race, but, at the same time, the fidelity of the small fraction as well as the Incarnation itself brought down further blessing upon the race, on top of the blessing through their forefathers, which, according to St. Paul, was never revoked.

Later "Faithful Remnants"

In both Judaism and Christianity, the teaching and revelations about the role of "faithful remnants" has continued. Talmudic Judaism teaches that the continued existence of the entire world is being supported by the prayers of thirty-six righteous men.[3] This same principle—that for the sake of just a few faithful souls, entire countries or even the entire world are spared divine justice—is frequently reflected in private revelations made to Christian saints.[4]

[3] "The world must contain not less than thirty-six righteous men in each generation", Talmud Tract *Sanhedrin 97b*, *The Babylonian Talmud*, ed. Rabbi Dr. I. Epstein (London: Soncino Press, 1935), p. 659. This statement also appears in Sukkah 45b. The Talmud is the Jewish oral law, put in written form during the period around A.D. 200 to 600.

[4] Catholics are under no obligation to accept private revelations as true. Nevertheless the devotional life of the Church has always been heavily influenced by such revelations, especially those granted to saints. As the *Catechism of the Catholic Church* states: "Guided by the magisterium of the Church, the *sensus fidelium* knows how to discern and welcome in these [private] revelations whatever constitutes an authentic call of Christ or his saints to the Church" (no. 67).

The most dramatic private revelations of the last century were those of Fatima, in which first the Angel of Portugal, and then the Blessed Virgin Mary, appeared to three young shepherd children in a remote village of Portugal during 1916 and 1917. At his first appearance the Angel of Portugal exhorted the children to pray. When he appeared again some months later, he found them playing and reproved them: " 'What are you doing?' he asked. 'Pray! Pray very much! The Hearts of Jesus and Mary have designs of mercy on you. Offer prayers and sacrifices constantly to the Most High.... You will thus draw down peace upon your country.' " [5]

The prayers and sacrifices of these three young children were, at least in part, responsible for delivering the entire country of Portugal from the horrors of World War I. The historicity of the apparitions at Fatima was confirmed by the extraordinary fact that the culminating "miracle of the sun" of October 13, 1917, in which the sun was seen to dance in the sky and drop to earth, was announced in advance and witnessed by at least 70,000, including many skeptics and atheists as well as believing Catholics. [6]

Another, similar example is provided by the revelations made to the recently canonized Sister Faustina, in which Jesus revealed that as a result of her prayers, Poland would be spared total destruction during World War II. Some of Jesus' words to her about the power of her intercession include:

[5] Lucia's Fourth Memoir, reprinted in Sister Lucia, *Fatima in Lucia's Own Words* (Fatima, Portugal: Postulation Center, 1976), pp. 151–52.

[6] Among the books that provide detailed accounts of the Fatima apparitions are John De Marchi, I.M.C., *Fatima: The Full Story* (Washington, N.J.: AMI Press, 1986), and William Walsh, *Our Lady of Fatima* (New York: Doubleday, 1990).

For your sake I bless the entire country.[7]

My daughter, your confidence and love restrain My justice, and I cannot inflict punishment because you hinder Me from doing so.[8]

[L]et me tell you that there are [but a few] souls living in the world who love Me dearly. . . . They are a defense for the world before the justice of the Heavenly Father and a means of obtaining mercy for the world. The love and sacrifice of these souls sustain the world in existence.[9]

For your sake I will withhold the hand which punishes; for your sake I bless the earth.[10]

By your entreaties, you and your companions shall obtain mercy for yourselves and for the world.[11]

Through your prayers, you shall mediate between heaven and earth.[12]

The testimony about how God works with mankind is clear, both from Judaism and Christianity. The relationship between God and mankind is not established and maintained on the basis of "averages", or on the behavior of the majority. The majority of mankind, throughout all of human history, has always turned away from God, has failed Him, and will continue to do so. God's relationship with the

[7] Sister M. Faustina Kowalska, *Divine Mercy in My Soul: The Diary of Sister M. Faustina Kowalska* (Stockbridge, Mass.: Marian Press, 1987), p. 21 (para. 40).

[8] Ibid., p. 106, para. 198.

[9] Ibid., pp. 165–66, para. 367.

[10] Ibid., p. 191, para. 431.

[11] Ibid., p. 192, para. 435.

[12] Ibid., p. 194, para. 438.

entire human race is established and maintained on the basis of His relationship with a "chosen few", with those few souls who truly give their hearts to Him, in whom He can truly find delight. It is for the sake of these few that He pours out His mercy upon the rest. Just as it was in the days of Noah, in the days of Sodom and Gomorrah, in the days of Moses, so it was with the "faithful remnant" of the Jews at the time of Jesus who turned to the Messiah with faith and love, and so it will be with a faithful remnant among the Jews (as well as among the Gentiles) at the time of the Second Coming.

Witness of the Lemann Brothers

As an example of such a "faithful remnant", consider the case of two remarkable Jewish converts to the Catholic Church of the nineteenth century—the Lemann brothers. They were Jews, twin brothers orphaned at an early age, and raised by their uncles and aunts in a wealthy, aristocratic Jewish family in Lyons, France. They, on their own initiative and without the knowledge of their family, were baptized into the Catholic faith at the age of eighteen; when the family found out, they tried to get the boys to recant; when that failed, several of their uncles violently attacked them. At the point of death, one of the boys was able to struggle free sufficiently to cry for help, and they were rescued by the police. The incident, occurring as it did in one of the foremost families of the city, caused quite a scandal, and the family attempted to justify its behavior by accusing the boys of having been hoodwinked by the priest who baptized them, claiming he was only after their inheritance. To defend the priest the boys, then eighteen, sent the following letter to the local newspaper:

Sunday, September 17, 1854
Dear Editor:

We see ourselves in the necessity of breaking a silence which
we had determined to keep. The newspapers have spoken
enough about the unfortunate incident which has brought
us to the public's attention. If we alone were being accused, the condemnation that was placed on our conversion would be of little concern to us; our conscience belongs
to us alone, and we recognize no one else's right to it. But,
as certain people are circulating malicious insinuations with
respect to the clergy, it has become our duty to reveal the
truth and enlighten the opinions of reasonable men.

In our conversion, all has been the work of God. From
our childhood, the sight of Catholic services greatly impressed us, to the point that we felt regret that we were
not Christian. When we began school, this regret became
more acute; we saw, on one hand, a few Jews; on the
other hand, a great number of Christian children. This
difference struck us. When they went to Mass and we
heard the songs accompanied by the organ, we blushed to
be reduced to gathering in an ordinary classroom and go
through the motions of a pointless ritual.

But what shook us even more were the love and the devotion of the priests and religious who vowed themselves
to the service of the ill, a devotion which we compared with
the coldness and indifference of the others who surrounded
us. On top of that, one of us fell gravely ill. We were drawn
more and more to Catholicism. However, we dared not
broach the question; we wanted to study further. The further we advanced in our study, the more sharply we saw the
false position we were in. We opened up history, and we
could not avoid becoming aware of the present state of the
Jewish people as compared to its past.

More and more difficulties, which our Rabbi never
could resolve, piled up in our heads. The study of the

classics of Bossuet, of Fenelon, of Massillon, was able to prepare our hearts to receive the grace of a God of mercy. Then we searched the Holy Scriptures. From the start, we understood that we could not walk alone; we must find a holy Priest. Every day from then on, he gave us instruction, dissipated our doubts, explained to us the prophecies, and enabled us to grasp the link between the old and the new law.

Then, we said to ourselves "If the Messiah has already come, it is Jesus Christ, and we must become Christians. If he has not yet come, we must nevertheless no longer remain Jews, because the time of the promise has passed and our books have lied."

He made us wait over a year. After we graduated from high school, we insisted on being baptized; we had been out of school over a month.

He could not refuse our request; we became Christians, and we became happy.

No one can make us renounce our faith; we are resolved to die first.

It seems to us that the age of eighteen is old enough to discern the true from the false. Furthermore, the Jews have demanded freedom of religion for themselves and for Protestants; they can hardly refuse it to us.

P.S. Sir, we rely on your fairness to print this letter in your next issue.[13]

The twin brothers went on to become priests, theologians, and canons of the Church; they became good friends of Pope Pius IX and played an active role at the First Vatican Council. At that council, they circulated a "*Postulatum*" that was

---

[13] Father Theotime de St. Just, O.M.C., *Les Frères Lemann: Juifs Convertis* (Paris: Librarie St. François, 1937), pp. 43–45 (translation by author).

signed by almost all of the Fathers of the Council and that was heartily endorsed by Pope Pius IX. Only the outbreak of the Franco-Prussian war, which prematurely terminated the Council, prevented the official proclamation of the *Postulatum*. It consisted of a warm invitation to the Jews to join the Catholic Church; the text follows:

> The undersigned Fathers of the Council humbly yet urgently beseechingly pray that the Holy Ecumenical Council of the Vatican deign to come to the aid of the unfortunate nation of Israel with an entirely paternal invitation; that is, that it express the wish that, finally exhausted by a wait no less futile than long, the Israelites hasten to recognize the Messiah, our Savior Jesus Christ, truly promised to Abraham and announced by Moses; thus completing and crowning, not changing, the Mosaic religion.
>
> On one hand, the undersigned Fathers have the very firm confidence that the holy Council will have compassion on the Israelites, because they are always very dear to God on account of their fathers, and because it is from them that the Christ was born according to the flesh.
>
> On the other hand, the same Fathers share the sweet and intimate hope that this ardent desire of tenderness and honor will be, with the aid of the Holy Spirit, well received by many of the sons of Abraham, because the obstacles that have held them back until now appear to be disappearing more and more, the ancient wall of separation now having fallen.
>
> Would that they then speedily acclaim the Christ, saying "Hosanna to the Son of David! Blessed be He who comes in the name of the Lord!"
>
> Would that they hurl themselves into the arms of the Immaculate Virgin Mary, even now their sister according

to the flesh, who wishes likewise to be their mother according to grace as she is ours![14]

Seed and Blessing

Any serious consideration of a continuing special role for Jews in the economy of salvation after the coming of Christ must deal with the complex issue of the blessing that was given to the Jews as the "seed of Abraham". This blessing to the "seed of Abraham" should be familiar to many Catholics, for it appears in the Magnificat of the Blessed Virgin Mary. The Magnificat is Mary's spontaneous hymn of praise of God taken directly from Scripture (Luke 1:46–55) and recited daily by priests and religious throughout the world as part of the evening prayers of the Divine Office.[15] This hymn closes with the words: "As he spoke to our fathers, to Abraham and to his seed for ever" (Douay-Rheims translation).[16] These words are an allusion to Genesis 22:17–18, in which after Abraham offered to sacrifice Isaac in obedience to God's request, God promised Abraham "... and in your seed shall all the nations of the earth be blessed". In numerous later passages in the Old Testament, God repeats His promise of a special relationship with the "seed of

[14] Augustin and Joseph Lemann, *La Cause des Restes d'Israel Introduite au Concile Oecumenique du Vatican* (Paris: Librarie Lecoffrre, 1912), pp. 79–81 (translation by author).

[15] By Canon Law (CIC, canons 276, no. 3, and 663, no. 3), all Catholic priests and many religious must recite daily the Divine Office, which consists of specific prayers, psalms and readings to be prayed at various times of the day and at night. Others are also, of course, encouraged to pray it.

[16] Some modern translations translate the original Greek "seed" as "children" or "posterity". (The current English language Divine Office uses "children".)

Figure 2-1: Augustin and Joseph Lemann later in life, priests and canons of the Church

Abraham"; for instance Deuteronomy 32:9–10 (here Jacob, as Abraham's grandson, represents the "seed of Abraham"): "For the LORD's portion is his people, Jacob his allotted heritage. He found him in a desert land, and in the howling waste of the wilderness; he encircled him, he cared for him, he kept him as the apple of his eye."

Let us begin by considering the meaning and use of the concept of "seed" in the Old Testament. When one reads the account of God's creation of plant life in Genesis 1:11–12 in a literal translation (or the original Hebrew), one cannot help but be struck with the emphasis placed on the word "seed" followed by the phrase "each according to its kind". In the original, in each of the two verses the word "seed" appears three times, followed by "each according to its kind" (Genesis 1:11–12):

> And God said, "Let the earth put forth vegetation, plants seeding seed, and fruit trees bearing fruit in which is their seed, each according to its kind, upon the earth." And it was so. The earth brought forth vegetation, plants seeding seed according to their own kinds, and trees bearing fruit in which is their seed, each according to its kind. And God saw that it was good.[17]

This is echoed a few verses later, with a repetitive insistence on all creatures reproducing "according to their kinds" (Genesis 1:21–25):

> So God created the great sea monsters and every living creature that moves, with which the waters swarm, according to their kinds, and every winged bird according

---

[17] RSV translation with modifications to more closely reflect the original Hebrew.

to its kind. And God saw that it was good.... And God said, "Let the earth bring forth living creatures according to their kinds: cattle and creeping things and beasts of the earth according to their kinds." And it was so. And God made the beasts of the earth according to their kinds and the cattle according to their kinds, and everything that creeps upon the ground according to its kind. And God saw that it was good.

It is almost as though God, knowing in advance that in the latter days the theory of evolution would appear, wanted to nip the false and pernicious theory in the bud,[18] by emphasizing that when He created each different type of plant or animal life, He gave it the property of reproducing only within its own kind; that the faculty of producing seed resulting only in reproduction truly "according to its own kind" is intrinsic in the very nature of life itself. In fact, despite all of the attempts to the contrary, no one has ever succeeded in showing a single example of life producing seed *not* "after its own kind"; no mutation into another species has *ever* been observed. This sense of immutability is intrinsic to the very concept of "seed" in the Bible, in which the entire mystery of the reproduction of life "according to its own kind" is contained. The concept of "seed" lies at the very heart of God's creation of life itself.

---

[18] This is the author's opinion based on the scientific evidence. For a good discussion of the scientific merits of the theory of evolution, see Philip E. Johnson, *Darwin on Trial* (Downers Grove, Ill.: InterVarsity Press, 1993). Catholic doctrine is not incompatable with some forms of the theory of evolution (cf. Pope Pius XII's 1950 encyclical *Humani Generis* and Pope John Paul II's October 22, 1996, address to the Pontifical Academy of Sciences, *L'Osservatore Romano*, October 23, 1996).

Thus we see that the idea of seed encompasses the idea of generation according to its own kind; that God has initiated the chain of creation, creating the "parent" with the ability to produce seed; and that ability to produce seed entails a reproduction after its own kind. This identity extends even into the moral domain; later in Genesis we encounter "seed" again, in reference to the battle between Eve and her offspring and the serpent (Genesis 3:15): "I will put enmity between you and the woman, and between your seed and her seed; he shall bruise your head, and you shall bruise his heel."

Here we see that "seed" carries a very strong sense of literal, physical line of descent as well as a strong notion of identity-in-character, of being "according to its kind", extending into the moral, as well as physical, domain. For the moral characteristics of the relationship between the woman and the serpent, the mutual enmity, was to flow down through the generations, through "your seed and her seed", much the same as physical characteristics.

Yet we also see in the Old Testament that God's blessing, intended to flow through the "seed of Abraham" from father to first-born son, did not always do so, but often bypassed the eldest son and went, instead, to a younger one. The original intention of God appeared to be that in each generation a special blessing, a sort of spiritual patrimony, would be passed from the father to the first-born son. However, in each of the generations of the three Patriarchs—who are so central to Judaism that God Himself is identified as "the God of Abraham, the God of Isaac, the God of Jacob—this rule was overturned, with the blessing going to a younger son instead. It was Abraham's second son, Isaac, who received the blessing instead of the elder Ishmael; then it was

Jacob, the second-born of Isaac's sons, who ended up "steal-
ing" the blessing from his elder brother, Esau; and then in
turn Jacob withdrew the blessing of preeminence from his
eldest son, Reuben, because he had lain with his father's con-
cubine and gave it to Joseph instead (Genesis 49). Over the
centuries this typology has been applied to the situation of
the Jews versus the Gentiles—the Jews were the "eldest sons"
and in principle held the right to the special blessing of the
father (in this case God), but because of their unworthiness
this blessing was withdrawn and conferred to the "younger
sons", the Gentiles. A number of passages in the New Testament are sometimes cited to support the idea that the special blessing that had been given to the Jews had been revoked.
One such is John the Baptist's statement in Matthew 3:9:
"Do not presume to say to yourselves, 'We have Abraham as
our father'; for I tell you, God is able from these stones to
raise up children to Abraham."

Another is St. Paul in Romans 9:6−8: "For all are not Israelites that are of Israel, neither are all they that are the seed
of Abraham, children; but 'in Isaac shall thy seed be called.'
That is to say, not they that are the children of the flesh, are
the children of God, but they, that are the children of the
promise are accounted for the seed." [19]

The question is how these statements can be reconciled
with God's often repeated promises to the Jews, which seemed
to be eternal and irrevocable in nature. As St. Paul states in
Romans 11:28−29: "but as regards election they [the Jews]
are beloved for the sake of their forefathers. For the gifts and
the call of God are irrevocable."

[19] Douay-Rheims translation.

The apparent contradiction can be resolved when one makes a few careful distinctions. In the passage from Matthew, John the Baptist is not talking about lowering the Jews from their status, but of raising up others. In so doing, God would not be violating His promise; He would simply be sovereignly extending extraordinary graces to others, a right that Jesus emphasizes in an exactly apropos parable: "Am I not allowed to do what I choose with what belongs to me? Or do you begrudge my generosity?"(Matthew 20:15). Thus the threat of John the Baptist is not that God will remove the Jews from their position in God's order, but that He might well raise others to the same level.

The other distinction that should be made is between a "blessing by choice", such as that passed on from father to eldest son by the Patriarchs, and a "blessing by nature", that is, one that is incorporated into the nature of the individual as an inherited characteristic. It is this latter that is suggested by the concept of seed in the Old Testament and emphasized by the repeated use of the phrase "seed of Abraham" (an emphasis that is unfortunately often lost in modern translations). Thus it seems as though the former sort of blessing, a blessing of special grace somewhat analogous to that passed down from father to (in principle) eldest son, and which had belonged to the Jews prior to the coming of Christ, was extended to the faithful Gentiles with the advent of Christianity, perhaps being taken away from the Jews who refused to believe in Christ. Yet a second sort of blessing, a blessing by nature promised to "the seed of Abraham", would continue to flow through the propagation "according to its own kind" suggested by the word "seed", and thus would remain with the Jewish race, despite their lack of faith in Christ. St. Paul seems to be alluding to this duality of blessing in his famous metaphor of the branches grafted onto the olive tree (Romans 11:16–24):

> [I]f the root is holy, so are the branches. But if some of the branches were broken off, and you, a wild olive shoot, were grafted in their place to share the richness of the olive tree, do not boast over the branches. If you do boast, remember it is not you that support the root, but the root that supports you. You will say, "Branches were broken off so that I might be grafted in." That is true. They were broken off because of their unbelief, but you stand fast only through faith. So do not become proud, but stand in awe. . . . For if you have been cut from what is by nature a wild olive tree, and grafted, contrary to nature, into a cultivated olive tree, how much more will these natural branches be grafted back into their own olive tree.

In this metaphor, the sap of the olive tree is the "blessing by choice", while the intrinsic nature of the branch (cultivated vs. wild) is the "blessing by nature". The Gentiles are described as wild branches, that is, not sharing the blessing by nature, which have been grafted onto the tree, thus receiving the blessing by choice, just as a grafted limb receives the circulating sap of the tree. On the other hand, the Jews—the "cultivated branches" because of their blessing by nature— have been cut off for their disbelief, thus being separated from the flow of the sap, that is, from receiving the blessing by choice. However, they still maintain their character as cultivated branches, since the blessing by nature belongs to the "seed" that reproduces "according to its kind". Therefore when they do come to the faith and thus are grafted back on to "their own" olive tree, how blessed they will be, since they will then receive the blessing by choice originally intended for them, which is perfectly matched to their blessing by nature from which they were never separated. The duality of this blessing by nature and by grace is paralleled in the closing words of the *Postulatum* from the First Vatican Council inviting the Jews into the Church. In it the Blessed Virgin Mary, the Mediatrix of all Graces, is appropriately seen as the channel of both blessings:

> Would that they [the Jews] hurl themselves into the arms of the Immaculate Virgin Mary, even now their sister according to the flesh, who wishes likewise to be their mother according to grace. . . !

CHAPTER THREE

Jew, Gentile, and the Church

At the time of Jesus, to be a Jew was not only to belong to a religion, but also to be a member of an extended tribe or ethnic group that was a nation-state as well, although currently under foreign domination. Those not a member of the tribe were "Gentiles". A few Gentiles had adopted the Jewish religion; these were known as "proselytes". Initially all of Jesus' followers were Jews; shortly after His death, they were joined by some Gentiles, but for some time His followers were seen simply as a new sect within Judaism, somewhat like the earlier Essenes or the later followers of the would-be Messiah Bar Kochba. In fact, for almost two decades it was an active issue of contention whether one had to first convert to Judaism before being allowed to become a follower of Jesus. (The Council of Jerusalem was called about fifteen years after the death of Jesus precisely to address this issue.) This diffusion of Christianity outwards, from the Jews to the Gentiles, is the topic of this chapter.

For the sake of the following discussion, the word "Jew" will be used to refer to members of the ethnic or national group, "Gentile" for anyone not a member of the Jewish ethnic group, and "Christian" and "Christianity" for belief in the Messiahhood of Jesus, although this is anachronistic since the term "Christian" was introduced only later.

Jews, God, Gentiles, and Demons

In order to understand the reaction that Jews of the day would have had to the inclusion of Gentiles into the early Church, one must first consider what distinguished Judaism from the gentile religions of the day. Today we think of the difference between religions as being a difference of beliefs, primarily about who God is, how He acts, and how He has revealed Himself. The set of beliefs that one accepts determines the religion to which one belongs.

In Old Testament times, the difference between religions was of a different character. Everyone, Jew and Gentile (or pagan, a more value-laden word for the same people), recognized that there exists a large host of supernatural beings whom one can worship and serve as "gods", and who, in turn, render service to their followers. One's religion was defined by one's choice of "god" or "gods" to serve. Today we tend to think that the pagan "gods" were figments of a superstitious imagination; we even think that the ancient Jews believed the same thing, and that the revelation of "Jehovah" [1] as the one true God was simply in contrast to such false superstition. However, that is not the case.

The "gods" that the pagans worshipped truly existed and truly fulfilled the role of gods to their adherents—that is, in return for adoration, reverence, and sacrifice they returned services to their adherents. However, rather than being "God" in the meaning of the uncreated creator of all that is, they were merely spirits, in fact, fallen angels (otherwise known as demons or devils). This is made entirely explicit

---

[1] When "the Lord" appears in the Bible, it represents the English translation of the Hebrew "tetragammon", that is, JHVH, which is the name of the one true God revealed to the Jews in the Old Testament. This is commonly vocalized in English as "Jehovah", or, more correctly, "Yahweh".

in Psalm 96:5: "For all the gods of the Gentiles are devils: but
the LORD made the heavens".[2] The pagans thought that
that was all that there were for potential gods, and that the
Jews' Jehovah was just the particular spirit that the Jews
chose to worship, just as Baal, Astarte, etc., or some combi-
nation might be the spirit(s) that the pagans chose to worship and who in return met their needs for protection, for
control over nature, for victory in war, etc. And it is clear,
both from the Old Testament and from today's accounts of
satanism and occultism, that such fallen spirits are able to
provide some supernatural[3] services for their adherents.

The unique revelation of Judaism was that in addition to
these "gods", there is one true God, a different sort of god,
absolutely unique and absolutely sovereign, Himself uncreated who created all the other gods as well as everything else
that exists, and that this incomprehensibly sovereign and
exalted God is willing to enter into a personal god/man relationship with those who follow Him. That is what Judaism
was—the religion of following the Creator-God as god rather
than a fallen spirit.

The entire Old Testament reflects this true understanding
of God and of gods. Whenever there is a reference to serving "the LORD" versus serving "other gods", this is what is
meant; for instance Joshua 24:15:

"[C]hoose this day whom you will serve, whether the
gods your fathers served in the region beyond the River,

[2] Douay-Rheims translation.
[3] Technically the correct word is "preternatural"; in precise theological ter-
minology "supernatural" is restricted to workings of God whereas "preternatural" refers to the workings of fallen spirits, but the less precise and more
common usage will be followed here.

or the gods of the Amorites in whose land you dwell; but as for me and my house, we will serve the LORD."

This meaning is often "explained away" by commentators who do not recognize the existence of the supernatural world in its full complexity and power. Yet the verses that focus on this relationship between "the LORD" and the other gods are sometimes quite explicit:

Psalm 82:1–8: God has taken his place in the divine council; in the midst of the gods he holds judgment.... I say, "You are gods, sons of the Most High, all of you; nevertheless, you shall die like men, and fall like any prince." Arise, O God, judge the earth; for to thee belong all the nations!

Psalm 95:3: For the LORD is God, the mighty God, the great King over all the gods.[4]

The fact that when the Jewish people were unfaithful and offered sacrifice to the gods of the pagans they were sacrificing to demons is explicitly stated:

Deuteronomy 32:16–17: They stirred him to jealousy with strange gods; with abominable practices they provoked him to anger. They sacrificed to demons which were no gods, to gods they had never known....

Baruch 4:6–8: [Y]ou were handed over to your enemies because you angered God. For you provoked him who made you, by sacrificing to demons and not to God. You forgot the everlasting God, who brought you up, and you grieved Jerusalem, who reared you.

---

[4] Translation from *Christian Prayer: The Liturgy of the Hours* (Boston: St. Paul Editions, 1976).

The underlying Hebrew word that is here translated "demons" is "שֵׁדִים", "*shadim*". It has the same root consonants as a word that means destruction, violence, havoc, or devastation, which is appropriate, for that is what the demons are—agents of destruction and devastation. And that is what the pagans, then and now, serve as "gods", whether they are aware of it or not.

It was in order to avoid being spiritually contaminated by these demons that God commanded the Jews to destroy all of the pagans in the land they were to take over. When they failed to do so, the results were disastrous. Psalms 106:34–41 recounts:

> They did not destroy the peoples, as the LORD commanded them, but they mingled with the nations[5] and learned to do as they did. They served their idols, which became a snare to them. They sacrificed their sons and their daughters to the demons; they poured out innocent blood, the blood of their sons and daughters, whom they sacrificed to the idols of Canaan; and the land was polluted with blood. Thus they became unclean by their acts, and played the harlot in their doings. Then the anger of the LORD was kindled against his people, and he abhorred his heritage; he gave them into the hand of the nations, so that those who hated them ruled over them.

When the Jews failed to eliminate the pagans, they ended up serving the pagans' demons as gods. This was the reason for the intensity of the separation enforced in Judaism between the Jews and the Gentiles, for the impurity and spiritual pollution associated with them and for the catastrophic

---

[5] The underlying Hebrew word, "*goyim*", which is translated here as "nations", is elsewhere variously translated as "pagans", "Gentiles", or "heathen".

implications of the intermingling between Jews and Gentiles in any context, but most extremely in worship. What might appear as the extreme "xenophobia" of the Jews was not a peculiar fault of their own, but was imposed on them by God to enable them to fulfill the mission for which they had been chosen. This is what God meant when He so frequently proclaimed Himself to be a "jealous God" (Deuteronomy 6:14–15):

> "You shall not go after other gods, of the gods of the peoples who are round about you; for the LORD your God in the midst of you is a jealous God; lest the anger of the LORD your God be kindled against you, and he destroy you from off the face of the earth."

To be a follower of a god is to invite that god "into" the human soul. It would be unspeakably repugnant to the purity of God to have to cohabit a soul with the filth of a demon—a so-called pagan god. Thus, the "jealousness" of God. This might even be reflected in the central prayer of Judaism, the "Shm'a", although it is not the most common interpretation. The Shm'a comes from Deuteronomy 6; it begins:

שְׁמַע יִשְׂרָאֵל יְהוָה אֱלֹהֵינוּ יְהוָה אֶחָד
Shm'a Yisrael Adonai Elohenu Adonai Echod

This is the "first and greatest" commandment cited by Jesus in Mark 12:29. The usual translation is "Hear, O Israel: The LORD our God, the LORD is one!" This reading places the emphasis on the unity of the LORD and stands in opposition to Christianity's doctrine of the trinitarian nature of God ("one God in three persons"[6]); the translation may, in fact,

---

[6] *Catechism of the Catholic Church*, no. 253.

be a reaction to it. An alternative rendering is "Hear O Israel, the LORD is our God, the LORD alone." [7] This places the emphasis on serving *only* the LORD, to the exclusion of any other gods.

Jews and Gentiles in the Early Church[8]

At its inception the Church was *entirely* Jewish. *All* of the very first members of the Church—the apostles, the disciples, and the center and heart of the church, the Blessed Virgin Mary—were Jews. During his life and ministry, Jesus repeatedly stated that the salvation which he brought was meant, at least at first, preferentially for Jews. We see that when he commissioned the disciples to go out and preach the good news, he restricted the evangelization to the Jews (Matthew 10:1–7):

> And he called to him his twelve disciples and gave them authority over unclean spirits, to cast them out, and to heal every disease and every infirmity.... These twelve Jesus sent out, charging them, "Go nowhere among the Gentiles, and enter no town of the Samaritans, but go rather to the lost sheep of the house of Israel. And preach as you go, saying, 'The kingdom of heaven is at hand.'"

[7] This translation is a correct one for both the underlying Hebrew text and the Latin Vulgate and is used in *The New American Bible*. Although generally "*echod*" means "one", in a few instances—e.g., Joshua 22:20, 1 Chronicles 29:1, and Isaiah 51:2—it means "alone" or "only"; however it is not the usual way to express "alone".

[8] Readers familiar with the U.S. Bishops' Committee for Ecumenical and Interreligious Affairs August 2002 *Reflections on Covenant and Mission* will recognize this section as a refutation, in part, of that document.

On another occasion, when a non-Jew tried to approach Jesus for healing, Jesus again stated in no uncertain terms that His mission was only to the Jews (Matthew 15:21–24):

> And Jesus went away from there and withdrew to the district of Tyre and Sidon. And behold, a Canaanite woman from that region came out and cried, "Have mercy on me, O Lord, Son of David; my daughter is severely possessed by a demon." But he did not answer her a word. And his disciples came and begged him, saying, "Send her away, for she is crying after us." He answered, "I was sent only to the lost sheep of the house of Israel."

This incident serves as an archetype for what ended up being the characteristic pattern for the spread of the Gospel. For the story of the Canaanite woman did not end there— when she showed greater faith in Jesus than the Jews did, He relented and extended His mission to her. Let us continue (Matthew 15:25–28):

> But she came and knelt before him, saying, "Lord, help me." And he answered, "It is not fair to take the children's bread and throw it to the dogs." She said, "Yes, Lord, yet even the dogs eat the crumbs that fall from their master's table." Then Jesus answered her, "O woman, great is your faith! Be it done for you as you desire." And her daughter was healed instantly.

"It is not fair to take the children's bread and throw it to the dogs"—the children clearly represent the Jews, and Jesus' mission was initially intended to be directed to them. Yet "even the dogs eat the crumbs that fall from their masters' table"; when the children (the Jews) are so careless or unappreciative that they let the food drop (do not take advantage of what Jesus is offering them), then the right to it passes to the Gentiles. This theology was also explicitly stated by St. Paul:

"the gospel ... is the power of God for salvation to every one who has faith, *to the Jew first* and also to the Greek" (Romans 1:16, emphasis added) shows that the Jews were the initial target of Jesus' mission, and "their [the Jews'] rejection [of the Gospel] means the reconciliation of the world ..." (Romans 11:15) states that the "reconciliation of the world"—that is, the inclusion of the Gentiles into the New Covenant—has come about as a result of the Jews' rejection of Jesus.

Another example in which Jesus makes clear that although Jews were the ones initially chosen to receive the Gospel, Gentiles could supplant them by showing greater receptiveness and faith, is found in Matthew 8 (verses 5–12):

> As he entered Capernaum, a centurion came forward to him, beseeching him and saying, "Lord, my servant is lying paralyzed at home, in terrible distress." And he said to him, "I will come and heal him." But the centurion answered him, "Lord, I am not worthy to have you come under my roof; but only say the word, and my servant will be healed. For I am a man under authority, with soldiers under me; and I say to one, 'Go,' and he goes, and to another, 'Come,' and he comes, and to my slave, 'Do this,' and he does it."
>
> When Jesus heard him, he marveled, and said to those who followed him, "Truly, I say to you, not even in Israel have I found such faith. I tell you, many will come from east and west and sit at table with Abraham, Isaac, and Jacob in the kingdom of heaven, while the sons of the kingdom will be thrown into the outer darkness; there men will weep and gnash their teeth."

The centurion's faith and humility is such a model for all Christians that it is embedded in the Mass, as the response of the communicant before receiving Jesus in the Blessed Sacrament:

> "Domine, non sum dignus, ut intres sub tectum meum, sed tantum dic verbo, et sanabitur anima mea." [9]

> ("Lord, I am not worthy to receive you under my roof, but only say the word, and my soul shall be healed.") [10]

This pattern, that although the Jews were to be the first recipients of Christianity they failed to accept it and the Gentiles took their place, is in fact an echo of the principle repeated over and over again in the Old Testament of the eldest son being the "son of the blessing" but proving unworthy and being supplanted by a younger sibling. Perhaps it would be more correct to say that the pattern in the Old Testament was but a foreshadowing of the ultimate expression of the principle—that the ultimate blessing of salvation history, the New Covenant brought by the Jewish Messiah Jesus, was rejected (in large part) by the elder son, the Jews, who were entitled to it by right, and thus passed on to the younger, the Gentiles.

Jesus had made it so clear that He had come first and foremost for the Jews that the burning question which remained at His death was whether the New Covenant was *restricted* to the Jews, or whether Gentiles too could enter in. Given Jesus' teachings, as well as the severely exclusive nature of the Old Covenant, it is not surprising that it took a while for the early disciples, all Jews, to accept that the Church was open to Gentiles as well as Jews, not *only* as an extraordinary ex-

---

[9] *Missale Romanum*, Editio Typica Tertia (Vatican: Typis Vaticanis, 2002).
[10] This is the literal translation of the Latin text. The current English translation alters it somewhat.

ception and not *only* on the condition that they first become proselytes. In fact it took a number of miracles and special revelations and an Apostolic Council,[11] before this was finally resolved.[12]

We see the unfolding of this development in the book of Acts, which chronicles the early days of the Church. The Church is considered to have been born on Pentecost, when the Holy Spirit fell on a large group of disciples gathered in the Upper Room. Only Jews and Jewish proselytes were present at this initial "birth" of the Church (Acts 2:1–41):

> When the day of Pentecost had come, they were all together in one place. And suddenly a sound came from heaven like the rush of a mighty wind, and it filled all the house where they were sitting. And there appeared to them tongues as of fire, distributed and resting on each one of them. And they were all filled with the Holy Spirit and began to speak in other tongues, as the Spirit gave them utterance.
>
> Now there were dwelling in Jerusalem Jews, devout men from every nation under heaven ... both Jews and proselytes.... Peter, standing with the eleven, lifted up his voice and addressed them, "Men of Judea and all who dwell in Jerusalem, ... this is what was spoken by the prophet Joel: 'And in the last days it shall be, God declares, that I will pour out my Spirit upon all flesh, and your sons and your daughters shall prophesy, and your young men shall see visions, and your old men shall dream

---

[11] The Apostolic Council of Jerusalem (about A.D. 49), described in Acts 15.

[12] This stands in stark contrast to the suggestion made by the *Reflections* document that Jesus intended His mission primarily for the Gentiles and *not* for the Jews, a sort of extension of Judaism to non-Jews. The words of Jesus Himself, the theology expounded by St. Paul, and the history of the early Church show that to be anything but the case.

dreams; yea, and on my menservants and my maidser-
vants in those days I will pour out my Spirit; and they
shall prophesy."

"Men of Israel, hear these words: Jesus of Nazareth, a
man attested to you by God with mighty works and wonders and signs which God did through him in your midst,
as you yourselves know—this Jesus, delivered up according to the definite plan and foreknowledge of God, you
crucified and killed by the hands of lawless men. But God
raised him up, having loosed the pangs of death, because
it was not possible for him to be held by it. . . . This Jesus
God raised up, and of that we all are witnesses. . . ."

"Let all the house of Israel therefore know assuredly
that God has made him both Lord and Christ, this Jesus
whom you crucified." Now when they heard this they
were cut to the heart, and said to Peter and the rest of the
apostles, "Brethren, what shall we do?" And Peter said to
them, "Repent, and be baptized every one of you in the
name of Jesus Christ for the forgiveness of your sins; and
you shall receive the gift of the Holy Spirit. . . . So those
who received his word were baptized, and there were added
that day about three thousand souls.

Repeatedly this passage points out that those involved were
all Jewish. It took place when Jews from all over the world
were gathered in Jerusalem to celebrate the Jewish "Feast of
Weeks", one of the three annual Jewish festivals for which
Jews were to make a pilgrimage to the Temple in Jerusalem.
That is why "there were dwelling in Jerusalem Jews, devout
men from every nation", "both Jews and proselytes", that is,
converts to Judaism. Peter addressed his speech to "Men of
Judea and all who dwell in Jerusalem" and "Men of Israel".
It was from among these—Jews and converts to Judaism, men
of Judea and Israel and the diaspora—that came the 3,000
who were baptized, the first mass influx into the Church.

The book of Acts continues with the story of the propagation of Christianity outward from its origin among Jews in the Holy Land to the wider world. As it recounts it, the revelation that Christianity was meant for the whole world was made in stages. During the life of Jesus, it was really only the Jews, and only those in the Holy Land, who were evangelized. At the first Pentecost, Jews and proselytes from the diaspora were brought into the Church. The next divine intervention had one of the apostles, Philip, preach the good news to the Ethiopian eunuch. He was most probably a proselyte—after all, he had come to Jerusalem for the feast and he was reading the Hebrew Scriptures—but one from the diaspora as well as one of another race. Furthermore, as a eunuch he was excluded from the synagogue by the laws of the Torah (Deuteronomy 23:1: "He whose testicles are crushed or whose male member is cut off shall not enter the assembly of the Lord"). Thus he was as much of an outsider as possible without actually being a Gentile. Yet it was to this consummate outsider that a most dramatic divine intervention came to bring him into the Church (Acts 8:26–39):

> An angel of the Lord said to Philip, "Rise and go toward the south to the road that goes down from Jerusalem to Gaza." And he rose and went. And behold, an Ethiopian, a eunuch, a minister of the Candace, queen of the Ethiopians, in charge of all her treasure, had come to Jerusalem to worship and was returning; seated in his chariot, he was reading the prophet Isaiah. And the Spirit said to Philip, "Go up and join this chariot."
>
> So Philip ran to him, and heard him reading Isaiah the prophet, and asked, "Do you understand what you are reading?" And he said, "How can I, unless some one guides me?" And he invited Philip to come up and sit with him. Now the passage of the scripture which he was reading

was this: "As a sheep led to the slaughter or a lamb before its shearer is dumb, so he opens not his mouth. In his humiliation justice was denied him. Who can describe his generation? For his life is taken up from the earth." And the eunuch said to Philip, "About whom, pray, does the prophet say this, about himself or about some one else?" Then Philip opened his mouth, and beginning with this scripture he told him the good news of Jesus.

And as they went along the road they came to some water, and the eunuch said, "See, here is water! What is to prevent my being baptized?" Then Philip said, "If you believe with all your heart, you may." And he answered and said, "I believe that Jesus Christ is the Son of God." And he commanded the chariot to stop, and they both went down into the water, Philip and the eunuch, and he baptized him. And when they came up out of the water, the Spirit of the Lord caught up Philip; and the eunuch saw him no more, and went on his way rejoicing.

One can imagine the impression that this incident made on the other disciples when Philip told them. After this, only the final stage in the outward propagation of the Gospel, going out to the Gentiles, was left. We read how that was done in the book of Acts (Acts 10:1—11:18, summarized):

At Caesarea there was a centurion named Cornelius, a devout man who feared God, gave alms liberally, and prayed constantly to God. In a vision he saw an angel of God coming in and saying to him, "Cornelius." And he stared at him in terror, and said, "What is it, Lord?" And he said to him, "Your prayers and your alms have ascended as a memorial before God. And now send men to Joppa, and bring one Simon who is called Peter; he is lodging with Simon, a tanner, whose house is by the seaside."

So he sent three servants to Joppa. As they were coming near the city, Peter went up on the housetop to pray.

And he became hungry and desired something to eat; but while they were preparing it, he fell into a trance and saw the heaven opened, and something descending, like a great sheet, let down by four corners upon the earth. In it were all kinds of animals and reptiles and birds of the air. And there came a voice to him, "Rise, Peter; kill and eat." But Peter said, "No, Lord; for I have never eaten anything that is common or unclean." And the voice came to him again a second time, "What God has cleansed, you must not call common." This happened three times, and the thing was taken up at once to heaven.

Now while Peter was inwardly perplexed as to what the vision which he had seen might mean, behold, the men that were sent by Cornelius arrived. And while Peter was pondering the vision, the Spirit said to him, "Behold, three men are looking for you. Rise and go down, and accompany them without hesitation; for I have sent them." He rose and went off with them, and on the following day they entered Caesarea. Cornelius was expecting them and had called together his kinsmen and close friends and he [Peter] said to them, "You yourselves know how unlawful it is for a Jew to associate with or to visit any one of another nation; but God has shown me that I should not call any man common or unclean. So when I was sent for, I came without objection. Truly I perceive that God shows no partiality, but in every nation any one who fears him and does what is right is acceptable to him." While Peter was still saying this, the Holy Spirit fell on all who heard the word. And the believers from among the circumcised who came with Peter were amazed, because the gift of the Holy Spirit had been poured out even on the Gentiles. For they heard them speaking in tongues and extolling God. Then Peter declared, "Can any one forbid water for baptizing these people who have received the Holy Spirit just as we have?" And he commanded them to be baptized in the name of Jesus Christ.

When Peter returned to Jerusalem, the circumcision party criticized him, saying, "Why did you go to uncircumcised men and eat with them?" But Peter explained to them, and they were silenced. And they glorified God, saying, "Then to the Gentiles also God has granted repentance unto life."

The chain of miracles used to bring about Cornelius' entry into the Church emphasized further to the Jewish disciples that Gentiles, too, were to be included. First, an angel was sent to the Gentile centurion. Then, Peter received a vision in which he was explicitly told not to keep to the Jewish dietary laws, "not to call common what God has cleansed"; by extension, referring also to the Gentiles themselves. Then Peter was explicitly instructed by the Spirit to go to Cornelius' house (an action that hitherto would have been forbidden to a Torah-observant Jew: "You yourselves know how unlawful it is for a Jew to associate with or to visit any one of another nation" [Acts 10:28]). Then the Holy Spirit fell on them in a dramatically visible way and they began speaking in tongues, eliminating all possible doubt about their equal membership in the Church. So although the other disciples initially criticized Peter upon his return for eating with Gentiles, when he recounted the story to them, "they glorified God, saying, 'Then to the Gentiles also God has granted repentance unto life'" (Acts 11:18). Thus was it made known to all that the Gentiles, too, were to be included.

So we see that the message of Christianity originated within the bosom of the Jewish people and was restricted to Jews during Jesus' life. Only after His death was it radiated outward stage by stage—Holy Land Jews, diaspora Jews, proselytes, and finally Gentiles. Although this should be obvious from sacred Scripture, it is sufficiently absent from today's consciousness that many well-meaning people, both Jews and Christians, somehow have the impression that Jesus came "for the Gentiles" and never intended for Jews to become Christian. Nothing could be further from the truth or from the evidence of the historical record. Jesus, as a Jew, came into the very center of the Jewish world precisely to bring them, the Jews, to the fullness of their promised covenant with God through the Jewish Messiah (Jesus), actually restricting His mission and that of His disciples explicitly to Jews until after His death, at which point, by stages, it was propagated outward to the Gentile world.

Following Peter's revelation and the conversion of the centurion and his household, the disciples were open, on their missionary journeys, to making converts from among the Gentiles as well as from among the Jews. Often they met less resistance from Gentiles than from Jews—for instance, as recounted in Acts 11:19–24:

> Now those who were scattered because of the persecution that arose over Stephen traveled as far as Phoenicia and Cyprus and Antioch, speaking the word to none except Jews. But there were some of them, men of Cyprus and Cyrene, who on coming to Antioch spoke to the Greeks also, preaching the Lord Jesus. And the hand of the Lord was with them, and a great number that believed turned to the Lord. News of this came to the ears of the church in Jerusalem, and they sent Barnabas to Antioch. When he came and saw the grace of God, he was glad; and he exhorted them all to remain faithful to the Lord with steadfast purpose; for he was a good man, full of the Holy Spirit and of faith. And a large company was added to the Lord.

Another example is given in Acts 13:44–50:

> The next sabbath almost the whole city [Antioch] gathered together to hear the word of God. But when the Jews saw the multitudes, they were filled with jealousy, and contradicted what was spoken by Paul, and reviled him. And Paul and Barnabas spoke out boldly, saying, "It was necessary that the word of God should be spoken first to you. Since you thrust it from you, and judge yourselves unworthy of eternal life, behold, we turn to the Gentiles. For so the Lord has commanded us, saying, 'I have set you to be a light for the Gentiles, that you may bring salvation to the uttermost parts of the earth.'"
>
> And when the Gentiles heard this, they were glad and glorified the word of God; and as many as were ordained to eternal life believed. And the word of the Lord spread throughout all the region. But the Jews incited the devout women of high standing and the leading men of the city, and stirred up persecution against Paul and Barnabas, and drove them out of their district.

The influx of a large number of Gentiles into the Church caused no small confusion, including whether the new entrants were to keep the Mosaic law with respect to dietary restrictions and, potentially more cripplingly, with respect to circumcision. This problem was serious enough to require the convening of the first council for the new Church, the Council of Jerusalem, circa A.D. 49. What happened is related in Acts 15:1–31 (condensed):

> But some men came down from Judea and were teaching the brethren, "Unless you are circumcised according to the custom of Moses, you cannot be saved." The apostles and the elders gathered together to consider this matter. And after there had been much debate, Peter rose and said to them, "Brethren, you know that in the early days

God made choice among you, that by my mouth the Gentiles should hear the word of the gospel and believe. And God who knows the heart bore witness to them, giving them the Holy Spirit just as he did to us; and he made no distinction between us and them, but cleansed their hearts by faith. Now therefore why do you make trial of God by putting a yoke upon the neck of the disciples which neither our fathers nor we have been able to bear? But we believe that we shall be saved through the grace of the Lord Jesus, just as they will."

Then it seemed good to the apostles and the elders, with the whole church, to choose men from among them and send them to Antioch with the following letter: "It has seemed good to the Holy Spirit and to us to lay upon you no greater burden than these necessary things: that you abstain from what has been sacrificed to idols and from blood and from what is strangled and from unchastity. If you keep yourselves from these, you will do well. Farewell."

So when they were sent off, they went down to Antioch; and having gathered the congregation together, they delivered the letter. And when they read it, they rejoiced at the exhortation.

Thus under the guidance of the Holy Spirit the Council determined that Gentile Christians were under no obligation to be circumcised or to keep the Jewish dietary laws.[13]

The Gospel, which was being extended to the Gentiles, had been rejected by the great majority of the Jews. Even during His life only a small minority had accepted Jesus as the Messiah, and many of those were turned away by His shameful death. One need just compare the vast throngs that

---

[13] It did not, however, address the issue of whether the obligations of Mosaic law were still binding on Jewish Christians.

hailed Jesus' triumphal entry into Jerusalem on Palm Sunday with "Hosanna to the Son of David! Blessed is he who comes in the name of the Lord! Hosanna in the highest!" (Matthew 21:9) with the crowd, most probably consisting of many of the very same persons, which only a few days later shouted, "Away with him, away with him, crucify him!" (John 19:15). Fortunately, the working of the Holy Spirit on Pentecost brought "many thousands"(Acts 21:20) of Jews again to become believers in Jesus. Without such a special grace it would have been very difficult for Jews to accept that Jesus could have been the Messiah, given their erroneous understanding about what would happen when the Messiah came.[14]

The Jewish Drive to Remain Separate

To understand the drive that the Jewish people had, and still have, to maintain their distinct identity separate from the Gentiles, it is necessary to consider the intrinsic difference between the Old Covenant, which God made with the Jews through Abraham, and the New Covenant, which came through Jesus.

The New Covenant is a covenant through faith. It is by faith that one becomes, and remains, a member. Although the sacraments strengthen and confirm membership in the covenant, as well as bring untold graces, they are not the foundation per se of it, as is evidenced by the fact that "baptism by desire" has existed since the early days of the Church.

In contrast to this, the Old Covenant, that given to the Jews, is a covenant through blood, through descent, through membership in the genealogical clan that began with

---

[14] These misconceptions are discussed at length in Chapter 4, "The Messianic Idea in Judaism".

Abraham's son Isaac. It constitutes an ethnic identity more than it characterizes a set of beliefs. Conversion to Judaism consists not so much in subscribing to a set of beliefs (although that too is necessary), as by being adopted into the clan, into the community of Israel. To become a Jew by conversion is to be adopted into the Jewish community, much as being a Jew is to be born into the Jewish community; in both cases, it is defined more by membership than by faith.

This pattern is still seen today. There are many atheist Jews and agnostic Jews, but neither they nor others consider them to not be Jews as a consequence. This pattern is even a part of the law of today's state of Israel. Israel's "Law of Return" grants Jews from anywhere in the world automatic citizenship in the country of Israel, extending to all Jews whatever their personal beliefs. The only exception is Jews who are members of another different, well-defined religious community; at that point, they are no longer considered Jews because they have forfeited membership in the Jewish community by accepting membership in an alternative one.[15]

It is easy to see this characteristic of Jews and Judaism in a negative light: as "elitist" or "separatist" or, at best, unfriendly. So it is important to realize that this central aspect of Judaism was designed into the religion, and perhaps even into the people themselves, by God Himself for good and necessary reasons. It was God who restricted the covenant to the Jews and had them zealously protect it through rigid separation from all Gentiles; it was God who was the source of the Jewish laws in the Old Testament that defined ritual

---

[15] See for instance, the 1990 *Beresford* case in which the Israeli Supreme Court denied the rights of *aliyah* (i.e., of a Jew to immigrate to Israel) to a South African couple who called themselves Hebrew Christians. (See Elias Friedman, *Jewish Identity* [New York: Miriam Press, 1987], pp. 11–25.)

purity and impurity and prevented Jews from mingling with Gentiles; and it was God who in the Old Testament commanded the Jews to wipe out all of the Gentiles in the territory that the Jews were to occupy.

This exclusionary aspect of Judaism was required for the Jews to be able to fulfill the role for which they had been chosen—that of bringing the Messiah, God born as man, into the world. The Jews had to remain a separate and distinct people, remaining true to the worship of the one true God, remaining (relatively) free from spiritual pollution coming from the worship of other gods, and above all maintaining their eugenic identity as the "seed of Abraham" in order to bring about the promise that God made to the "seed of Abraham" (Genesis 12 and 22), to bring blessing to all mankind through bearing the Messiah. They were able to maintain this necessary distinctness for the two thousand years between Abraham and Jesus, a truly miraculous circumstance for an insignificant nomadic tribe in the ancient Near East, one unduplicated in history, and one that required all of the aids that God had given them in both their laws and their character.

This is the basic reason for the peculiarly exclusionary nature of Judaism. It also provides the context for understanding why the first Christians, all of them Jews, had so much trouble grasping that Christianity was for Gentiles as well.

It is clear that the fierce protectiveness of their separate identity which God "built-in" to the Jewish people has not gone away, despite the fact that the Messiah has already come. The survival of the Jews as a distinct people for another two thousand years, without a land and under continual persecution, is no less miraculous. It raises a key question to the Christian understanding of Judaism; one that lies at the heart of Christian missionary activity among Jews, at the heart of Christian theology about Judaism, and even figures in Christian eschatology. That question is: Do the Jews continue to have a role to play in salvation history following Christ, that is, between the first and the Second Coming?[16]

If one takes seriously the words of Jesus in the New Testament, the way of salvation provided for the Jews by Judaism was unambiguously supplanted by the way of salvation offered by Christ. As Jesus said to Jews who rejected Him:

> "Truly, truly, I say to you, he who hears my word and believes him who sent me, has eternal life; he does not come into judgment, but has passed from death to life. . . . You search the scriptures, because you think that in them you have eternal life; and it is they that bear witness to me; yet you refuse to come to me that you may have life. . . . Do not think that I shall accuse you to the Father; it is Moses who accuses you, on whom you set your hope. If you believed Moses, you would believe me, for he wrote of me. But if you do not believe his writings, how will you believe my words?" (abridged from John 5:24–47).

There can be no question about whether Jesus "intended" Christianity to be adopted by Jews in place of Judaism; the fact that He did is continually explicit throughout the New Testament. That God wished for the Jews to accept Christ is evident—remember Jesus' weeping over the tragedy that they, by and large, failed to (Matthew 23:37–39):

---

[16] Among those who believe that they do is Cardinal Ratzinger, Prefect of the Congregation for the Doctrine of the Faith: "Israel still has a mission to accomplish today. We are in fact waiting for the moment when Israel, too, will say Yes to Christ, but we also know that while history still runs its course even this standing at the door fulfills a mission, one that is important for the world" (Cardinal Ratzinger, *God and the World* [San Francisco: Ignatius Press, 2002], pp. 149–50).

"O Jerusalem, Jerusalem, killing the prophets and stoning those who are sent to you! How often would I have gathered your children together as a hen gathers her brood under her wings, and you would not! Behold, your house is forsaken and desolate. For I tell you, you will not see me again, until you say, 'Blessed is he who comes in the name of the Lord.' " [17]

What arrangements God makes to bring Jews to heaven despite their failure to accept Jesus, we leave to His mercy, and the understanding of the Church is that such arrangements exist. However, His *intention* that they follow Jesus is certain.

This still, though, leaves open the question of whether God would like Jews who *do* become followers of Christ to continue to maintain their distinct ethnic identity even after entry into the Church.

This was a very lively issue among the first Christians, and it remains one today among Jews who enter the Church. In the first few centuries of the Church, there were a number of sects of Jewish Christians who held to this belief and kept themselves separate, usually continuing to follow the Jewish ritual laws. The best known among these were the Karaites and the Ebionites. It was in part in reaction to them that the Marcion heresy, which took an incorrectly hostile view toward the Jewish religion, arose. Whenever there is a "mass" influx of Jews to Christianity, the issue arises over again. In the seventeenth century, a large group of Jews converted to Christianity *en masse* following their disillusionment with the false messiah Sabbatai Zevi; they became known as the Frankists and persisted in maintaining themselves as a separate Jewish sect within Christianity with their own practices, surviving

---

[17] This passage is discussed at greater length in Chapter 8, "The Jews and the Second Coming".

as such into the twentieth century. Over the past decades there has been a sizable influx of Jews into the Catholic Church;[18] within this Jewish-Catholic community there is a lively debate about whether or not Jews should maintain a distinct community within the Church.

Three different lines of thought can lead to the conclusion that Jews should remain as a visibly separate community within the Church. (There are parallel issues among non-Catholic "Messianic Jews", but this discussion will focus on Jews who accept the Catholic faith.) The first reason for Jews to continue as a distinct community within the Church is the belief that God still wishes Jews to follow the Jewish laws and festivals, even after they become Christian. This view, however, must be rejected by Jews who enter the Catholic Church as inconsistent with Church doctrine[19] as well as with a number of passages in the New Testament, including Mark 7:19, Acts 10:15, 1 Corinthians 10:27, and Galatians 5:6. (Some non-Catholic, "Messianic" Jews do believe that Jewish law remains binding on Jews who become Christian and have alternative interpretations of the Scripture passages in question.[20])

The second reason is a pragmatic one—that it would facilitate Jewish entry into the Church. As discussed, Jews frequently have a strong inner drive to maintain their Jewish

[18] This subject is further discussed in Chapter 9, "The Return of the Jews".

[19] For instance, Eugenius IV's Papal Bull *Cantata Domino*, from the Council of Florence in 1442 (Denzinger 712). The issue is also addressed by St. Augustine in *Contra Faustum*, bk. 19, chap. 16; by St. Thomas Aquinas in the *Summa Theologica*, II, 1, question 103; and by St. Jerome in his commentary on Galatians (*Super Galat.* ii, 1). All the aforementioned concur that the efficacy of Jewish ritual observance ended with the coming of Christ.

[20] For instance "Jesus and the Food Laws: A Reassessment of Mark 7:19b", by David Rudolph, a Messianic Jew, in *The Evangelical Quarterly*, October 2002, pp. 291–311.

identity, independent of their religious convictions. This drive in itself can make them unwilling to enter the Church even once they believe in Jesus, because they are unwilling to give up their self-identity as Jews. Sometimes they even feel strongly that they want their children to carry on the Jewish identity. Why not allow them to "have their cake and eat it too", so to speak, by establishing a distinct, visible community of Jewish Catholics? This argument claims that it would have several beneficial effects. It would allow Jews who become Catholic to celebrate their Catholic faith while still feeling culturally "at home" in their liturgies. They could satisfy the desire they still have in their hearts to celebrate the major Jewish holidays, worshipping the Most Holy Trinity in forms and contexts with which their "Jewish souls" resonate. And, perhaps most importantly, it could serve as a powerful evangelistic tool to draw other Jews to the faith, by demonstrating that, yes, there are Jews who believe in Christ and the Church, and one does not have to stop being a Jew to be Christian. In summary, this rationale accepts that there is a deep drive, for whatever reason, for Jews to maintain their Jewish identity and tries to accommodate that drive in such a way that it does not prevent Jews from entering the Church.

The third reason is eschatological. Most of the prophecies in the Bible that describe the end times make it clear that the Jews will continue as an identifiable, distinct people until the end of the world—in Christian terms, until the Second Coming. There are even specific prophecies that appear to say that in the last days the Jews will be gathered in from the four corners of the world and brought back to their own homeland in and around Jerusalem.[21] The question is: Does

---

[21] These prophecies are discussed at length in Chapter 8, "The Jews and the Second Coming".

this mean that God *wants* the Jews to remain identifiable as a distinct people, or just that He knows that they *will*? If the former, then the Jews have a religious duty not to disappear *en masse* into the Church. Since God wants Jewish entry into the Church, this would imply that He wants Jews to maintain their distinct identity even after entry into the Church. On the other hand, the prophecies could simply reflect the fact that God knows that the Jewish people will remain as a distinct entity until the Second Coming.

The fact that the Jews have a special role to play until the Second Coming does not *necessarily* imply that Jews who convert should avoid "disappearing" into the Church. It is useful to consider the parallel with yeast and bread. For yeast to do any good in making bread, it must be kept separate from the other ingredients until it is time to use it. However, at that point in the process one must take some of the yeast away from where it has been kept separate and mix it in with the other ingredients until it becomes indistinguishable from the rest of the dough. Perhaps that is the case with the Jews. God gave them unique qualities that have a needed leavening effect on the entire Church. But for those qualities to have their effect, when God grants the grace of conversion to the Jew, He separates him from the rest of the "yeast" and mixes him in with the "dough", that is, removes him from the Jewish community and mixes him into the Church. Just as the yeast does not lose its importance in disappearing into the dough but rather achieves it, so might the Jewish charism realize its unique importance in "disappearing" into the Church. And God in His providence, and in His timing in providing the grace of conversion, knows that the separate supply of yeast—the unconverted Jews—will last until the right time. In this light, let us again consider the words of St. Paul (Romans 11:15–26):

For if their rejection means the reconciliation of the world, what will their acceptance mean but life from the dead? If the dough offered as first fruits is holy, so is the whole lump; and if the root is holy, so are the branches. . . . You will say, "Branches were broken off so that I might be grafted in." That is true. . . . If you have been cut from what is by nature a wild olive tree, and grafted, contrary to nature, into a cultivated olive tree, how much more will these natural branches be grafted back into their own olive tree. . . . I want you to understand this mystery, brethren: a hardening has come upon part of Israel, until the full number of the Gentiles come in, and so all Israel will be saved.

CHAPTER FOUR

The Messianic Idea in Judaism

The Centrality of the Messiah in Judaism

The fact that Judaism has historically defined itself, in large part, around the coming of the Messiah should not be a matter of contention. It has been the consistent testimony of Jews and Judaism, starting with the graphic prophecies of the Old Testament, maintained in the apocryphal writings of the Second Temple period (about 500 B.C. to A.D. 70), continued in the Talmud and by the great Jewish sages of medieval times and into our times by traditional Jews. Consider, for instance, the following, which is taken from a tract on the Messianic hope in Judaism published by the Lubavitchers, one of the largest Hasidic (ultra-orthodox Jewish) sects in the world:

Moshiach Tutorial
(based on classical Torah sources)

Belief in the Era of Moshiach[1] has accompanied the Jewish Nation since its earliest days. It is mentioned countless times in the Torah, in the writings of the prophets, and in the Mishnah and Talmud.[2]

[1] Hebrew for "Messiah".
[2] "Mishnah" refers to a part of the Talmud.

Maimonides[3] includes this tenet in his "Thirteen Principles of Faith" which form the foundation of Jewish belief. Many congregations include these principles at the
conclusion of their morning prayers and say: "I believe
with complete faith in the coming of Moshiach and,
although he may tarry, nonetheless I await his coming
every day."

The theme of Geulah (=Redemption) is found throughout Jewish teachings.... Mention of Moshiach is found
frequently in the prophets, particularly in the prophecies
of Isaiah, aptly named "the Prophet of Redemption". He
provides a detailed description of future events; of the arrival and accomplishments of Moshiach, and of the Geulah process itself.

The belief in the Redemption permeates our rich heritage. Its central role can be assessed by studying the prayer
texts, replete with references to Moshiach and the New
Age. Three times daily we recite the Amidah—a central
prayer composed of nineteen benedictions in which we
ask for all our needs. Six of these are devoted to Geulah;
the ingathering of exiles, the reinstallation of the High
Court, Jerusalem and the Temple rebuilt, the arrival of
Moshiach, and so on.

Three times a day we pray:

"Speedily cause the scion of David your servant to flour-
ish, and increase his power by your salvation, for we hope
for Your salvation every day."

Waiting for Moshiach, anticipating his coming, is not simply
a virtue but a religious obligation. Rambam (Maimonides)
thus rules that whoever does not believe in—and whoever

---

[3] Maimonides (died 1204) was the greatest Jewish rabbi of medieval times.
His codification of Jewish law, *Guide to the Perplexed*, remains authoritative to
this day. He was also known as "Rambam", an acronym formed from his full
name, "Rabbi Moses Ben Maimon".

does not await (eagerly look forward to)—the coming of Moshiach, in effect denies the whole Torah, all the prophets beginning with Moses. (Rambam, *Hilchot Melachim* 11:1)

As stated above, in the popular formulation of his thirteen Principles of Faith (the hymn of Ani Ma'amin), this is put as follows: "I believe with complete faith in the coming of Moshiach and, although he may tarry, nonetheless I await his coming every day, that he will come."

Some authorities view this principle as an integral part of the first of the Ten Commandments ("I am G-d, your G-d,[4] who has taken you out of the land of Egypt, from the house of bondage;" Exodus 20:2), which charges us with the belief of G-d.

In view of this legal obligation to await Moshiach, therefore, one of the first questions an individual is asked on the Day of Divine Judgment is "Did you look forward to salvation?" (*Shabbat* 31a).

This tract relies in large part on the writings of Maimonides, perhaps the greatest single authority of Rabbinic Judaism. In his codification of Jewish law, Maimonides emphasized the obligation for all Jews to believe in the Messiah:

The Messiah will arise and restore the kingdom of David to its former might. He will rebuild the sanctuary and gather the dispersed of Israel.... But whoever does not believe in him or does not await his coming denies not only the rest of the prophets, but also the Torah and our teacher Moses.

This obligation is even one of his fundamental "Thirteen Principles" of the Jewish faith:

[4] Many Jews use this spelling out of reverence for the holiness of God's name.

The twelfth principle concerns the Days of the Messiah. It consists of believing and recognizing as true that he will come and not thinking that he will delay. "Though he tarry, wait for him." One should . . . believe in him . . . magnify and love him, and pray for him, in accordance with the words of all the prophets from Moses to Malachi. And whoever is in doubt concerning him or belittles his glory, he has denied the Torah which explicitly promises his coming.

According to Maimonides this belief in the coming of the Messiah is the central duty of the Jew:

When a man believes in all these fundamental principles, and his faith is thus clarified, he is then part of that "Israel" whom we are to love, pity, and treat, as God commanded, with love and fellowship. Even if a Jew should commit every possible sin out of lust or mastery by his lower nature, he will be punished for his sins but will still have a share in the world to come. He is one of the "sinners in Israel." But if a man gives up any one of these fundamental principles, he has removed himself from the Jewish community. He is an atheist, a heretic, an unbeliever who "cuts among the plantings." We are commanded to hate him and to destroy him. Of him it is said "Shall I not hate these who hate You, O Lord?" (Psalm 139:21).[5]

Unfortunately, in recent times there has been an attempt in some quarters to rewrite the history of Judaism with the intention of showing that Judaism, including Judaism at the

---

[5] Maimonides, *Helek: Sanhedrin, Chapter 10*, trans. Arnold J. Wolf, in "Maimonides on Immortality and the Principles of Judaism", *Judaism*, 1966, cited in *A Maimonides Reader*, Isadore Twersky, ed. (New York: Behrman House, 1972), p. 422.

time of Christ, *never* focused on the coming of the Messiah. Some of this is inspired by the modernist spirit, which has great difficulty in acknowledging the role of supernatural intervention in the affairs of mankind. However, it may also, in part, be motivated by a desire to deter Jews from considering the claims of Christianity. Explicit consideration of the Messianic expectations of Judaism leads to some dangerous questions. How did Jesus' claims compare to the Jewish prophecies? When the Messiah comes, how will he be like Jesus, and how will he differ? Do the necessary conditions for the coming of the Messiah still exist? If not, when did they end? How might that relate to Jesus' death? And so forth. On the other hand, if Jews can be convinced that Judaism never expected the coming of a personal Messiah, then they need give scant consideration to the claims of Christianity. Thus, excising the notion of a personal Messiah from Judaism is a way of protecting it from missionary approaches.

Those who would like to eliminate the expectation of a personal Messiah from Judaism must find an alternative way to deal with the many Messianic texts in Judaism. Some attempt to do so by redefining the Messianic hope as a general hope for the betterment of society and recasting the Jewish nation as a whole as a sort of corporate Messiah that will bring about this social progress. Such was the approach of Moses Hess, an influential Jewish nationalist of the mid-nineteenth century who is credited with converting Karl Marx to socialism. Hess wrote:

Every Jew has the making of a Messiah in himself. . . . Our religion has as its point of departure the enthusiasm of a race who from its appearance on the stage of history has foreseen the final purposes of mankind and which had the foreboding of a messianic time in which the spirit of

humanity will be fulfilled, not only in this or that individual or only partially, but in the social institutions of all
mankind.[6]

This is a very common interpretation of Messianism in
Judaism today. It, however, is contradicted by the evidence
provided by 4,000 years of Jewish writings. Let us turn to
some of those writings.

The Messiah in the Old Testament

There are a great many prophecies of the coming of the Messiah in the Old Testament. Some of these simply announce
His coming—that there will be a Messiah, that He will be
descended from David, that He will "restore" Israel, although the nature of that restoration is at times ambiguous.
Sometimes it seems to be a matter of a restoration of the
sovereignty of the nation, sometimes of peace and tranqui-
lity, sometimes of the relationship with God. Other prophecies in the Old Testament give specific details about the
coming Messiah's life and ministry—that He will come from
Bethlehem, that He will be born of a virgin, that He will
heal the sick and give sight to the blind, and so forth. Finally,
some describe His suffering to atone for the sins of others,
and even give details of His Passion and death.

Most of these passages were seen within Judaism, too, as
referring to the Messiah to come, at least through the time
of the Talmudic sages. However, as the passages were used in

---

[6] Moses Hess, *Rome and Jerusalem* (New York: Philosophical Library, 1958),
pp. 10, 324; quoted in Richard Wurmbrand, *Marx and Satan* (Bartlesville, Okla.:
Living Sacrifice, 1986), pp. 88, 91.

later centuries by Christian apologists[7] to try to convert the Jews, Jewish authorities began to deny that some were Messianic in meaning, despite the unwavering testimony of earlier Jewish authorities. Furthermore for some passages—such as Psalm 22, which is discussed below—Jewish Bibles made use of a different textual variant[8] than that used by Christian Bibles, yielding a very different meaning.

Christian apologists cite over one hundred passages[9] in the Old Testament as Messianic prophecies fulfilled by Jesus. Most of these are acknowledged by Jewish authorities as Messianic prophecies, but many are pointed out to be ambiguous in their predictions or to make predictions not fulfilled by Jesus. Frequently, in the light of faith a prophecy's application to Jesus will be obvious, but a critical eye will see it as not having been fulfilled by Him. Some Jewish apologists claim that the Gospels are fictional accounts written to convert Jews, and so naturally they portray Jesus as fulfilling the Old Testament Messianic prophecies. This leaves unexplained, however, why writers of such fictional Gospels allowed themselves to be martyred for their faith in a Messiah who was a product of their own fiction. Furthermore, the Gospel accounts that we have were circulating widely within the lifetimes of people who witnessed Jesus' ministry and of many more who heard accounts from eyewitnesses. Just as we are

[7] An apologist is someone who presents the reasons for believing a certain point of view (from the Greek "*apologia*" meaning "defense" or "answer"). Hence a Christian apologist is one who gives the reasons for believing in Christianity; a Jewish apologist one who refutes those reasons in favor of Jewish beliefs.

[8] All Bibles are based on hand-copied, ancient manuscripts, which show minor differences in the text. These differences are called "textual variants".

[9] Some go much higher. Alfred Edersheim in his *The Life and Times of Jesus the Messiah* (Grand Rapids, Mich.: Eerdmans, 1953), 2:710–41, puts his count of Messianic prophecies in the Old Testament at 456.

unlikely to accept a fictionalized account of the first man landing on the moon or of Kennedy's assassination, events which occurred 35 to 40 years ago, so too would someone in A.D. 70 be unlikely to accept a fictional account of the crucifixion.

The meanings of some of the Messianic prophecies in the Old Testament are immediately apparent, while others require some effort to understand. In general the understanding of the Messiah builds as one progresses through the Old Testament. This reflects a universal aspect of divine revelation itself. Theological revelation is always progressive in nature—that is, over time, man is granted a fuller and fuller knowledge of God in general, including a fuller understanding of the meaning of prior revelation. This was true in the strictly Jewish context, as well as in the Christian revelation that followed. Abraham was given a fuller knowledge of God, and a greater intimacy with Him, than any of his predecessors had since the fall. Then, when God revealed Himself to Moses in the burning bush, He gave Moses a yet fuller revelation of the divine name, which had been withheld from mankind until then. As God said to Moses: "I appeared to Abraham, to Isaac, and to Jacob, as God Almighty, but by my name the LORD [i.e., Yahweh] I did not make myself known to them" (Exodus 6:3).

And so it is throughout salvation history. God's trinitarian nature was hinted at, but not revealed, in the Old Testament. Many of the central doctrines of Christianity, including the trinitarian nature of God, the divinity of Jesus, and the perpetual virginity of Mary, only gradually became clear in the centuries following Jesus' death. As Jesus Himself said at the Last Supper, "I have yet many things to say to you, but you cannot bear them now. When the Spirit of truth comes, he will guide you into all the truth" (John 16:12–13).

Similarly, the Messianic prophecies in the Old Testament often contain veiled information about the Messiah that became clear only later, through the inspiration of the Talmudic sages, of the Gospel writers, or through the life of Jesus Himself.

When the Messiah would come

In a class by itself is the prophecy found in Daniel 9, which appears to predict that the Messiah will appear about A.D. 26, precisely the date that many scholars give for Jesus' baptism by John and hence the beginning of His public ministry. The prophecy then states that He will be killed between three and four years later—also precisely fulfilled, since Jesus was crucified three and one-third years after His baptism by John. The prophecy concludes with the prediction that a short time later the Temple would be destroyed—again fulfilled by the destruction of the Temple by the Romans in A.D. 70.[10] The passage, however, takes a bit of effort to understand (Daniel 9:24–27):

[10] Some consider Daniel 9 to refer to the persecution of the Jews under Antiochus IV, which began about 171 B.C. (for instance *The New American Bible* [New York: Catholic Book, 1986], footnote to Daniel 9, p. 1035), although (in the words of the same footnote): "The fathers of the Church almost unanimously understood the reference to be to Christ." These are not necessarily mutually exclusive, for a prophecy may have multiple applications, as the footnote to this verse in the Confraternity of Christian Doctrine version explains: "Others ... distinguish three different times of desolation: viz., that under Antiochus; that when the temple was destroyed by the Romans; and the last near the end of the world under Antichrist. To all which, as they suppose, this prophecy may have a relation" (*The Holy Bible*, Douay/ Confraternity Version [New York: P.J. Kenedy and Sons, 1961], p. 965).

Seventy weeks are shortened upon thy people and upon
thy holy city, that transgression may be finished, and sin
may have an end, and iniquity may be abolished; and everlasting justice may be brought; and vision and prophecy
may be fulfilled, and the saint of saints may be anointed.
Know thou therefore, and take notice, that from the going forth of the word to build up Jerusalem again, unto
Christ, the prince, there shall be seven weeks, and sixty-
two weeks. . . . And after sixty-two weeks Christ shall be
slain: and the people that shall deny him shall not be his.
And a people with their leader that shall come, shall destroy the city and the sanctuary; and the end thereof shall
be waste, and after the end of the war the appointed desolation. And he shall confirm the covenant with many, in
one week: and in the half of the week the victim and the
sacrifice shall fail: and there shall be in the temple the
abomination of desolation: and the desolation shall continue even to the consummation, and to the end (Douay-
Rheims translation).

A few keys are necessary to decipher this passage. The Hebrew for "week" is the same word as for "seven", and a day
represents one year; hence "seven weeks" is 49 years, "sixty-
two weeks" is 434 years, and "seventy weeks" is 490 years.
The "going forth of the word to restore and build Jerusalem" refers to the order of King Artaxerxes to rebuild Jerusalem recorded in Ezra 7:11–26, which was given in 458 B.C.
It took exactly "seven weeks", or 49 years, to complete the
building of the walls of Jerusalem, indicated by the fact that
49 years after Artaxerxes' decree, or in 409 B.C., Nehemiah
ended his appointment as governor of Judah. Adding another sixty-two weeks, or 434 years, brings us to A.D. 26,
which is the year which many, including the ancient Church
historian Bishop Eusebius, give as the date of Jesus' baptism

in the Jordan by John and the beginning of His public ministry. Then, in the "half of the week"—that is, three and a half years later—the "the victim and the sacrifice shall fail". And it was about three years and four months after Jesus' baptism that He was crucified, at which time the Temple veil was rent in two as a sign that the Temple sacrifices would henceforth fail. (The fact that the Temple sacrifices failed at the time of the crucifixion is further confirmed in a passage in the Talmud—in *Rosh Hashanah 31b*—which will be discussed later.) Then within a generation, the Romans came and destroyed the Temple and the entire city of Jerusalem and sent the Jews into exile, fulfilling the verse "a people with their leader that shall come, shall destroy the city and the sanctuary; and the end thereof shall be waste, and after the end of the war the appointed desolation".

Where and from whom the Messiah would be born

Passages dealing with from whom and from where the Messiah would come include:

—He will be descended from Judah (Genesis 49:10): "The scepter shall not depart from Judah, nor the ruler's staff from between his feet, until he comes to whom it belongs; and to him shall be the obedience of the peoples."

—He will be a descendant of Jacob (Numbers 24:17): "I see him, but not now; I behold him, but not nigh: a star shall come forth out of Jacob, and a scepter shall rise out of Israel. . . ."

—He will be a descendent of Jesse, the father of King David (Isaiah 11:1–2): "There shall come forth a shoot from the stump of Jesse, and a branch shall grow out of his roots. And the Spirit of the LORD shall rest upon him."

This is fulfilled in Jesus being a descendent of Jesse, which is reflected in the genealogies given in Matthew 1:1–16 and Luke 3:23–38. This prophecy is explicitly cited in Romans 15:12: "and further Isaiah says, 'The root of Jesse shall come, he who rises to rule the Gentiles; in him shall the Gentiles hope.'"

—He will be a descendant of King David (2 Samuel 7:12–13, God speaking to King David): "When your days are fulfilled and you lie down with your fathers, I will raise up your offspring after you, who shall come forth from your body, and I will establish his kingdom. He shall build a house for my name, and I will establish the throne of his kingdom for ever."

His descent from David is also prophesied in Jeremiah 23:5: "Behold, the days are coming, says the LORD, when I will raise up for David a righteous Branch, and he shall reign as king and deal wisely, and shall execute justice and righteousness in the land."

—He will be born in Bethlehem (Micah 5:2): "But you, O Bethlehem Ephrathah, who are little to be among the clans of Judah, from you shall come forth for me one who is to be ruler in Israel, whose origin is from of old, from ancient days."

This was fulfilled by Jesus' birth in Bethlehem, as made explicit in Matthew 2:1–6:

Now when Jesus was born in Bethlehem of Judea in the days of Herod the king, behold, wise men from the East came to Jerusalem, saying, "Where is he who has been born king of the Jews? For we have seen his star in the East, and have come to worship him." When Herod the king heard this, he was troubled, and all Jerusalem with him; and assembling all the chief priests and scribes of the people, he inquired of them where the Christ was to be born. They told him, "In Bethlehem of Judea; for so it is written by the prophet: 'And you, O Bethlehem, in the land of Judah, are by no means least among the rulers of Judah; for from you shall come a ruler who will govern my people Israel.'"

— He will be born of a virgin (Isaiah 7:14): "Therefore the Lord himself will give you a sign. Behold, the virgin shall conceive and bear a son, and shall call his name Immanuel."

This prophecy is explicitly cited in Matthew 1:22–23: "All this took place to fulfill what the Lord had spoken by the prophet: 'Behold, the virgin shall conceive and bear a son, and his name shall be called Emmanuel' (which means, God with us)."

Jewish apologists argue that the underlying Hebrew word for "virgin" in this verse, עַלְמָה ("almah"), is ambiguous and could alternatively simply mean "young woman"; however, a young woman giving birth would hardly constitute a miraculous sign. Furthermore, in the centuries before the birth of Christ an official Jewish translation of the Old Testament into Greek was made for the use of Jews who no longer spoke Hebrew. This translation, known as the Septuagint, uses the Greek word παρθένος ("parthenos"), which unambiguously means "virgin".[11]

---

[11] Jewish apologists argue that the original Septuagint translators (around 250 B.C.) probably translated only the first five books of the Old Testament (the Torah), and the translation of Isaiah was made later. This is, however, a

—Kings would come bringing Him gifts (Psalm 72:1–11): "Give the king thy justice, O God, and thy righteousness to the royal son! May he judge thy people with righteousness, and thy poor with justice! . . . May the kings of Tarshish and of the isles render him tribute, may the kings of Sheba and Seba bring gifts! May all kings fall down before him, all nations serve him!"

This was fulfilled when the three magi from the East came bringing gifts at Jesus' birth (Matthew 2:9–11): "[L]o, the star which they had seen in the East went before them, till it came to rest over the place where the child was. When they saw the star, they rejoiced exceedingly with great joy; and going into the house they saw the child with Mary his mother, and they fell down and worshiped him. Then, opening their treasures, they offered him gifts, gold and frankincense and myrrh."

Prophecies about the Messiah's mission

—His way would be prepared by a precursor (Isaiah 40:3–5, NKJ[12]): "The voice of one crying in the wilderness: 'Prepare the way of the LORD; make straight in the desert a highway for our God. Every valley shall be exalted and every mountain and hill brought low; the crooked places shall be made straight and the rough places smooth. The glory of the LORD shall be revealed, and all flesh shall see it together; for the mouth of the LORD has spoken.' "

---

distinction without a difference, since it is in any case certain that the entire translation was made by Jews for Jews and completed by 150 B.C. at the latest.

[12] NKJ = New King James version.

The precursor is also prophesied in Malachi 3:1: "Behold, I send my messenger to prepare the way before me, and the Lord whom you seek will suddenly come to his temple; the messenger of the covenant in whom you delight, behold, he is coming, says the LORD of hosts."

This role was fulfilled by John the Baptist. Matthew explicitly cites Isaiah 40 (Matthew 3:1–3): "In those days came John the Baptist, preaching in the wilderness of Judea, 'Repent, for the kingdom of heaven is at hand.' For this is he who was spoken of by the prophet Isaiah when he said, 'The voice of one crying in the wilderness: Prepare the way of the Lord, make his paths straight.' "

—He would heal the sick (Isaiah 35:4–7): "Be strong, fear not! Behold, your God will come with vengeance, with the recompense of God. He will come and save you. Then the eyes of the blind shall be opened, and the ears of the deaf unstopped; then shall the lame man leap like a hart, and the tongue of the dumb sing for joy. For waters shall break forth in the wilderness, and streams in the desert; the burning sand shall become a pool, and the thirsty ground springs of water. . . ."

One method used by Jewish apologists to "prove" that Jesus was not the Messiah is to interpret a prophecy like the one contained here, "then shall the lame man leap like a hart, and the tongue of the dumb sing", as being universal in scope. Thus some Rabbis argue that when the Messiah comes *all* the lame and dumb will be healed, rather than just those for whom the Messiah performs the miracle.

Similarly, the following line, "for waters shall break forth in the wilderness, and streams in the desert", is taken in a purely literal, physical sense, rather than in a spiritual one; thus, since Jesus did not perform this miracle, He was not the Messiah. Yet when Jesus spoke to the Samaritan woman at the well He made clear that it referred to "living waters" irrigating the desert of the soul: "Every one who drinks of this water will thirst again, but whoever drinks of the water that I shall give him will never thirst; the water that I shall give him will become in him a spring of water welling up to eternal life" (John 4:13–14).

—He would free the captives (Isaiah 61:1–2): "The Spirit of the Lord GOD is upon me, because the LORD has anointed me to bring good tidings to the afflicted; he has sent me to bind up the brokenhearted, to proclaim liberty to the captives, and the opening of the prison to those who are bound; to proclaim the year of the LORD's favor, and the day of vengeance of our God; to comfort all who mourn."

Jesus explicitly applied this prophecy to Himself in Luke 4:16–21:

> And he came to Nazareth, where he had been brought up; and he went to the synagogue, as his custom was, on the sabbath day. And he stood up to read; and there was given to him the book of the prophet Isaiah. He opened the book and found the place where it was written, "The Spirit of the Lord is upon me, because he has anointed me to preach good news to the poor. He has sent me to proclaim release to the captives and recovering of sight to the blind, to set at liberty those who are oppressed, to proclaim the acceptable year of the Lord." And he closed the book, and gave it back to the attendant, and sat down; and the eyes of all in the synagogue were fixed on him. And he began to say to them, "Today this scripture has been fulfilled in your hearing."

—Where He would live (Isaiah 9:1–2): "But there will be no gloom for her that was in anguish. In the former time he brought into contempt the land of Zebulun and the land of Naphtali, but in the latter time he will make glorious the way of the sea, the land beyond the Jordan, Galilee of the nations. The people who walked in darkness have seen a great light; those who dwelt in a land of deep darkness, on them has light shined."

This was fulfilled when Jesus dwelt in Capernaum, which is in the land of Zebulun and Naphtali. This is made explicit in Matthew 4:13–16: "[A]nd leaving Nazareth he went and dwelt in Capernaum by the sea, in the territory of Zebulun and Naphtali, that what was spoken by the prophet Isaiah might be fulfilled: 'The land of Zebulun and the land of Naphtali, toward the sea, across the Jordan, Galilee of the Gentiles— the people who sat in darkness have seen a great light, and for those who sat in the region and shadow of death light has dawned.' "

—When He came many would resist believing in Him (Isaiah 6:9–10): "Go, and say to this people: 'Hear and hear, but do not understand; see and see, but do not perceive.' Make the heart of this people fat, and their ears heavy, and shut their eyes; lest they see with their eyes, and hear with their ears, and understand with their hearts, and turn and be healed."

Jesus Himself applied this verse to those whose who heard Him but did not become His disciples: (Matthew 13:14–15): "With them indeed is fulfilled the prophecy of Isaiah which says: 'You shall indeed hear but never understand, and you shall indeed see but never perceive. For this people's heart has grown dull, and their ears are heavy of hearing, and their eyes they have closed, lest they should perceive with their eyes, and hear with their ears, and understand with their heart, and turn for me to heal them.' "

And St. John in his Gospel explicitly applies this verse, along with Isaiah 53:1, to Jesus (John 12:37–41): "Though he [Jesus] had done so many signs before them, yet they did not believe in him; it was that the word spoken by the prophet Isaiah might be fulfilled: 'Lord, who has believed our report, and to whom has the arm of the Lord been revealed?' Therefore they could not believe. For Isaiah again said, 'He has blinded their eyes and hardened their heart, lest they should see with their eyes and perceive with their heart, and turn for me to heal them.' Isaiah said this because he saw his glory and spoke of him."

—His character was prophesied (Isaiah 9:6): "For to us a child is born, to us a son is given; and the government will be upon his shoulder, and his name will be called 'Wonderful Counselor, Mighty God, Everlasting Father, Prince of Peace.' "

—His spirit was also prophesied (Isaiah 11:2–4):

And the Spirit of the LORD shall rest upon him, the spirit of wisdom and understanding, the spirit of counsel and might, the spirit of knowledge and the fear of the LORD. And his delight shall be in the fear of the LORD. He shall not judge by what his eyes see, or decide by what his ears hear; but with righteousness he shall judge the poor, and decide with equity for the meek of the earth; and he shall smite the earth with the rod of his mouth, and with the breath of his lips he shall slay the wicked.

Prophecies of the Passion and death

ZECHARIAH

In Chapter 9, Zechariah prophesies that the Messiah will enter Jerusalem in triumph, riding on the colt of an ass (Zechariah 9:9): "Rejoice greatly, O daughter of Zion! Shout aloud, O daughter of Jerusalem! Lo, your king comes to you; triumphant and victorious is he, humble and riding on an ass, on a colt the foal of an ass."

This prophecy was fulfilled on Palm Sunday and explicitly cited as such in John 12:12–16:

> The next day a great crowd who had come to the feast heard that Jesus was coming to Jerusalem. So they took branches of palm trees and went out to meet him, crying, "Hosanna! Blessed is he who comes in the name of the Lord, even the King of Israel!" And Jesus found a young ass and sat upon it; as it is written, "Fear not, daughter of Zion; behold, your king is coming, sitting on an ass's colt!" His disciples did not understand this at first; but when Jesus was glorified, then they remembered that this had been written of him and had been done to him.

Zechariah 12 and 13 contain several stunning prophecies intimately tied to Jesus' crucifixion. On the simplest level, Zechariah 12:10 is a straightforward reference to the crucifixion of Jesus: "[W]hen they look on him whom they have pierced, they shall mourn for him, as one mourns for an only child, and weep bitterly over him, as one weeps over a first-born."

The Gospel of John quotes this verse as fulfilled at the crucifixion (John 19:37): "And again another scripture says, 'They shall look on him whom they have pierced.'"

Yet one can legitimately point out, as contemporary Jewish anti-missionaries do,[13] that Zechariah 12:10 was not fulfilled at the crucifixion, since those who pierced Jesus did *not* mourn over Him, but in fact rejoiced at His fate. However, this simply draws attention to the fact that this prophecy is even more impressive than it initially appears—it not only refers to the first coming of Jesus and His crucifixion, but also to His Second Coming, which will be preceded by the large scale conversion of the Jews. This final conversion of the Jews[14] was prophesied by Jesus Himself on the eve of His crucifixion, when He said (Matthew 23:37–39): "O Jerusalem, Jerusalem ... you will not see me again, until you say, 'Blessed is he who comes in the name of the Lord.' "

It was also predicted by St. Paul in Romans 11:25–26: "I want you to understand this mystery, brethren: a hardening has come upon part of Israel, until the full number of the Gentiles come in, and so all Israel will be saved."

It is *then* that they will "look on him whom they have pierced, ... mourn for him, ... and weep bitterly over him".[15]

The fact that Zechariah 12:10 takes place at the time of the Second Coming, rather than at the time of the crucifixion, is made clear by the verses that precede and follow it, for they beautifully describe Israel's final, miraculous victory

---

[13] For instance, Rabbi Michael Skobac of Toronto, *Jews for Judaism* Education Director, in his counter-missionary audiotape on Zechariah 12, available from *Jews for Judaism*, P.O. Box 15059, Baltimore, MD.

[14] The conversion of the Jews that is to precede the Second Coming is discussed at length in Chapter 9, "The Return of the Jews".

[15] It is also true that the one who most literally did "pierce" Jesus, the centurion at the foot of the cross who thrust a lance into Jesus' side, experienced an instantaneous conversion and "mourned for him": "Truly this man was the Son of God!" (John 19:34–37; Matthew 27:37; Mark 15:39).

followed by the Lord's coming in glory. Zechariah 12:6–14:9 reads (extracts):

"On that day I will make the clans of Judah like a blazing pot in the midst of wood, like a flaming torch among sheaves; and they shall devour to the right and to the left all the peoples round about, while Jerusalem shall still be inhabited in its place, in Jerusalem. And the LORD will give victory to the tents of Judah. . . . On that day the LORD will put a shield about the inhabitants of Jerusalem so that the feeblest among them on that day shall be like David, and the house of David shall be like God, like the angel of the LORD, at their head. And on that day I will seek to destroy all the nations that come against Jerusalem. And I will pour out on the house of David and the inhabitants of Jerusalem a spirit of compassion and supplication, so that, when they look on him whom they have pierced, they shall mourn for him, as one mourns for an only child, and weep bitterly over him, as one weeps over a first-born. On that day the mourning in Jerusalem will be as great as the mourning for Hadadrimmon in the plain of Megiddo. . . .

"And if one asks him, 'What are these wounds on your back?' he will say, 'The wounds I received in the house of my friends.' Then the LORD will go forth and fight against those nations as when he fights on a day of battle. On that day his feet shall stand on the Mount of Olives which lies before Jerusalem on the east; and the Mount of Olives shall be split in two from east to west by a very wide valley; so that one half of the Mount shall withdraw northward, and the other half southward. . . . Then the LORD your God will come, and all the holy ones with him. . . . And there shall be continuous day (it is known to the LORD), not day and not night, for at evening time there shall be light. . . . And the LORD will become king over all the earth; on that day the LORD will be one and his name one."

Note the reference to the "wounds on [his] back . . . received in the house of [his] friends". This is, of course, a prophecy of Jesus' scourging, which is also prophesied in Isaiah 53:5: "But he was wounded for our transgressions, he was bruised for our iniquities; upon him was the chastisement that made us whole, and with his stripes we are healed."

BOOK OF WISDOM

The book of Wisdom contains a beautiful, profound prophecy about what will cause the Messiah to be persecuted (Wisdom 2:12–24):

[12] "Let us lie in wait for the righteous man, because he is inconvenient to us and opposes our actions; he reproaches us for sins against the law, and accuses us of sins against our training.

[13] He professes to have knowledge of God, and calls himself a child of the Lord.

[14] He became to us a reproof of our thoughts;

[15] the very sight of him is a burden to us, because his manner of life is unlike that of others, and his ways are strange.

[16] We are considered by him as something base, and he avoids our ways as unclean; he calls the last end of the righteous happy, and boasts that God is his father.

[17] Let us see if his words are true, and let us test what will happen at the end of his life;

[18] for if the righteous man is God's son, he will help him, and will deliver him from the hand of his adversaries.

[19] Let us test him with insult and torture, that we may find out how gentle he is, and make trial of his forbearance.

[20] Let us condemn him to a shameful death, for, according to what he says, he will be protected."

[21] Thus they reasoned, but they were led astray, for their wickedness blinded them,

[22] and they did not know the secret purposes of God, nor hope for the wages of holiness, nor discern the prize for blameless souls;

[23] for God created man for incorruption, and made him in the image of his own eternity,

[24] but through the devil's envy death entered the world, and those who belong to his party experience it.

Since virtually every line is fulfilled by Jesus, let us go through the passage verse by verse:

[12] "Let us lie in wait for the righteous man, because he is inconvenient to us and opposes our actions; he reproaches us for sins against the law, and accuses us of sins against our training."

Jesus made many such reproaches, such as (Matthew 23: 23–28):

"Woe to you, scribes and Pharisees, hypocrites! for you tithe mint and dill and cumin, and have neglected the weightier matters of the law, justice and mercy and faith;

these you ought to have done, without neglecting the others. You blind guides, straining out a gnat and swallowing a camel! Woe to you, scribes and Pharisees, hypocrites! for you cleanse the outside of the cup and of the plate, but inside they are full of extortion and rapacity. You blind Pharisee! first cleanse the inside of the cup and of the plate, that the outside also may be clean. Woe to you, scribes and Pharisees, hypocrites! for you are like whitewashed tombs, which outwardly appear beautiful, but within they are full of dead men's bones and all uncleanness. So you also outwardly appear righteous to men, but within you are full of hypocrisy and iniquity."

Continuing with the passage from Wisdom 2:

[13] "He professes to have knowledge of God, and calls himself a child of the Lord.

[14] He became to us a reproof of our thoughts. . . ."

Jesus frequently reproved others for their unspoken thoughts, such as in Matthew 9:2–4:

And behold, they brought to him a paralytic, lying on his bed; and when Jesus saw their faith he said to the paralytic, "Take heart, my son; your sins are forgiven." And behold, some of the scribes said to themselves, "This man is blaspheming." But Jesus, knowing their thoughts, said, "Why do you think evil in your hearts?"

Verse 16 in Wisdom 2:

[16] "[H]e calls the last end of the righteous happy, and boasts that God is his father."

This was obviously fulfilled by Jesus; consider Jesus' words from the Sermon on the Mount (Matthew 5:10): "Blessed are those who are persecuted for righteousness' sake, for theirs

THE MESSIANIC IDEA IN JUDAISM

is the kingdom of heaven." The Greek word here translated as "blessed" (μακάριοι) can also be translated "happy".

Jesus also not only "boast[ed] that God is his father", but John makes clear that that was one of the reasons His death was sought (John 5:18): "This was why the Jews sought all the more to kill him, because he not only broke the sabbath but also called God his Father, making himself equal with God."

Verses 17 and 18 were also perfectly fulfilled in the Passion and death of Jesus:

> [17] "Let us see if his words are true, and let us test what will happen at the end of his life;

> [18] for if the righteous man is God's son, he will help him, and will deliver him from the hand of his adversaries."

For when Jesus was dying on the Cross (Matthew 27:39–43)

> those who passed by derided him, wagging their heads and saying, "You who would destroy the temple and build it in three days, save yourself! If you are the Son of God, come down from the cross." So also the chief priests, with the scribes and elders, mocked him, saying, "He saved others; he cannot save himself. He is the King of Israel; let him come down now from the cross, and we will believe in him. He trusts in God; let God deliver him now, if he desires him; for he said, 'I am the Son of God.' "

The next section was all too obviously fulfilled in the Passion:

> [19] "Let us test him with insult and torture, that we may find out how gentle he is, and make trial of his forbearance.

> [20] Let us condemn him to a shameful death, for, according to what he says, he will be protected."

²¹ Thus they reasoned, but they were led astray, for their wickedness blinded them,

²² and they did not know the secret purposes of God, nor hope for the wages of holiness, nor discern the prize for blameless souls;

²³ for God created man for incorruption, and made him in the image of his own eternity,

²⁴ but through the devil's envy death entered the world, and those who belong to his party experience it.

Both Matthew and Mark explicitly mention Jesus' silence as well as the underlying motive of envy. From Matthew 27:12–18:

> But when he was accused by the chief priests and elders, he made no answer. Then Pilate said to him, "Do you not hear how many things they testify against you?" But he gave him no answer, not even to a single charge; so that the governor wondered greatly. . . . For he knew that it was out of envy that they had delivered him up.

The Lemann brothers[16] made the touching point that Jesus' silence before the High Priest was motivated by His profound respect for the office of the Jewish Priesthood. Mosaic law forbids compelling a witness to testify against himself. It was because Jesus did not want to put the High Priest in the position of sinning against that law that He refused to answer the High Priest's questions even though beaten for it (John 18:19–23):

---

[16] In Augustin and Joseph Lemann, *Valeur de l'Assemblee qui Prononca la Peine de la Mort contre Jesus-Christ*, reprint: Villegenon, France: Editions Ste. Jeanne d'Arc, 1997.

The high priest then questioned Jesus about his disciples and his teaching. Jesus answered him, "I have spoken openly to the world; I have always taught in synagogues and in the temple, where all Jews come together; I have said nothing secretly. Why do you ask me? Ask those who have heard me, what I said to them; they know what I said." When he had said this, one of the officers standing by struck Jesus with his hand, saying, "Is that how you answer the high priest?" Jesus answered him, "If I have spoken wrongly, bear witness to the wrong; but if I have spoken rightly, why do you strike me?"

Jesus acquiesced only when the High Priest ordered Him to answer in the name of God.

ISAIAH 53—THE SUFFERING SERVANT

Many consider Isaiah 53 to hold the most beautiful and stirring depiction of Jesus and His Passion in the Old Testament, or, indeed, in all of Scripture (Isaiah 53:1–12):

> [1] Who has believed what we have heard? And to whom has the arm of the LORD been revealed?

> [2] For he grew up before him like a young plant, and like a root out of dry ground; he had no form or comeliness that we should look at him, and no beauty that we should desire him.

> [3] He was despised and rejected by men; a man of sorrows, and acquainted with grief; and as one from whom men hide their faces he was despised, and we esteemed him not.

⁴ Surely he has borne our griefs and carried our sorrows; yet we esteemed him stricken, smitten by God, and afflicted.

⁵ But he was wounded for our transgressions, he was bruised for our iniquities; upon him was the chastisement that made us whole, and with his stripes we are healed.

⁶ All we like sheep have gone astray; we have turned every one to his own way; and the LORD has laid on him the iniquity of us all.

⁷ He was oppressed, and he was afflicted, yet he opened not his mouth; like a lamb that is led to the slaughter, and like a sheep that before its shearers is dumb, so he opened not his mouth.

⁸ By oppression and judgment he was taken away; and as for his generation, who considered that he was cut off out of the land of the living, stricken for the transgression of my people?

⁹ And they made his grave with the wicked and with a rich man in his death, although he had done no violence, and there was no deceit in his mouth.

¹⁰ Yet it was the will of the LORD to bruise him; he has put him to grief; when he makes himself an offering for sin, he shall see his offspring, he shall prolong his days; the will of the LORD shall prosper in his hand;

¹¹ he shall see the fruit of the travail of his soul and be satisfied; by his knowledge shall the righteous one, my servant, make many to be accounted righteous; and he shall bear their iniquities.

¹² Therefore I will divide him a portion with the great, and he shall divide the spoil with the strong; because he

poured out his soul to death, and was numbered with the transgressors; yet he bore the sin of many, and made intercession for the transgressors.

In his narrative of the Passion, John cites verse 1 (John 12:37–38): "Though he had done so many signs before them, yet they did not believe in him; it was that the word spoken by the prophet Isaiah might be fulfilled: 'Lord, who has believed our report, and to whom has the arm of the Lord been revealed?'"

Matthew 8:16–17 applies verse 4 to Jesus: "That evening they brought to him many who were possessed with demons; and he cast out the spirits with a word, and healed all who were sick. This was to fulfill what was spoken by the prophet Isaiah, 'He took our infirmities and bore our diseases.'"

Mark explicitly applies verse 12 to Jesus (Mark 15:27–28): "And with him they crucified two robbers, one on his right and one on his left. And the scripture was fulfilled which says, 'He was reckoned [numbered] with the transgressors.'"

The rest of this passage was also stunningly fulfilled in Jesus' Passion and death. He was certainly despised and rejected by men (John 19:15): "Away with him, away with him, crucify him! . . . We have no king but Caesar." From the extensive beating and scourging He certainly "had no form or comeliness . . . no beauty"(v. 2). The scourging was the "stripes [by which] we are healed" (v. 5). Before the High Priest's accusation Jesus was silent (Matthew 26:62–63): "And the high priest stood up and said, 'Have you no answer to make? What is it that these men testify against you?' But Jesus was silent", thus fulfilling verse 7. After dying between the two thieves, Jesus was buried in a grave provided by the wealthy Joseph of Arimathea (Matthew 27:57–60): "When it was

evening, there came a rich man from Arimathea, named Joseph, who also was a disciple of Jesus. He went to Pilate and
asked for the body of Jesus. Then Pilate ordered it to be
given to him. And Joseph took the body and wrapped it in
a clean linen shroud and laid it in his own new tomb", thus
fulfilling verse 9, "[making] his grave with the wicked and
with a rich man in his death".

This chapter of Isaiah, known as the "Suffering Servant"
passage, has been used for centuries to demonstrate to Jews
that Jesus was the Messiah foretold in the Old Testament.
The passage was always seen by ancient Rabbinic commentators as referring to the person of the Messiah; however,
more recently Jews have asserted that the "suffering servant"
in the passage refers not to an individual, but to the Jewish
nation as a whole. This, however, is contradicted by the fact
that within the passage itself a contrast is drawn between the
Jewish nation (the "*we*"), and the one who bore our stripes
to make "*us*" whole.

PSALM 22

This psalm is a lengthy and beautiful description of Jesus'
agony:

> [1] My God, my God, why hast thou forsaken me? Why
> art thou so far from helping me, from the words of my
> groaning? . . .
>
> [6] But I am a worm, and no man; scorned by men, and
> despised by the people.
>
> [7] All who see me mock at me, they make mouths at me,
> they wag their heads;

[8] "He committed his cause to the LORD; let him deliver him, let him rescue him, for he delights in him!" . . .

[14] I am poured out like water, and all my bones are out of joint; my heart is like wax, it is melted within my breast;

[15] my strength is dried up like a potsherd, and my tongue cleaves to my jaws; thou dost lay me in the dust of death.

[16] Yea, dogs are round about me; a company of evildoers encircle me; they have pierced my hands and feet—

[17] I can count all my bones—they stare and gloat over me;

[18] they divide my garments among them, and for my raiment they cast lots. . . .

The identification of this psalm with the Passion is made explicit by the fact that the first verse is actually quoted by Jesus on the cross (Matthew 27:46): "And about the ninth hour Jesus cried with a loud voice, 'Eli, Eli, lama sabachthani?' that is, 'My God, my God, why hast thou forsaken me?'"

Verse by verse, every image and incident was played out in the crucifixion just as described in this psalm. It is hard to imagine a prophetic description of Jesus' agony more specific than verse 16, "they have pierced my hands and feet". Yet Jewish editions of the Bible translate this verse very differently; it will be instructive to look in some detail at the controversy that surrounds the translation.

Prior to the sixteenth century, all copies of the Old Testament were, of course, handwritten,[17] which although remarkably accurate, showed occasional small—sometimes a

[17] Johann Gutenberg invented the printing press around the year 1450.

single letter—differences one from another. These differences
are known as "textual variants". The Jewish translation of
the Old Testament is based on copies of the Old Testament
that show a different textual variant than the Christians use.
The word for "they pierced" in the Christian version—כארו
(phonetically "*cah-roo*")—differs by just a single letter (actually, just a part of a single letter) from the one in the Jewish
version, כְּאֲרִי ("*ca-ah-ree*"), which means "like a lion."

The difference is very small—just the length of the tail on
the final letter of the word, which in the Christian version is
a "*vav*" (ו) and in the Jewish version a "*yod*" (י).[18] Some
medieval Hebrew manuscripts show one, some the other,
and yet others, כרו, which would be a more correct spelling
for "they pierced". Since even the oldest manuscripts we
have date only from around the eleventh century and thus
have themselves been copied and recopied numerous times
since the days of Jesus (for a copy typically lasts only a few
hundred years), there have been ample opportunities for the
introduction of both intentional and accidental errors.

Since such errors are a frequent issue in Old Testament
textual criticism, the standard practice is to look at early Greek,
Syriac, and Latin translations. These were based on much
older Hebrew originals than we have today. Furthermore,
the Greek and Syriac translations were made by Jews *before*
Christ and hence are free from the danger of having been
influenced by Christian/Jewish polemics. Both the Greek
and Syriac translations read "they pierced", as does Jerome's
Latin Vulgate, which dates from the fourth century. It is
difficult to understand how the Greek and Syriac transla-

---

[18] Hebrew is written from right to left, the reverse of English.

tions, made in the period between the Old and the New Testaments, could be incorrect.[19] Furthermore, one can legitimately ask what sense "like a lion, my hands and my feet" makes, and suspect that, at some point in the repeated recopying of the text between the first and the eleventh centuries, an enterprising Jewish scribe might have taken it upon himself to make the slight change of shortening of the stroke of the "*vav*" (ו) to turn it into a "*yod*" (י), and so change "they pierced" into "like a lion". This inevitably calls to mind the words of Jesus (Matthew 5:17–18): "Do not think that I have come to abolish the law or the prophets; I have come not to abolish but to fulfill. For truly I tell you, until heaven and earth pass away, not one letter, *not one stroke of a letter*, will pass from the law until all is accomplished" (NRSV, emphasis added).

Verse 18, "they divide my garments among them, and for my raiment they cast lots", was equally literally fulfilled at the crucifixion (John 19:23–24):

> When the soldiers had crucified Jesus they took his garments and made four parts, one for each soldier; also his tunic. But the tunic was without seam, woven from top to bottom; so they said to one another, "Let us not tear it, but cast lots for it to see whose it shall be." This was to fulfill the scripture, "They parted my garments among them, and for my clothing they cast lots."

---

[19] Unless they were intentionally distorted by Christians, which is the accusation sometimes made by Jewish apologists. They point out that the spelling of "they pierced" is incorrect, and it is not the usual word used for "to pierce" in the Old Testament. For a good analysis of the underlying linguistic issues, see Walter Kaiser, *The Messiah in the Old Testament* (Grand Rapids, Mich.: Zondervan, 1995), p. 115, note.

PSALM 34

Psalm 34 contains the line, referring to a "righteous" man being sorely afflicted: "He keeps all his bones; not one of them is broken" (v. 20).

St. John associates this line with Jesus on the Cross. Soldiers had been sent out by Pilate to break Jesus' legs, that He might die more quickly (John 19:31): "Since it was the day of Preparation, in order to prevent the bodies from remaining on the cross on the sabbath (for that sabbath was a high day), the Jews asked Pilate that their legs might be broken, and that they might be taken away."

Death by crucifixion could take several days. However, if the victim's legs were broken death would come almost immediately, since he would be unable to push up with his legs to breathe. St. John explicitly quotes Psalm 34 in his account of the crucifixion (John 19:33–36):

> [B]ut when they came to Jesus and saw that he was already dead, they did not break his legs. But one of the soldiers pierced his side with a spear, and at once there came out blood and water. He who saw it has borne witness—his testimony is true, and he knows that he tells the truth—that you also may believe. For these things took place that the scripture might be fulfilled, "Not a bone of him shall be broken."

The Messiah in the Pseudo-Epigraphia

The pseudo-epigraphia are Jewish writings that did not make it into the canon of Scripture—that is, they were not accepted by the Jewish authorities as authentic Scripture when the Jewish canon was decided on. Most were written in the

Second Temple period (approximately 400 B.C. to A.D. 70). Even though not genuine sacred Scripture, they must necessarily reflect the beliefs generally held by Jews during that period. Thus the Messianic prophecies in the pseudo-epigraphia provide evidence of the Messianic beliefs held by Jews in the Second Temple period.

The Ethiopic book of Enoch is highly Messianic in tone, as shown in following passage from Chapter 46:

> I saw there the Ancient of Days, and his head was like pure wool, and with Him was another, whose countenance was like the visage of a Son of Man, and whose face was full of graciousness like one of the holy angels. And I asked one of the angels who went with me, and he showed me all the hidden things concerning the Son of Man: who he was, whence he came, and why he went with the Ancient of Days. And he answered me and said unto me: This is the Son of Man who hath righteousness, with whom dwelleth righteousness, and who revealeth all the treasures of hidden things; for the God of spirits hath chosen him, and his lot hath surpassed everything before the God of spirits in uprightness forever. This Son of Man, whom you have seen, will raise up the kings and the mighty from their seats, and the strong from their thrones. He will loosen the bands [loins] of the strong and break the teeth of sinners. He will expel kings from their thrones and their kingdoms, because they do not extol and praise [God], and do not acknowledge whence the kingdom was bestowed upon them. He will make vain the arrogance of tyrants and shame will fill them. Darkness will be their dwelling and worms will be their bed (46:1–6).[20]

[20] Joseph Klausner, *The Messianic Idea in Israel* (New York: MacMillan, 1955), p. 291.

Messianic prophecies also run through the Psalms of Solomon, probably written shortly after 48 B.C. Christians will have no difficulty seeing Jesus depicted in the following passage:

> Behold, O LORD and raise up unto them their king,
>   the son of David,
> At the time in which thou seest, O God, that he
>   may reign over Israel Thy servant.
> Gird him with strength to shatter unrighteous rulers,
> And to purge Jerusalem from the nations that trample
>   her down to destruction.
> Wisely, righteously he shall thrust out sinners from
>   their inheritance,
> He shall destroy the pride of the sinner as a potter's
>   vessel.
> With a rod of iron he shall break in pieces all their
>   substance,
> He shall destroy the godless nations with the word
>   of his mouth;
> At his rebuke nations shall flee before him,
> And he shall reprove sinners for the thoughts of their
>   heart.
> He shall gather together a holy people, whom he
>   shall lead in righteousness,
> And he shall judge the tribes of the people
>   that has been sanctified by the LORD his God . . .
> For all shall be holy and their king—the anointed of
>   the LORD . . .
> For he will smite the earth with the word of his
>   mouth forever.
> He will bless the people of the LORD with wisdom
>   and gladness,

And he himself will be pure from sin, so that he may
   rule a great people,
So that he may rebuke rulers, and remove sinners by
   the might of his word.
Throughout his days he will not stumble before his
   God;
For God will make him mighty by means of [His]
   holy spirit,
And wise in the counsel of understanding, with
   strength and righteousness. . . .
He will be shepherding the flock of the LORD
   faithfully and righteously,
And will suffer none among them to stumble in their
   pasture.
He will lead them aright, and there will be no pride
   in them in doing violence in their midst.
This will be the majesty of the king of Israel whom
   God knoweth
To raise him up over the house of Israel to instruct
   them.
His words [shall be] more refined than choicest
   gold,
In the assemblies he will judge the peoples, the tribes
   of the sanctified.
His words like the words of the holy ones in the midst
   of sanctified peoples.
Blessed be they that shall be in those days,
To see the good fortune of Israel, which God shall
   bring to pass in the gathering together of the
   tribes! (17:21–44).[21]

---

[21] Ibid., pp. 319–22.

The Assumption of Moses, written around A.D. 4–6, contains a prophecy of what the Messiah will find when He comes. Quoting from a Jewish scholar's description of this prophecy:

> [When the Messiah comes], over the people of Judea will rule evil and sinful men, gluttons and drunkards, who will be, besides all this, flatterers and hypocrites. They will be "removers of the landmark, provokers of strife, men of deceit," and "devourers of the inheritance of the poor" (or "of widows")—yet they will boast about their deeds of mercy: "Their hands and their minds are busy with unclean things, and their mouth speaks arrogance, while they furthermore say, 'Do not touch me, lest you pollute me!'" (7:9–10).[22]

These accusations against the "rulers of Judea" in the time of the Messiah are strongly reminiscent of the accusations that Jesus made against the Jewish rulers of His day. Consider, for instance:

> Matthew 23:23–28: "Woe to you, scribes and Pharisees, hypocrites! for you tithe mint and dill and cumin, and have neglected the weightier matters of the law, justice and mercy and faith; these you ought to have done, without neglecting the others. You blind guides, straining out a gnat and swallowing a camel! Woe to you, scribes and Pharisees, hypocrites! for you cleanse the outside of the cup and of the plate, but inside they are full of extortion and rapacity. You blind Pharisee! first cleanse the inside of the cup and of the plate, that the outside also may be clean. Woe to you, scribes and Pharisees, hypocrites! for you are like whitewashed tombs, which outwardly appear

---

[22] Ibid., pp. 325–26.

beautiful, but within they are full of dead men's bones and all uncleanness. So you also outwardly appear righteous to men, but within you are full of hypocrisy and iniquity."

Luke 20:46–47: "Beware of the scribes, who like to go about in long robes, and love salutations in the market places and the best seats in the synagogues and the places of honor at feasts, who devour widows' houses and for a pretense make long prayers. They will receive the greater condemnation."

The Messiah in the Talmud

The Talmud is the Jewish oral law, put in written form during the period around A.D. 200 to 600.[23] It consists largely of Rabbinic discussions on a wide range of theology, ethics, and law, based on the Torah, and is supposed to represent oral teaching received by Moses and passed on by him. In Judaism, it holds an authority second only to the canonical Jewish Scriptures. In fact, the Talmud itself says: "My son, be more careful in the observance of the words of the Scribes [i.e., the Talmud] than in the words of the Torah" (*Erubin 21b*).[24] The Talmud makes very clear that the expectation for the coming Messiah is for an *individual*. It also contains other prophetical insights about the Messiah that are of particular interest to Christians. Let us then turn to the Talmud to examine some of what it has to say about the Messiah.

The Talmud consists of sixty-three separate books, or "tractates". The one that deals most with the coming of the

---

[23] Jacob Neusner, *Introduction to Rabbinic Literature* (New York: Doubleday, 1994), p. xx.

[24] All Talmud quotations are from *The Babylonian Talmud*, Rabbi Dr. Epstein, ed. (London: Soncino Press, 1935–1938).

Messiah is the tractate *Sanhedrin*; it is from there that most of the following extracts have been drawn. The following discussion does not exhaust the Talmud's commentary on the Messiah; it simply represents some that is of particular interest from a Christian perspective.

When the Messiah will come

There is extensive discussion in the Talmud about when the Messiah will appear. Although the precise time cannot be known—"three things come unawares: Messiah, a found article and a scorpion" (*Sanhedrin 97a*)—the prevailing conditions at the time He comes are known:

> Thus hath Rabbi Johanan said: In the generation when the son of David [i.e., the Messiah] will come, scholars will be few in number, and as for the rest, their eyes will fail through sorrow and grief. Multitudes of trouble and evil decrees will be promulgated anew, each new evil decree will be promulgated anew, each new evil coming with haste before the other has ended.
>
> It has been taught, Rabbi Judah said: In the generation when the son of David comes, the house of assembly will be for harlots, Galilee in ruins, Gablan lie desolate, the border inhabitants wander about from city to city, receiving no hospitality, the wisdom of the scribes in disfavor, God-fearing men despised, people be dog-faced [i.e., as shameless as dogs], and truth entirely lacking.
>
> It has been taught: Rabbi Nehemiah said: In the generation of Messiah's coming impudence will increase, esteem be perverted, the vine yield its fruit, yet shall wine be dear, and the Kingdom will be converted to heresy with none to rebuke them (*Sanhedrin 97a–b*).

I leave it up to the reader to decide how closely these conditions were fulfilled at the time that Jesus came, based on the descriptions in the Gospels. How "few in number" were the true "scholars" prepared to recognize Him? How multitudinous were the "evil decrees", beginning (perhaps) with Herod's slaughter of the innocents and ending with Pilate's condemnation? Were the "houses of assembly" for harlots? What state was the "wisdom of the scribes" in? Were Jesus and the disciples "God-fearing men" who were "despised"? Was "truth entirely lacking" (Pilate: "What is truth?"—John 18:38)? Could the description of a "Kingdom converted to heresy with none to rebuke them" refer to the rejection of the Messiah itself ?

There is also speculation in the Talmud about the date when the Messiah is to appear. Some of it is particularly interesting for those who accept that Jesus was the prophesied Messiah. According to Jewish reckoning, the world was created in what is in our calendar 3762 B.C. In that light, consider the following:

> The Tanna debe Eliyyahu teaches: The world is to exist six thousand years. In the first two thousand there was desolation; two thousand years the Torah flourished; and the next two thousand years is the Messianic era, but through our many sins all these years have been lost (*Sanhedrin 97a–b*).

By Jewish reckoning, the world was created about 4,000 years before Christ (our 3762 B.C.). About 2,000 years later Judaism began with Abraham, and after another 2,000 years Jesus came. Hence 2,000 years of desolation (between Adam and Abraham, the start of the Jewish covenant); 2,000 years of Torah (the Jewish covenant); and then 2,000 years of the Messianic era (Christianity), to be followed by the final redemption (the Second Coming). Thus this teaching works out almost perfectly from a Christian perspective, if the Second Coming is near. Poignantly, the Talmud goes on to say, "[B]ut through our many sins all these years have been lost." Were those years lost in that the Messiah did not come, or were they lost in that He was not recognized by those to whom He came?

The discussion of when the Messiah is to appear concludes with: "Rab said: All the predestined dates [for redemption] have passed" (*Sanhedrin 97b*). If only they drew the logical conclusion—as the Lemann brothers did—from this observation!

What will happen when the Messiah comes

A common objection that Jews make against Jesus being the Messiah is that the Jewish expectations for what will happen when the Messiah comes—their expectations for "the Messianic Age"—have not occurred. These expectations are largely based on the exposition of the Old Testament in the Talmud. Yet in the Talmud there is a fundamental ambiguity about what will happen when the Messiah comes. "This world" (*Ha-Olam Hazeh*) is repeatedly contrasted with "the world to come" (*Ha-Olam HaBah*), but it is highly ambiguous whether "the world to come" refers to the world after the Messiah comes (Redemption) or the world after the resurrection of the dead (in Christian eschatology the world after the Second Coming). The Old Testament prophecies in this area are quite cryptic. As the editor of the Soncino edition of the Talmud puts it:

> The conception of what is to be understood by the future world is rather vague in the Talmud. In general, it is the

opposite of "HaOlam Hazeh," this world. In Ber I, 5 "this world" is opposed to the days of the Messiah. Whether the Messianic era is thus identical with the future world, and these again with the period of resurrection, is a moot point. The following quotation from G. Moore, *Judaism* (vol. 2, p. 389), is apposite: "Any attempt to systematize the Jewish notions of the hereafter imposes upon them an order and consistency which does not exist in them." [25]

Similarly, Joseph Klausner in his *The Messianic Idea in Israel* states:

> [T]hroughout the post-Biblical literature the Messianic age, the life after death, and the New World that is to follow the resurrection of the dead are constantly interchanged. For the two latter conceptions (the life after death and the New World) the Talmudic and Rabbinic literature has only one phrase, "the World to Come" (*"Ha-Olam HaBah"*), . . . "The World to Come" is frequently interchanged or confused with "the Days of the Messiah". [26]

Since even Jewish scholars admit that no consistent distinction is made between the various senses of "the world to come" in Rabbinic writings, it is somewhat unfair when Jewish apologists make the argument that Jesus could not have been the Messiah because He did not fulfill the "required" prophecies—that the dead will arise, that there will be no more illness or war or suffering or death, etc. Yet it is frequently done. For instance, the prophecy in Isaiah: "He will destroy death for ever, and the Lord God will wipe away tears from all faces" (Isaiah 25:8) is taken by Jewish

---

[25] Sanhedrin, vol. II, *The Babylonian Talmud*, p. 601, note 3.
[26] Klausner, *Messianic Idea*, pp. 408–9.

apologists as referring to "in the days of the Messiah" rather than after the resurrection. However, later Christian revelation makes it clear that it refers to after the resurrection of the dead (Revelation 21:1–4):

> Then I saw a new heaven and a new earth; for the first heaven and the first earth had passed away, and the sea was no more. And I saw the holy city, new Jerusalem, coming down out of heaven from God, prepared as a bride adorned for her husband; and I heard a loud voice from the throne saying, "Behold, the dwelling of God is with men. He will dwell with them, and they shall be his people, and God himself will be with them; he will wipe away every tear from their eyes, and death shall be no more, neither shall there be mourning nor crying nor pain any more, for the former things have passed away."

Already in the twelfth century Maimonides himself tried to clarify this distinction between the "Messianic Age" and the final redemption. He wrote:

> The ultimate and perfect reward, the final bliss which will suffer neither interruption nor diminution is the life in the world to come. The Messianic era, on the other hand, will be realized in this world, which will continue in its normal course except that independent sovereignty will be restored to Israel. The ancient sages already said, "The only difference between the present and the Messianic era is that political oppression will then cease." [27]

He made the same point in his discussion of another Messianic prophecy often used by anti-missionaries to discredit Jesus' claim. It is sometimes argued that Jesus could not have

---

[27] Maimonides, *Mishneh Torah: The Book of Knowledge*, trans. Moses Hyamson (New York: Bloch, 1938), p. 92a.

been the Messiah since according to Isaiah 11:6, when the
Messiah comes: "The wolf shall dwell with the lamb, and
the leopard shall lie down with the kid", yet wolves still eat
lambs. But Maimonides wrote about this very verse:

> Let no one think that in the days of the Messiah any of
> the laws of nature will be set aside, or any innovation be
> introduced into creation. The world will follow its nor-
> mal course. The words of Isaiah: "And the wolf shall dwell
> with the lamb, and the leopard shall lie down with the
> kid" (Isaiah 11:6) are to be understood figuratively, mean-
> ing that Israel will live securely among the wicked of the
> heathens who are likened to wolves and leopards, as it is
> written: "A wolf of the deserts does spoil them, a leopard
> watches over their cities" (Jeremiah 5:6). They will all
> accept the true religion. and will neither plunder nor de-
> stroy, and together with Israel earn a comfortable living
> in a legitimate way, as it is written: "And the lion shall
> eat straw like the ox" (Isaiah 11:7). All similar expres-
> sions used in connection with the Messianic age are
> metaphorical. In the days of King Messiah the full mean-
> ing of those metaphors and their allusions will become
> clear to all.[28]

In the light of the subsequent revelation of the New Testament, we know there are very good reasons for this confusion about what will happen on earth when the Messiah
comes. For the Messiah will in fact come twice, the first
time for Redemption and the second time to put an end to
"this world" and to usher in the "New Jerusalem". When
He came the first time, the changes made on the face of the

[28] Maimonides, *The Code of Maimonides (Mishneh Torah), Book 14: The Book
of Judges*, trans. Abraham Hershman (New Haven: Yale University Press, 1949),
p. 240.

earth, among those who were living, were of a spiritual nature—profound changes within the souls of men and in the relationship between man and God, rather than physical changes to the state of life on earth. Yet at the same time, when He came the first time, the changes made *in the world of the dead*, that is, for souls that had already passed away, were immense, universal, and very "physical" within that realm. For prior to Jesus' descent to the dead, every single soul "of the just"—the souls of all of the saints from Adam on—were "trapped" in limbo,[29] awaiting the coming of the Messiah to be released into heaven. They were released upon Jesus' descent to the dead, the day following the crucifixion. It is very understandable that Jewish prophecy should contain the image of all the just being freed from their struggle and entering paradise when the Messiah comes, for this is precisely what did happen—only for those who had already died, not for those still living. So we see that because of these two complexities—that of the two comings of the Messiah, and that of the effects in the world of the living versus in the world of those who have passed away—the Messianic prophecies of the Old Testament easily can be misunderstood, leading to the incorrect conclusion that Jesus did not fulfill them.

"Messiah ben Joseph" and "Messiah ben David"

The apparent contradictions between Old Testament Messianic prophecies that describe a Messiah who suffers and dies (such as Zechariah 12 and Isaiah 53) and those that depict one who comes in power and glory were resolved by

---

[29] The *"limbus patrum"*, or "limbo of the fathers".

the Talmudic Rabbis proposing two Messiahs rather than one. The first, *Messiah ben Joseph* (or "son of Joseph"), will be defeated by his enemies, suffer, and die. The second, *Messiah ben David*, will lead Israel to its final victory. For instance, the following passage from the Talmud[30] identifies Zechariah 12 as referring to Messiah ben Joseph: "What is the cause of the mourning [in Zechariah 12:10]. . . . The cause is the slaying of Messiah the son of Joseph . . . that well agrees with the scriptural verse, 'and they shall look upon me because they have thrust him through, and they shall mourn for him as one mourneth for his only son.' " In fact, according to Jewish Talmud scholar Joseph Klausner: "The idea of the 'suffering Messiah' has its source in this verse of Zechariah together with Isaiah 53."[31]

Although most of the details of the life of Messiah ben Joseph in the Talmud do not correspond with those of the life of Jesus, it is nevertheless haunting that the Messiah who suffers and dies is "Messiah ben Joseph"—Messiah son of Joseph. Jesus will, of course, come a second time in power and glory to usher in the Messianic Kingdom in its fullness. The first time He came, He came to suffer and die—and He was, quite literally, known as Jesus the son of Joseph.[32] In the Scriptures, He was sometimes identified as the son of Joseph precisely to emphasize His human nature in which He was to suffer and die: "They were astonished, and said, 'Where did this man get this wisdom and these mighty works? Is not this the carpenter's [i.e., Joseph's] son?' " (Matthew 13:54–55).

---

[30] *Sukkah 52a.*

[31] Klausner, *Messianic Idea*, p. 204.

[32] This would have been his formal name, since at the time Jews used a patronymic rather than a family name. "Christ", of course, was not part of His name, but a title, "the Anointed One".

The title "son of Joseph" becomes even more poignant when one considers the life of Joseph in the Old Testament and compares it to that of Jesus. Joseph was sold into slavery in Egypt so that, in God's plan, he could later save all of his people by providing them with bread. Jesus too became a servant, a slave, in the "Egypt" of man's sinful state: "Christ Jesus, who, though he was in the form of God, did not count equality with God a thing to be grasped, but emptied himself, taking the form of a servant, being born in the likeness of men. And being found in human form he humbled himself and became obedient unto death, even death on a cross" (Philippians 2:5–8).

He did this so that He could save all of humanity by feeding them with the true bread of life, His flesh in the Eucharist: "I am the bread of life. Your fathers ate the manna in the wilderness, and they died. This is the bread which comes down from heaven, that a man may eat of it and not die. I am the living bread which came down from heaven; if any one eats of this bread, he will live for ever; and the bread which I shall give for the life of the world is my flesh.... [H]e who eats this bread will live for ever" (John 6:48–58). Thus Jesus the son of Joseph fulfilled, in providing the "bread of life" that brings salvation to the Church, that which was foreshadowed in the first Joseph providing the physical bread that saved the chosen people.

Jesus also mirrored Joseph in being falsely condemned for a "crime" exactly opposite to His actual virtue. Joseph was condemned for attempted rape precisely because he refused to sleep with Potiphar's wife (Genesis 39); Jesus was condemned to death for the blasphemy of "falsely" claiming to be God's son, precisely because He *was* God's son (Matthew 26).

The parallels go on. Joseph initially tried to reveal himself to his brothers, to his own family, but they did not believe him; his brothers mocked and persecuted him and even planned to kill him, finally selling him for twenty pieces of silver instead (Genesis 37). Jesus also initially tried to reveal Himself to His own family, both literally His own relatives who did not believe Him (John 7:5) and, in a larger sense, the Jews, who also did not, in general, believe in Him. He too was rejected by His own people, the leaders of whom sought to have Him killed; He too was sold for, in this case, thirty pieces of silver (Matthew 26:15).

However, the end results of Joseph's brothers' rejection of him and attempt to kill him was that he saved "all the earth" (Genesis 41:57) from death—first the foreigners, and finally his own people. Similarly the end result of Jesus' rejection, Passion, and death is the salvation of all mankind from the death due to sin, purchasing for them the opportunity for eternal life. And as in the case of Joseph, it seems that it will be Jesus' own family—again, the Jews— who will end up being the "last" to be saved (in a general, corporate sense); or at least that is one common understanding of St. Paul's words in Romans 11:25–26: "I want you to understand this mystery, brethren: a hardening has come upon part of Israel, until the full number of Gentiles come in, and so all Israel will be saved." (This passage is discussed at length in Chapter 9, "The Return of the Jews").

As a Jew who has entered the Catholic Church, how sweet it is to read the words of Joseph when he is finally recognized by his brothers and breaks down, weeping with love; for it is easy to imagine them being spoken to us by our Savior, Jesus, when we, too, finally recognize Him (summarized from Genesis 45):

> Then Joseph could not control his feelings in front of all his retainers, and he exclaimed "Let everyone leave me."

No one therefore was present with him while Joseph made himself known to his brothers, but he wept so loudly that all the Egyptians heard. Joseph said to his brothers, "Come closer to me." When they had come closer to him he said, "I am your brother, Joseph whom you sold into Egypt. But now do not grieve, do not reproach yourselves for having sold me here, since God sent me before you to preserve your lives.[33] So it was not you who sent me here, but God. [Y]ou shall dwell in the land, and you shall be near me, and I will provide for you. And now your eyes see." And he kissed all his brothers and wept upon them.

The other name given to the Messiah, "Messiah ben David", is as perfect a name for Jesus in His second coming as "Messiah ben Joseph" is in His first. Even during His lifetime, He was sometimes referred to as "son of David" to emphasize His divine nature, His power and glory, rather than His humanity, as for instance by the two blind men whose sight He restored: "And as Jesus passed on from there, two blind men followed him, crying aloud, 'Have mercy on us, Son of David.' . . . Jesus said to them, 'Do you believe that I am able to do this?' They said to him, 'Yes, Lord.' Then he touched their eyes. . . . And their eyes were opened" (Matthew 9:27–30).

He was also called the "Son of David" by the jubilant crowds during Jesus' "victorious" entrance into Jerusalem on Palm Sunday: "And the crowds that went before him and that followed him shouted, 'Hosanna to the Son of David! Blessed is he who comes in the name of the Lord! Hosanna in the highest!' And when he entered Jerusalem, all the city

---

[33] Translation to this point is from the *Daily Roman Missal* (Princeton: Scepter Press, 1992), Reading for Thursday of Fourteenth Week in Ordinary Time; remainer RSV.

was stirred, saying, 'Who is this?' And the crowds said, 'This is the prophet Jesus from Nazareth of Galilee'" (Matthew 21:9–11).

For King David served to foreshadow the Messiah who was to come in glory. In the words of St. Augustine, "As the City of God moved along in the course of history, the first king to rule in that earthly Jerusalem, which foreshadowed the one that was to come, was David." [34] Thus the one who will come to inaugurate the glorious reign of the heavenly Jerusalem is known as Messiah ben David. This heavenly Jerusalem is described in Revelation 21–22 (extracts):

He showed me the holy city Jerusalem coming down out of heaven from God, having the glory of God, its radiance like a most rare jewel, clear as crystal. It had a great, high wall, with twelve gates, and at the gates twelve angels, and on the gates the names of the twelve tribes of the sons of Israel were inscribed.... [T]he street of the city was pure gold, transparent as glass. And I saw no temple in the city, for its temple is the Lord God the Almighty and the Lamb. And the city has no need of sun or moon to shine upon it, for the glory of God is its light, and its lamp is the Lamb.... And night shall be no more; they need no light of lamp or sun, for the Lord God will be their light, and they shall reign for ever and ever.

How fitting to call the "Lamb" who suffered and died to take away the sin of the world (John 1:29) Messiah ben Joseph; and how fitting to call Jesus in His glorious Second Coming Messiah ben David.

[34] St. Augustine, *City of God* (Garden City, N.Y.: Doubleday Image Books, 1958), p. 383.

Confirmation of Christianity in the Talmud

The Talmud, needless to say, does not set out to confirm Christianity—quite the opposite. There are, nonetheless, several passages in the Talmud that inadvertently confirm some of the claims of Christianity.

Two of these passages occur in the context of the destruction of the Jerusalem Temple in A.D. 70—referred to as the Second Temple, to distinguish it from Solomon's Temple destroyed in 586 B.C. during the Babylonian invasion. It was the center of Jewish worship and the only place where the animal sacrifices that were required for the atonement for sins under the Old Covenant could take place. Its destruction by the Romans in A.D. 70 was in many ways the greatest disaster ever to occur in Judaism, putting an end to the religion as it had been known until then, and as it had been laid out by God in the Old Testament.

"Hatred Without Cause" (Yoma 9b)

The Talmud describes the destruction of the Temple as a punishment of God. What was the sin for which the Jewish nation was punished in A.D. 70, about 40 years after the rejection and crucifixion of Jesus? (from the Talmud, *Yoma 9b*): "But why was the second Sanctuary destroyed, seeing that in its time they [the Jews] were occupying themselves with the Torah, the precepts, and the practice of charity? Because therein prevailed *hatred without cause*" [emphasis added].

"Hatred without cause" is a very telling phrase. Consider Jesus' words at the Last Supper (John 15:18–25):

> If the world hates you, know that it has hated me before it hated you. If you were of the world, the world would love its own; but because you are not of the world, but I

chose you out of the world, therefore the world hates
you. . . . He who hates me hates my Father also. . . . [N]ow
they have seen and hated both me and my Father. It is to
fulfill the word that is written in their law, 'They *hated me
without a cause*' [emphasis added].

When Jesus uses these very same words, "hatred without
cause", to portray His rejection and crucifixion, He is citing
Psalm 69. This Psalm has always been seen by the Church as
a portrayal of Jesus' Passion:

Save me, O God! . . . I am weary with my crying; my
throat is dry; my eyes fail while I wait for my God. Those
who hate me without a cause are more than the hairs of
my head; they are mighty who would destroy me, being
my enemies wrongfully . . . because for Your sake I have
borne reproach; shame has covered my face. I have become a stranger to my brothers, and an alien to my mother's children; because zeal for your house has eaten me
up, and the reproaches of those who reproach You have
fallen on me. . . . Reproach has broken my heart, and I
am full of heaviness; I looked for someone to take pity,
but there was none; and for comforters, but I found none.
They also gave me gall for my food, and for my thirst they
gave me vinegar to drink.

The verse "zeal for Your house has eaten me up" is cited in
John 2:17 as referring to Jesus, and the Gospels recount that
in His thirst on the Cross, Jesus was given wine mixed with
gall and vinegar to drink, thus fulfilling that prophecy.

So when the Talmud attributes the destruction of the Second Temple to "hatred without cause", it is exhibiting a gift
of prophecy, stating a profound truth that unknowingly
confirms Jesus' identity as the Messiah, although unaware of
the fact. The same sort of inadvertent gift of prophecy was

exhibited by the Jewish authorities centuries earlier when just before the crucifixion, Caiaphas, the Jewish High Priest, prophesied concerning Jesus' death:

> But one of them, Caiaphas, who was high priest that year, said to them, "You know nothing at all; you do not understand that it is expedient for you that one man should die for the people, and that the whole nation should not perish." He did not say this of his own accord, but being high priest that year he prophesied that Jesus should die for the nation, and not for the nation only, but to gather into one the children of God who are scattered abroad. So from that day on they took counsel how to put him to death (John 11:49–53).

This "hatred without cause", which brought about the death of Jesus and the destruction of the Second Temple just as the Talmud said, is well described in the Gospels. It is also beautifully depicted in the part of the traditional Good Friday liturgy known as "The Reproaches", in which Jesus says:

> My people, what have I done to you? How have I offended you? Answer me! Is it because I led you out of the land of Egypt, that you have led your Savior to the Cross?
>
> My people, what have I done to you? How have I offended you? Answer me! Is it because I led you through the desert for forty years and fed you with manna and brought you into a land of plenty, that you have led your Savior to the Cross?
>
> My people, what have I done to you? How have I offended you? Answer me! What more could I have done for you? I planted you as my most precious vine, and you became most bitter to me, even giving me vinegar to drink in my thirst, and with a lance piercing the side of your Savior.

My people, what have I done to you? How have I offended you? Answer me! For your sake I scourged Egypt
through its firstborn, and you have scourged and betrayed me.

My people, what have I done to you? How have I offended you? Answer me! I led you out of Egypt and
drowned Pharoah in the Red Sea, and you have handed
me over to the High Priest.

My people, what have I done to you? How have I offended you? Answer me! I opened the sea before you,
and you have opened my side with a spear.

My people, what have I done to you? How have I offended you? Answer me! I went before you in a pillar
of cloud, and you have led me to Pilate's court.

My people, what have I done to you? How have I offended you? Answer me! I filled you up with manna in
the desert, and you have struck me down with blows
and scourges.

My people, what have I done to you? How have I offended you? Answer me! I gave you to drink the water
of salvation from the rock, and you have given me to
drink gall and vinegar.

My people, what have I done to you? How have I offended
you? Answer me! For you I struck down the kings of the
Canaanites, and you have struck my head with a reed.

My people, what have I done to you? How have I offended you? Answer me! I gave you a royal scepter, and
you have placed on my head a crown of thorns.

My people, what have I done to you? How have I offended
you? Answer me! I raised you high with great strength,
and you have hanged me from the gibbet of the Cross.

My people, what have I done to you? How have I offended you? Answer me![35]

---

[35] *Missale Romanum*, translated from the Latin by author.

There is a haunting parallel, certainly not coincidental, between this part of the Catholic Good Friday liturgy and
one of the central prayers of the Jewish Passover Seder[36], the
"*Dayenu*" (Hebrew for "it would have been enough for us").
The "Dayenu" is a hymn in which the Jews express their
gratitude to God for the many saving miracles He performed to bring them safely out of Egypt and into the Promised Land. In the Reproaches, Jesus reproaches the Jews for
their *in*gratitude toward Him, naming many of the very same
miracles which He performed in bringing them out of Egypt,
and for which he received, in place of the gratitude due him,
"hatred without cause". From the "Dayenu":

> How many favors God has bestowed on us!
> If He had led us forth from Egypt but not executed
>   judgement on the Egyptians, it would have
>   been enough for us!
> If He had executed judgement on the Egyptians . . .
>   but not slain their first-born, it would have been
>   enough for us!
> If He had slain their first-born . . . but not opened
>   the Red Sea for us, it would have been enough
>   for us!
> If He had opened the Red Sea for us . . . but not
>   led us through the desert for forty years, it would
>   have been enough for us!

---

[36] The Passover Seder is the ritual meal that inaugurates Passover. Good
Friday itself, of course, took place on the eve of Passover (John 18–19), and
the Last Supper itself was a Passover Seder (Matthew 26). The apparent contradiction is resolved by the fact that, because of the number of pilgrims in
Jerusalem for the Passover Feast, some were permitted to celebrate their Seder
the preceding evening.

> If He had led us through the desert for forty years . . .
>   but not fed us with Manna, it would have been
>   enough for us!
> If He had fed us with Manna . . . but not led us
>   into the Land of Israel, it would have been enough
>   for us!
> If He had led us into the Land of Israel . . . but not
>   given us the High Priesthood, it would have been
>   enough for us![37]

How tragically these are echoed in Jesus' reproaches! It is as
though in this Good Friday liturgy Jesus Himself is pointing
out the contrast, verse by verse, between the gratitude that
Jews verbally acknowledge toward Him at the Passover Seder,
and the "hatred without cause" they actually showed Him.

The Miracle of the Scarlet Thread (Rosh Hashanah 31b)

With the destruction of the Second Temple in A.D. 70, the
Jewish people lost the ability to perform sacrifices for the
atonement of sins. Yet according to Christianity the efficacy
of such sacrifices should already have ended at the time of
the crucifixion, about forty years earlier. For it was then that
the Old Covenant, with its animal sacrifices for the atonement for sins, was replaced by the New Covenant, in which
Jesus shed His blood once and for all for the atonement of
sins. As the Letter to the Hebrews puts it:

> Now even a first covenant had ordinances of divine ser-
> vice, and its sanctuary, a sanctuary of this world.
>   For there was a tabernacle prepared . . . the Holy of
> holies . . . [into which goes] the high priest alone, once in

[37] Translation by author.

the year, not without blood, which he offers for himself, and for the errors of the people . . . being only (with meats and drinks and divers washings) carnal ordinances, imposed until a time of reformation.

But Christ having come a high priest of the good things to come, through the greater and more perfect tabernacle, not made with hands, that is to say, not of this creation, nor yet through the blood of goats and calves, but through his own blood, entered in once for all into the holy place, having obtained eternal redemption. For if the blood of goats and bulls, and the ashes of a heifer sprinkling them that have been defiled, sanctify unto the cleanness of the flesh: how much more shall the blood of Christ, who through the eternal Spirit offered himself without blemish unto God, cleanse your conscience from dead works to serve the living God? . . .

For Christ entered not into a holy place made with hands, like in pattern to the true; but into heaven itself, now to appear before the face of God for us: . . . By which will we have been sanctified through the offering of the body of Jesus Christ once for all. . . . For by one offering he hath perfected for ever them that are sanctified (Hebrews 9:1—10:14, American Standard Version translation).

Both the Talmud and the Zohar[38] contain accounts of how, in the days of the Temple, the High Priest would once a year—on *Yom Kippur*, or the "Day of Atonement"—enter the Holy of Holies and offer sacrifice for the atonement of the sins of all Israel. Both mention the "miracle of the scarlet thread", in which a scarlet thread would miraculously turn

---

[38] The Zohar is a non-canonical book of Jewish mystical teachings that first surfaced in Spain at the end of the thirteenth century, although its proponents date it back to at least the second century A.D.

white as the sign that God had accepted the sacrifice. From the account in the Zohar (*Vayikra*, Section 3, condensed):

> All the sins are [taken] away ... on this day, the defile-
> ment of the soul and of the body.... All that day ... God
> makes atonement for Israel and purifies them from all their
> sins and they are not accused before Him.... On this day
> the priest ... makes atonement for himself and his house
> and the priests and the sanctuary and all Israel.... They
> used to know by a certain thread of scarlet if the priest
> had been successful.... [I]t was known by the thread
> changing its color to white, when there was rejoicing above
> and below. If it did not, however, all were distressed, know-
> ing that their prayer had not been accepted.[39]

The scarlet thread turning white would be the sign that God had accepted the sacrifice and forgiven the Jewish people their sins ("though your sins be like scarlet, they may be-come white as snow; though they be crimson red, they may become white as wool"—Isaiah 1:18[40]). Yet the Talmud it-self reports that forty years before the Temple was destroyed, this great miracle, which gave divine confirmation that the High Priest's sacrifice had been accepted taking away the sins of the Jewish people, ceased to occur. The passage from the Talmud reads (*Rosh Hashanah 31b*):

> Originally they used to fasten the thread of scarlet on
> the door of the [Temple] court on the outside. If it
> turned white the people used to rejoice, and if it did not
> turn white they were sad.... For forty years before the

[39] *The Zohar*, trans. Maurice Simon and Dr. Paul Levertoff (London: Soncino Press, 1949).

[40] Translation from *Christian Prayer: The Liturgy of the Hours* (Boston: St. Paul Editions, 1976).

destruction of the Temple the thread of scarlet never turned white but it remained red.[41]

The Temple was destroyed about A.D. 70; hence the miracle ceased to occur about A.D. 30, which is precisely when the crucifixion took place—the crucifixion that replaced the sacrifice of the Old Covenant with that of Jesus on the Cross. According to the New Testament at the very moment that Jesus died on the Cross the curtain of the Temple that separated off the Holy of Holies was rent in two, symbolizing the end of the efficacy of the sacrifices of the Old Covenant (cf. Matthew 27:51; Mark 15:38; Luke 23:45). It is the Talmud itself that unwittingly confirms this when it recounts that from that time on—forty years before the destruction of the Temple in A.D. 70—the scarlet thread never again turned white.

The Historicity of Jesus

The Talmud itself relates some of the basic details of Jesus' life, death, and ministry. It is true that many of the references in the Talmud to Jesus are disputed. Many are pejorative, and for many centuries such blasphemy was a criminal offense. Those who believe that the references in the Talmud are to Jesus say that His identity was veiled under a pseudonym for fear of persecution; those who deny it say that the identification of the miscreants described in the Talmud with Jesus is itself Christian persecution at work. Further complicating matters is the fact that copies of the Talmud printed after the 1578 Basel edition eliminate passages referring to Jesus that appeared in earlier copies. Nevertheless particularly clear references to Jesus include:

---

[41] The miracle of the scarlet thread, and the fact that it ceased to occur about A.D. 30, is also recounted in *Yoma 39b*.

"Jesus the Nazarene practiced magic and led astray and deceived Israel" (*Sanhedrin 107b*).[42]

"It was taught: On the eve of Passover Yeshu [i.e., Jesus] the Nazarene was hung. . . . A herald went forth and cried, 'He is going forth to be stoned because he has practised sorcery and enticed Israel to apostasy. Any one who can say anything in his favour, let him come forward and plead on his behalf.' But since nothing was brought forward in his favour he has hanged on the eve of Passover!" (*Sanhedrin 43a*, Sanhedrin, vol. I, *Babylonian Talmud*, pp. 136–37.)

Other passages that appear to refer to Jesus describe Him as illegitimate (*Sanhedrin 106a*), as having acquired His magical abilities in Egypt, where He grew up (*Shabbath 104b*), and as having been executed by hanging on the eve of Passover (*Sanhedrin 43a* and *67a*) at the age of thirty-three or -four (*Sanhedrin 106b*). To the objection that the Talmud might simply be acknowledging the widely circulated myths of Christianity rather than attesting to their basis in fact, one can reply that there was nothing to prevent the Rabbis of the Talmud from simply dismissing the story of Jesus as a fiction, rather than providing an alternative, disparaging version of His story. Thus the Talmud itself confirms at least the basics of Jesus' historical existence, which is more than some Jews (and, tragically, some "Christians", too) are willing to admit to.

Healings by Jesus' Disciples in the Talmud

The Talmud attests to the fact that the followers of Jesus were able to heal the sick, even at the point of death, but states emphatically that it is preferable to die than to benefit from such a healing. The followers of Jesus are referred to in the Talmud as "*Minim*", which means "heretics". The following story appears

---

[42] This verse is censored out in censored editions of the Talmud.

in several places in the Talmud in slightly varied versions. This version is from *Abodah Zarah 27b* in the Babylonian Talmud:

> No man should have any dealings with the Minim, nor is it allowed to be healed by them even [for] an hour's life. It once happened to Ben Dama the son of Rabbi Ishmael's sister that he was bitten by a serpent and Jacob of Kefar Sekinah [a disciple of Jesus][43] came to heal him but Rabbi Ishmael did not let him ... his soul departed and he died. Whereupon Rabbi Ishmael exclaimed, "Happy art thou Ben Dama for thou wert pure in body and thy soul likewise left thee in purity, nor hast thou transgressed. ..." One [having dealings with the Minim] may be drawn after them.

In other versions of the same story (*Abodah Zarah 40d, 41a*) when Jacob came in to cure Ben Dama he said, "We will speak to thee in the name of Jeshu [i.e., Jesus]."[44] This is the same well-known formula used by the disciples in the New Testament, for instance, when Peter healed the beggar at the gate of the Temple, who had been lame from birth: "And Peter directed his gaze at him ... and said ... 'In the name of Jesus Christ of Nazareth, walk.' ... [A]nd immediately his feet and ankles were made strong, and leaping up he stood and walked and entered the temple with them, walking and leaping and praising God" (Acts 3:4–8).

---

[43] Elsewhere the Talmud explicitly states that Jacob of Kefar Sekinah was a disciple of Jesus: "I came across one of the disciples of Jesus the Nazarene, Jacob of Kefar-Sekiniah by name. ...", *Abodah Zarah 17a.*

[44] R. Travers Herford, *Christianity in Talmud and Midrash* (London: Williams and Norgate, 1903), p. 104. The full name given here is "Jeshu Ben Pandira", which is one of the names given to Jesus of Nazareth in the Talmud. "There can be no reasonable doubt that the 'Jeshu' who is variously called Ben Stada and Ben Pandira is the historical Jesus, the founder of Christianity" (ibid., p. 37). Also *The Jewish Encyclopedia*, ed. Singer (New York: KTAV Publications, 1901), s.v. "Jesus": "It is certain, in any case, that the rabbinical sources also regard Jesus as the 'son of Pandera'."

CHAPTER FIVE

Judaism and the Holocaust

The Holocaust and Jewish Theology

It is with a great deal of trepidation that one approaches the task of writing on the Holocaust. There is no way to be sufficiently sensitive to the incomprehensible suffering that it entailed. Yet one cannot examine the role of Judaism in salvation history without addressing it, nor can one understand current thinking in Jewish theology without giving explicit consideration to the effects the tragedy of the Holocaust have had on that theology.

The intention in examining some of the effects that the Holocaust has had on Jewish theology is not to criticize—it is rather to defend the true Jewish ideal, the genuine Jewish conception of and faith in God, against contrary views that have emerged in response to the trauma and tragedy. It is only logical that a disaster of such proportions should occasion a deep reexamination of the fundamental theological tenets of Judaism and present an unprecedentedly great challenge to that faith. Yet should the end result be the destruction of the true Jewish theology, which sustained the Jews in their relationship to God for over 4,000 years, it would, in the words of one Jewish scholar, "destroy Judaism and give Hitler the posthumous victory we all wish to deny him".[1] It is in that spirit, in the defense of the nobility of Judaism and its true conception of the goodness and greatness of God, that this exploration is undertaken.

The Jewish understanding of the relationship between God and man, and more particularly between God and the Jews, is fundamentally based on the teaching of the Old Testament. The Old Testament, in many places, explicitly makes it clear that

1. God is all-good, all-loving, and all-powerful;
2. the Jews are the "chosen people", the special favorites of God;
3. the good will be rewarded in this life; evil people will be punished for their deeds in this life.

The only one of these three axioms with which Christianity would differ is the last. Yet it is logical that the Christian view of reward/punishment in this life, as opposed to in the afterlife, should differ from the Jewish view. For the very nature of man's reward and punishment changed with the coming of the Messiah (Jesus). Before Jesus came, the gates of heaven were closed to all mankind, even the righteous; there was thus no reward of heaven for them (yet), and they were held in a "limbo", known as the "limbo of the fathers", or as the "bosom of Abraham", awaiting the coming of the Messiah to enable them to enter heaven proper. This Jesus did, the day after the crucifixion and before the Resurrection, when He descended to the dead. It is not surprising that Jewish revelation, that is pre-Jesus revelation, should

---

[1] Dr. Michael Wyschogrod, quoted by Isaac C. Rottenberg, *Jewish Christians in an Age of Christian-Jewish Dialogue* (published by family and friends of the author, 1995), p. 20.

not know of the rewards of heaven, because pre-Jesus there were no such rewards! The revelation of what happens to the dead now that the "gates of heaven" have been opened by Christ's death and descent to the dead is intrinsically a Christian revelation to which Judaism is not privy. And it is not only a question of revelation, of what the ancient Jews *knew*—the underlying workings of God may actually have been different at that time. It seems reasonable to suppose that during the time when the gates of heaven were still closed, God exercised His justice differently and *did* punish sin and reward virtue during the lifetime of the individual.[2]

Since before Jesus the fullness of the afterlife was as yet unavailable to man, so too was any detailed knowledge about it. There are only a few hints about it in pre-Christian Jewish revelation. Among the clearest are those in Daniel and in Second Maccabees. They contain a vague promise, but no detail about what is to come:

> At that time . . . many of those who sleep in the dust of the earth shall awake, some to everlasting life, and some to shame and everlasting contempt. And those who are wise shall shine like the brightness of the firmament; and those who turn many to righteousness, like the stars for ever and ever (Daniel 12:2–3).

> He also took up a collection . . . and sent it to Jerusalem to provide for a sin offering. In doing this he acted very well and honorably, taking account of the resurrection. For . . . he was looking to the splendid reward that is laid up for those who fall asleep in godliness. . . . Therefore he

---

[2] This is not to imply that suffering was always a punishment from God, as the story of Job powerfully illustrates.

made atonement for the dead, that they might be delivered from their sin (2 Maccabees 12: 43–45).

Even in the absence of detailed knowledge, faithful Jews held an unwavering confidence in the ultimate reward (2 Maccabees 7:1–23):

> It happened also that seven brothers and their mother were arrested and were being compelled by the king, under torture with whips and cords, to partake of unlawful swine's flesh. One of them, acting as their spokesman, said, "What do you intend to ask and learn from us? For we are ready to die rather than transgress the laws of our fathers." The king fell into a rage, and gave orders that pans and caldrons be heated. These were heated immediately, and he commanded that the tongue of their spokesman be cut out and that they scalp him and cut off his hands and feet, while the rest of the brothers and the mother looked on. When he was utterly helpless, the king ordered them to take him to the fire, still breathing, and to fry him in a pan. The smoke from the pan spread widely, but the brothers and their mother encouraged one another to die nobly, saying, "The Lord God is watching over us and in truth has compassion on us...."
>
> After the first brother had died in this way, they brought forward the second for their sport. They tore off the skin of his head with the hair, and asked him, "Will you eat rather than have your body punished limb by limb?" He replied in the language of his fathers, and said to them, "No." Therefore he in turn underwent tortures as the first brother had done. And when he was at his last breath, he said, "You accursed wretch, you dismiss us from this present life, but the King of the universe will raise us up to an everlasting renewal of life, because we have died for his laws."

After him, the third was the victim of their sport. When it was demanded, he quickly put out his tongue and courageously stretched forth his hands, and said nobly, "I got these from Heaven, and because of his laws I disdain them, and from him I hope to get them back again." As a result the king himself and those with him were astonished at the young man's spirit, for he regarded his sufferings as nothing. When he too had died, they maltreated and tortured the fourth in the same way. And when he was near death, he said, "One cannot but choose to die at the hands of men and to cherish the hope that God gives of being raised again by him. But for you there will be no resurrection to life!"

The passage then relates the similar deaths of the fifth and sixth sons and closes with a description of the mother:

The mother was especially admirable and worthy of honorable memory. Though she saw her seven sons perish within a single day, she bore it with good courage because of her hope in the Lord. She encouraged each of them in the language of their fathers. Filled with a noble spirit, she fired her woman's reasoning with a man's courage, and said to them, "I do not know how you came into being in my womb. It was not I who gave you life and breath, nor I who set in order the elements within each of you. Therefore the Creator of the world, who shaped the beginning of man and devised the origin of all things, will in his mercy give life and breath back to you again, since you now forget yourselves for the sake of his laws."

In contrast to the scarcity of references to the afterlife, God's promises to reward virtuous behavior in *this* life run throughout the Old Testament. Leviticus 26 gives a full exposition of this theology; the *Shm'a*, the central prayer of Judaism, provides it in a summary form:

> If you will earnestly heed the commandments which I have you this day, to love the Lord your God, and to serve Him with all your heart and with all your soul, then I will favor your land with rain at the proper season—rain in autumn and rain in spring—so that you will have an ample harvest of grain and wine and oil. I will assure grass in the fields for your cattle. You will eat to contentment.
>
> Take care lest you be tempted to forsake God and turn to false gods and worship them. For then the wrath of the Lord will be directed against you. He will close up the heavens and there will be no rain; the earth will not yield her produce. You will soon disappear from the good land which the Lord is giving you.

Combining these three theological axioms one can see the difficulty that Jewish theology has faced in the light of the Holocaust. If God is all-powerful and all-good, if He especially loves the Jewish people, and if His rewards come in this life, then what can one make of the Holocaust? One of the three axioms has to go, and the most frequently chosen has been the first. Either God's goodness, or His power to affect human destiny, is denied.[3]

The second axiom is very rarely chosen. At the time of the Holocaust, the belief was sometimes expressed among orthodox Jews that the persecution was a punishment for

[3] The problem was expressed by Graham B. Walker, Jr., in his *Elie Wiesel: A Challenge to Theology* (Jefferson, N.C.: McFarland, 1988), as follows (p. 14): "How can God permit this? This question is one of the main internal struggles that Judaism faces after the Holocaust. This question challenges both the ability of God and the meaning of a covenant relationship in a post-Holocaust world."

the widespread apostasy of the Jewish people—including assimilation, the idolatry of Zionism, and the abandonment of Torah in favor of secularism or socialism.[4] However, the Holocaust itself wiped out most of the very religious Jews and destroyed almost all of the communities that tried diligently to follow all of the Jewish laws governing daily life. Jewish culture today overwhelmingly represents precisely those strains of less observant Judaism; the Jews who have followed that path are hardly going to see it as being a violation of the Jewish covenant with God.

The third axiom is usually not challenged because Judaism today does not stress the rewards and punishment, or even the existence, of the afterlife. The entire issue of "life after death" is to a large extent avoided—perhaps as a result of the influence of the same "modernism" and "enlightenment rationality", which has influenced Christianity, or perhaps in an effort to further distinguish Judaism from Christian thinking. The theology of heaven and hell might have become so associated with Christianity that the entire area is seen as tainted and to be avoided, despite its extensive presence in the Talmud. The topic of "salvation" itself may have become unwelcome as a result of the role it has played in efforts to convert the Jews. Typical is the reaction of one of the characters in Elie Wiesel's novel *The Gates of the Forest*: "Stop thinking about our salvation and perhaps the cemeteries won't be so full of Jews." [5]

---

[4] Gershon Greenberg, "Orthodox Theological Responses to Kristallnacht", paper presented to 18th Annual Scholar's Conference on the Church Struggle and the Holocaust, Washington, D.C., 1988, cited in Steven Jacobs, ed., *Contemporary Christian Responses to the Shoah* (Lanham, Md.: University Press of America, 1993), p. 47.

[5] Elie Wiesel, *The Gates of the Forest* (New York: Holt, Rinehart and Winston, 1966), p. 84.

The Talmudic teaching on the rewards of heaven and the pains of hell are well developed and graphic. Yet the same Talmudic sources that teach about heaven and hell hold to the necessity of strict ritual observance to gain the former and avoid the latter. It would be reasonable to suppose that as modern Judaism dismissed the need for strict ritual observance, it also moved away from the very concept of the reward and punishment that had been tied to it, much as many Catholics have ceased "believing" in hell as a result of dismissing the need to follow the traditional rules of moral behavior, particularly sexual behavior, that had always been associated with avoiding it.

Ironically, Maimonides taught that faith in the resurrection was itself a necessary condition for a Jew to "have a share in the world to come".[6] Yet the entire area is rarely mentioned in contemporary Judaism.

Since the second and the third axioms are rejected as candidates for revision to reconcile Jewish theology to the Holocaust, the first is chosen. In choosing the first axiom as the one that must go, either God's goodness, or His faithfulness, or His presence in human affairs is denied. All three of these variations can be found in post-Holocaust Jewish theology. Rabbi Arthur Hertzberg[7] is an example of giving up on God's fundamental goodness (if his own words can

---

[6] His thirteenth principle was "I believe with perfect faith that there will be a resurrection of the dead"; and he said that if a man gives up any of these fundamental principles he is an "atheist, an unbeliever", has removed himself from the Jewish community, and loses his share in the world to come. Cf. Isadore Twersky, ed., *A Maimonides Reader* (New York: Behrman House, 1972), pp. 401–23.

[7] Rabbi Hertzberg is the former president of the American Jewish Congress and the author of a number of best-selling books on Judaism. He is one of the foremost Rabbis of the United States.

be taken at face value). In his memoirs he recounts: "I was aware then, in 1948, that I could never return to the Orthodox faith in God. I would not forgive Him for the Holocaust, and I would not absolve Him by agreeing that the death camps had existed in a realm that he could not control." [8]

For an example of one who gives up on God's faithfulness to His covenant with the Jews, one can turn to Elie Wiesel: "I believe during the Holocaust the covenant was broken." [9] And the third variation, deciding that for all intents and purposes God does not exist, is represented by Jewish theologian Richard Rubenstein: "God really died at Auschwitz. . . . [N]othing in human choice, decision, value or meaning can any longer have vertical reference to transcendent standards. We are alone in a silent, unfeeling cosmos. . . . Though most of us will refrain from antisocial behavior, we do so because of fear of ourselves and others rather than fear of God. . . . Ultimately, as with all things, it will pass away, for omnipotent Nothingness is Lord of All Creation." [10]

Rubenstein came to this conclusion out of a conscious awareness of the bind that the "three axioms" placed him in: "If I believe in God as the omnipotent author of the historical drama and Israel as His chosen people, I had to accept [the] conclusion that it was God's will that Hitler committed

[8] From his memoirs, *A Jew in America* (San Francisco: Harper, 2002), excerpted in *New Jersey Jewish Standard*, June 8, 2001, p. 7.

[9] Elie Wiesel, cited in Harry James Cargas, *Harry James Cargas in Conversation with Elie Wiesel* (New York: Paulist, 1976), pp. 56–57. Also, "For the very first time in our history, this very covenant was broken. That is why the Holocaust has terrifying theological implications" (Elie Wiesel, "Jewish Values in the Post-Holocaust Future", *Judaism* 16 [1967], p. 282).

[10] Richard Rubenstein, *After Auschwitz* (Indianapolis: Bobbs-Merrill, 1966), pp. 224–25.

six million Jews to slaughter. I could not possibly believe in such a God nor could I believe in Israel as the chosen people of God after Auschwitz." [11]

Rubenstein did not *entirely* abandon belief in God; rather, he "replaces the biblical God of history with a God of nature. . . . The God of the land, fertility, and the cycles of life replaces the God of history for Rubenstein." [12]

This is ironic because this is precisely the paganism that the Jewish people were enjoined *not* to follow, time after time, in the Old Testament, under pain of death. To add insult to injury, he turns this nature-worship into the "real" meaning of the Jewish Messiah: "Messianism's real meaning is the proclamation of the end of history and the return to nature and nature's cyclical repetitiveness. . . . The deliberate turning of the people of the religion of history to the religion of nature is a moment of *kairos*[13] . . . earth's fruitfulness, its vicissitudes, and its engendering power will once again become the central spiritual realities of Jewish life. . . ." [14]

Does this rejection of the "biblical" God and of the Jews as a chosen people mean that, for Rubenstein, there is no reason for the Jewish people to continue as a distinct community? By no means, rather, "It is precisely the ultimate hopelessness and gratuity of our human situation which calls forth our strongest need for religious community. If all we have is one another, then assuredly we need one another more than ever." [15]

---

[11] Ibid., p. 46.
[12] Walker, *Challenge to Theology*, p. 17.
[13] Greek term used to mean, roughly, "due season" or "appropriate time".
[14] Rubenstein, *After Auschwitz*, pp. 135–36.
[15] Ibid., pp. 131–42; 227–43.

So rather than withdrawing from the Jewish community, Rubenstein clings to it all the more firmly, defining Judaism in terms of his denial of God and neo-paganism and centering its meaning entirely on man rather than on God, thus spreading his apostasy. With these three examples of the abandonment of belief in God's goodness and power by leading figures in contemporary Jewish theology, it is not hard to see the difficulties resulting from the turn taken by post-Holocaust Judaism.

There is a tragic irony in this, for the heart of being a Jew is fidelity to God and faith in His goodness. Remember that Judaism itself was founded on Abraham's fidelity to God and trust in His goodness in the face of what appeared to be the most unjust and cruel act of God imaginable—His requirement that he sacrifice his son Isaac. Contrast Abraham's attitude with this "post-Holocaust" one, that because something horribly unjust and cruel has happened, God must not be good or must not intervene in human affairs.

Having been founded on the basis of Abraham passing this test, it would be tragic if Judaism were to fail this similar test 4,000 years later. It is not as though all of the Jews who went through the Holocaust lost their faith in God's goodness. Wiesel himself concedes that rather than his theological response to the Holocaust being universal, "many Jews kept their faith or even strengthened it".[16] According to Jewish Holocaust theologian Irving Rosenbaum, it tended to be the more observant Jews who received the grace to sustain their faith despite the suffering: "Jews who observed the rites and rituals of tradition were 'able to face life with dignity, death with serenity—and sometimes ecstasy.' "[17] According to Jewish

---

[16] Wiesel, cited in in Cargas, *Conversation with Elie Wiesel*, pp. 56–57.

[17] Irving Rosenbaum, *The Holocaust and Halacha* (New York: KTAV Publications, 1976), p. 8, quoted in Walker, *Elie Wiesel*, p. 49.

scholar and Rabbi Joseph Telushkin, many even went to their deaths with a profession of faith on their lips (a profession of faith that Christians might even consider to be christological, given that "Christ" is simply the Greek for "Messiah"): " 'I believe with a full heart in the coming of the Messiah, and even though he may tarry I will still wait for him', many Jews sang while walking to the gas chambers."[18]

A beautiful example of Jewish faith surviving the Holocaust is provided in the autobiography of Mel Mermelstein, a seventeen-year-old Jew who survived Auschwitz. Having just found out from a stranger that all his sisters and parents had perished:

> I moved toward the gate where my uncle was waiting for me. Shocked and with tears in my eyes, I sat down upon the grass and covered my face with my hands. My uncle placed his hand upon my head and said, "God wanted it to be so, and His judgment is holy." Slowly I lifted my head, incredulous at the words he just uttered.
>
> "I know ... I know, Moishele. Listen, before you ask, before you question, repeat after me: 'Boruch dayen emess.' " I repeated the words that meant "Blessed is the Righteous Judge." The traditional Words on learning of a death seemed harshly inappropriate. But even as I said them, a softening set in.
>
> "Do you want me to bless God for this unbearable pain? Do you want me to call 'just' this hideous unrighteousness?" I don't recall the words I used, but my sense of being put-upon remains with me. To believe that God was anywhere to be found at Auschwitz was too much.

[18] Rabbi Joseph Telushkin, *Jewish Literacy* (New York: William Morrow, 1991), p. 545. Readers will recall this from Chapter 4 as one of Maimonides' Thirteen Principles of Faith.

"Moishele, Moishele, please ..." My uncle was crying now. "Your questions are just, but you're not the first to ask them. 'As we bless God for the good, so must we bless Him for the evil.' Those are the words of the Talmud. They're words beyond understanding, but if we cannot say them, we cannot hope. Bitterness, yes ... but hopelessness, no. The Jewish way is to bless and to hope, and to bless and to hope, until hope and blessing surmount the pain and even the bitterness, and the living learn how to go on."

My uncle continued saying, "God is righteous. God is good. It's people who sometimes forget; who let evil rule them; who lose the sense of the image of God with themselves and become beasts of prey."

"Maybe we should translate the prayers," he said. " 'Blessed is the God who will judge righteously.' He does not forget. Sometimes it seems as if He needs time to assimilate everything He has seen, and to react to it and give recompense. But you'll see it, Moishele, you're young enough. You'll see. *He does not forget!*" [19]

Should the tragedy of the Holocaust serve to alienate the Jews from their trust in and worship of God, that might be a tragedy as great as the deaths themselves. Some Jewish theologians have used the Holocaust to question traditional Jewish views of God; for instance, Rabbi Irving Greenberg's claim that traditional views of God the Redeemer must be abandoned "in the presence of the burning children". Others have recognized the danger of succumbing to this temptation; as Michael Wyschogrod warns in his response to Greenberg's statement, "Inserted at the heart of Judaism as a revelational event comparable to Sinai, the Holocaust will

[19] Mel Mermelstein, *By Bread Alone: The Story of A–4685*, Auschwitz Study Foundation (Los Angeles: Crescent Publications, 1979), pp. 239–40.

necessarily destroy Judaism and give Hitler the posthumous victory we all wish to deny him". [20]

After all, it was the Jews who, through Abraham, taught all of mankind what it means to trust God. As the Letter to the Hebrews puts it:

> By faith Abraham obeyed when he was called to go out to a place which he was to receive as an inheritance; and he went out, not knowing where he was to go. By faith he sojourned in the land of promise, as in a foreign land, living in tents with Isaac and Jacob, heirs with him of the same promise.... By faith Sarah herself received power to conceive, even when she was past the age, since she considered him faithful who had promised. Therefore from one man, and him as good as dead, were born descendants as many as the stars of heaven and as the innumerable grains of sand by the seashore....
>
> By faith Abraham, when he was tested, offered up Isaac, and he who had received the promises was ready to offer up his only son, of whom it was said, "Through Isaac shall your descendants be named." He considered that God was able to raise men even from the dead; hence, figuratively speaking, he did receive him back.
>
> By faith Isaac invoked future blessings on Jacob and Esau. By faith Jacob, when dying, blessed each of the sons of Joseph.... By faith Joseph, at the end of his life, made mention of the exodus of the Israelites and gave directions concerning his burial. By faith Moses, when he was born, was hid for three months by his parents.... By faith Moses, when he was grown up, refused to be called the son of Pharaoh's daughter, choosing rather to share ill-treatment with the people of God than to enjoy the fleet-

---

[20] Rottenberg, *Jewish Christians*, p. 20.

ing pleasures of sin. He considered abuse suffered for the Christ greater wealth than the treasures of Egypt, for he looked to the reward. By faith he left Egypt, not being afraid of the anger of the king; for he endured as seeing him who is invisible. By faith he kept the Passover and sprinkled the blood, so that the Destroyer of the first-born might not touch them.

By faith the people crossed the Red Sea as if on dry land; but the Egyptians, when they attempted to do the same, were drowned. By faith the walls of Jericho fell down after they had been encircled for seven days. . . . And what more shall I say? For time would fail me to tell of Gideon, Barak, Samson, Jephthah, of David and Samuel and the prophets—who through faith conquered kingdoms, enforced justice, received promises, stopped the mouths of lions, quenched raging fire, escaped the edge of the sword, won strength out of weakness, became mighty in war, put foreign armies to flight. . . .

And all these, though well attested by their faith, did not receive what was promised, since God had foreseen something better for us, that apart from us they should not be made perfect (Hebrews 11:8–40).

The paradigm for man's correct response in the face of apparent injustice on the part of God is provided in the story of Job. Job, not without apparent justification, accuses God of injustice and finally elicits a response from Him. God does not respond by explaining why He did what He did (although the reason appears in the initial narration in Job 1–2), or by assuring Job that he would be fully recompensed (although he was in Job 42); rather, God's reply was (to paraphrase the majestic poetry of Job 40–41), "Where were you when I made the world? I don't remember seeing you there. Who are you to think you know better than Me, to put yourself in judgment over Me?" Not without significance,

God's speech ends with a description of a terrible, huge rep-
tilian monster that breathes fire and has a heart "as hard as
stone" (Job 41:24), who, in the final line, is called the "king
over all the children of pride" (Job 41:34). The reference is
unmistakable—men who presume to judge God are children of pride, and their king is the devil himself.

The Holocaust presents a horribly difficult trial for Jewish
theology. When Christians are faced with great persecution
and suffering, they are theologically better equipped to deal
with them, since Jesus Himself was faced with the same apparent contradiction between God's goodness and sovereignty and the exorbitant demands of suffering He places on
His faithful servants. Martyrdom is a continuing presence in
Christianity, beginning at Jesus' birth with the capricious cruelty of the slaughter of the innocents, continuing through
the incomprehensibly painful Passion and death of the Son
of God Himself, and followed by periods of martyrdom
through our own day. For good reason it is said that "the
blood of martyrs is the seed of the Church." Sometimes Christians pass the test, sometimes they fail, but in either case they
have the advantage of the theology of suffering that St. Edith
Stein called "the science of the cross", and the supreme example of the Passion.

The theology of suffering contained in Christianity can
contribute a great deal to the understanding of God's providence in allowing the Holocaust to happen. One can say
that Christianity not only has a theology of suffering, but
that Christianity *is* a theology of suffering. After all, Christian theology revolves around the fact that when God became man He did so primarily in order to undergo suffering;
the central act of redemption for all of mankind was the torture and death of the God-man on the Cross. From the very
earliest days of Christianity, when Jesus' first disciples were

still living, the redemptive value of the Cross was understood as being further extended by the suffering of His followers. As St. Paul wrote: "Now I rejoice in my sufferings for your sake, and in my flesh I complete what is lacking in Christ's afflictions for the sake of his body, that is, the church" (Colossians 1:24).

The Second Vatican Council asserted that only Christianity can make sense out of the deeper mysteries of man's existence, certainly including that of suffering:

> [O]nly in the mystery of the Incarnate Word does the mystery of man take on light. In fact ..., Christ, the final Adam, *fully reveals man to himself* and makes his supreme calling clear.... Through Christ and in Christ, the riddles of sorrow and death grow meaningful.[21]

Pope John Paul II explicitly applied these words to the mystery of suffering. In discussing the passage, he wrote:

> If these words refer to everything that concerns the mystery of man, they certainly refer in a very special way *to human suffering*. Precisely at this point the "revealing of man to himself and making his supreme vocation clear" is particularly *indispensable*.[22]

Unfortunately, despite the wealth of this doctrine, some Christian theologians have fallen into the same trap; for instance, Catholic theologian John Shea:

> Shea distinguishes between the "interventionist God" and the "intentionalist God." The former is the God who is naively and unreflectively believed to change the course

---

[21] *Gaudium et spes*, no. 22, 1965.
[22] John Paul II, Apostolic Letter *On the Christian Meaning of Human Suffering* (*Salvifici Doloris*), Feb. 11, 1984, no. 31.

of nature and history by directly but intermittently inter-
rupting the workings of the world. This God is said to
cure cancer, bring rain, and save people from accidents.
After the Shoah, a Deity who could have rescued the six
million and did not is hardly the God who would turn
around a single person's lung cancer. Such a God seems to
be totally without credibility. And, as we have intimated
above, such a description of God may well be a misread-
ing of much of the Hebrew and Christian Scriptures.[23]

Protestant theologian Paul van Buren writes:

> Theology can shut its eyes and pretend that the Holo-
> caust never happened. . . . But if there are prospects for
> serious theology, for a theology not hopelessly blind to
> matters that pertain to the heart of its task, then the time
> has come for a reconsideration of the whole theological
> and Christian enterprise of the most radical sort.[24]

Such apostasy among Christians in response to the mystery
of suffering is scandalous and tragic and does a disservice
both to God and to the Jews themselves, who are entitled to
as full an explanation of the mystery as Christianity has to
offer.

Elie Wiesel

Elie Wiesel serves as an excellent illustration of the problem
prevalent in contemporary, "post-Holocaust" Jewish theology. Sent to Auschwitz at the age of fifteen with his family,
he saw his parents and a younger sister perish, but he sur-

[23] Jacobs, *Contemporary Christian Responses*, pp. 287, 135.
[24] Paul van Nuren, address to the American Academy of Religion, November 1, 1975, quoted in ibid., p. 92.

vived until liberation about a year later. (Like Mel Mermel-stein, Wiesel, too, was from a village in the Carpathian mountains.) He is perhaps the single most audible Jewish voice on the theological implications of the Holocaust, having written over fifteen books and hundreds of articles and essays. He was chairman of the President's Commission on the Holocaust, headed the U.S. Holocaust Memorial Council, and received the Nobel Peace Prize. He claims to have been the first to apply the word "Holocaust" to the tragedy (and that when he did so, he was explicitly alluding to Abraham's "sacrifice" of Isaac!). [25]

Yet consider the tragic abandonment of traditional Jewish theology evidenced in the following quotes of his:

> There is no Jewish theology for a very simple reason: God wants man to be concerned with human things, not with godly things. . . . Jewish theology is human relations. [26]

> Only the Jew knows that he may oppose God as long as he does so in defense of His creation. [27]

> Jewish tradition allows man to say anything to God, provided it be on behalf of man. Man's inner liberation is God's justification. [28]

> This was the meaning of the holocaust; it implicated not only Abraham or his son, but their God as well. [29]

[25] Elie Wiesel, interview June 29, 1996, Sun Valley, Idaho, on American Academy of Achievement website www.achievement.org.

[26] Lecture in 1974 at Stanford University, quoted in R. M. Brown, *Elie Wiesel: Messenger to All Humanity* (Notre Dame, Ind.: Notre Dame Press, 1983), p. 140.

[27] Elie Wiesel, *A Jew Today* (New York: Random House, 1978), p. 6.

[28] Elie Wiesel, *Souls on Fire: Portraits and Legends of Hasidic Masters* (New York: Random House, 1972), p. 111.

[29] Wiesel, *Gates*, p. 166.

In the endless engagement with God, we [the Jews] proved to Him that we were more patient than He, more compassionate, too.[30]

Wiesel's theology is summed up in his essay on the story of Job:

I was offended by [Job's] surrender in the text. Job's resignation as man was an insult to man. He should not have given in so easily. He should have continued to protest. He should have said to God: "By accepting Your inequities, do I not become your accomplice?"... By repenting sins he did not commit, by justifying a sorrow he did not deserve, [Job] communicates to us that he did not believe in his own confessions; they were nothing but decoys. Job personified man's eternal quest for justice and truth—he did not choose resignation. Thus he did not suffer in vain; thanks to him, we know that *it is given to man to transform divine injustice into human justice and compassion*[31] (emphasis added).

This theme—that man, not God, is the noble one—is at the heart of Wiesel's theology, and he repeats it over and over, in addresses:

[The Jewish survivors of the death camps] had every reason in the world to deny God, to deny anything sacred, to oppose all promises and abort all signs of hope; they had every reason in the world to become ferocious nihilists, anarchists, carriers of fear and nightmare. But what, in fact, did the Jewish survivors of the death camps do as soon as they were liberated? Believe it or not; they held

---

[30] Wiesel, *A Jew Today*, p. 147.

[31] Elie Wiesel's essay "Job: Our Contemporary", in his *Messengers of God: Biblical Portraits and Legends* (New York: Random House, 1976), pp. 234–35.

services. To give thanks to God? No, to defy him! To tell him, listen, as mere mortals, as members of the human society, we know we should seize weapons and use them in every place and in every way and never stop—because it is our right. But we are Jews and as such we renounce that right; we choose—yes, choose to remain human. And generous. [32]

The theme reappears in his autobiographical account of Auschwitz (the following takes place during a celebration of Rosh Hashanah, the Jewish New Year, in the concentration camp):

"What are You, my God," I thought angrily, "compared to this afflicted crowd, proclaiming to You their faith, their anger, their revolt? What does Your greatness mean, Lord of the universe, in the face of all this weakness, this decomposition, and this decay? Why do You still trouble their sick minds, their crippled bodies? ..."

Why, but why should I bless Him? ... Because He had had thousands of children burned in His pits? Because He kept six crematories working night and day, on Sundays and feast days? Because in His great might He had created Auschwitz, Birkenau, Buna, and so many factories of death? How could I say to Him: "Blessed art Thou, Eternal, Master of the Universe, Who chose us from among the races to be tortured day and night, to see our fathers, our mothers, our brothers, end in the crematory? Praised by Thy Holy Name, Thou Who hast chosen us to be butchered on Thine altar?"

This day I had ceased to plead. I was no longer capable of lamentation. On the contrary, I felt very strong. I was the accuser, God the accused. My eyes were open and I was alone—terribly alone in a world without God and

[32] "To Remain Human in Face of Inhumanity", condensed version of an address by Elie Wiesel, in *The Jewish Digest*, September 1972, p. 42.

without man. Without love or mercy. I had ceased to be anything but ashes, yet I felt myself to be stronger than the Almighty, to whom my life had been tied for so long.[33]

Wiesel also has this theme expressed by his fictional characters (in this case a Jewish wise man on the eve of Israel's Six Day War):

> If this time again You desert Your people, if this time again You permit the slaughterer to murder Your children and besmirch their allegiance to the covenant, if this time You let Your promise become mockery, then know, O Master of all that breathes, know that You no longer deserve Your people's love and their passion to sanctify You, to justify You toward and against all, toward and against Yourself; . . . before dying I shall shout as no victim has ever shouted, and know that each of my tears and each of my shouts will tarnish your glory, each of my gestures will negate You and will negate me as You have negated me."[34]

Not only is God portrayed as unfaithful and unjust, but at times far worse. Consider Wiesel's novel *The Accident*,[35] which revolves around Sarah, a twelve-year-old girl in a concentration camp (the following characterization is from R. M. Brown's laudatory *Elie Wiesel: Messenger to All Humanity*):

> What is history for one who enters Sarah's world? "A source of malediction," in the hands of a God who "tortures twelve-year-old children" (pp. 96–97). What is the

[33] Elie Wiesel, *Night* (New York: Hill and Wang, 1960), pp. 72–74.
[34] Elie Wiesel, *A Beggar in Jerusalem* (New York: Random House, 1970), p. 117.
[35] Elie Wiesel, *The Accident* (New York: Avon, 1970).

scene of our human activity? "The immense brothel we call the universe," whose doorkeeper is God (p. 98). Who is the God of such a world? After hearing Sarah's story, the narrator knows why God and death have been allied in human minds ("whoever sees God must die"). Savagely he writes, "Why should He want to kill a man who succeeded in seeing Him? Now everything became clear. God was ashamed. God likes to sleep with twelve-year-old girls. And doesn't want us to know" (p. 98). Conclusion: "Whoever listens to Sarah and doesn't change, whoever enters Sarah's world and doesn't invent new gods and new religions, deserves death and destruction (p. 96).[36]

Who is there to speak up for God, who would defend Him against such accusations? Wiesel gives the answer in his play *The Trial of God*, which is set in a small Ukrainian town in 1649 after a pogrom wiped out all but two of the town's Jews. A mock trial is held against God for allowing it to happen, but there is no one to play the defense attorney for God. Just then a stranger appears who steps forward to do so. In his defense of God, among other statements he says, "I'm His servant. He created the world and me without asking for my opinion; He may do with both whatever He wishes. Our task is to glorify Him, to praise Him, to love Him—in spite of ourselves."[37] Who does this mysterious stranger, who defends God with words worthy of Job or of St. Ignatius, turn out to be? None other than Satan himself. Thus, in the words of R.M. Brown (who discussed

[36] Brown, *Elie Wiesel*, p. 161.
[37] Elie Wiesel, *Trial of God* (New York: Schocken Books, 1995), p. 157.

the play with Wiesel): "The play insists that arguments justifying God in the face of evil are not only inadequate, they are diabolical." [38]

Elie Wiesel's "faith" is placed in humanity in general, and in the Jewish people in particular, instead of, if not actually in opposition to, God. This is reflected in the closing words of his essay "A Jew Today": "We owe it to our past not to lose hope.... We must show our children that in spite of everything, we keep our faith—in ourselves and even in mankind, though mankind may not be worthy of such faith. We must persuade our children and theirs that three thousand years of history must not be permitted to end with an act of despair on our part. To despair now would be a blasphemy—a profanation." [39] One must ask, is the "god" in whom Elie Wiesel places his faith the God of the Jewish people, or the Jewish people themselves?

Elie Wiesel presents this revolt against God as "Jewish theology"; yet contrast it to the words of the Prophet Isaiah (who certainly has at least as much claim to represent Jewish theology!):

> Truly with you God is hidden, the God of Israel, the savior!
> Those are put to shame and disgrace who vent their
>   anger against him....
> Before him in shame shall come all who vent their anger
>   against him (Isaiah 45:15–16, 24). [40]

[38] Brown, *Elie Wiesel*, pp. 150–53. The identification of the mysterious stranger as Satan is made explicit at the very end of the play (*Trial of God*, p. 161).

[39] Wiesel, *A Jew Today*, p. 149

[40] *Christian Prayer: The Liturgy of the Hours* (Boston: St. Paul Editions, 1976), pp. 638–39.

Or to the words of Psalm 100:

Know that he, the Lord, is God. . .
Go within his gates, giving thanks.
Enter his courts with songs of praise.
Give thanks to him and bless his name.
Indeed, how good is the Lord, eternal his merciful love.
He is faithful from age to age.[41]

The Christian response to Wiesel's angst is presented by the Catholic writer François Mauriac in his foreword to Elie Wiesel's autobiographical *Night*. In it he describes meeting with a young Elie Wiesel shortly after the end of the war. After Wiesel recounts the hanging of a young child in the camp, Mauriac thinks:

And I, who believe that God is love, what answer could I give my young questioner, whose dark eyes still held the reflection of that angelic sadness which had appeared one day upon the face of the hanged child? What did I say to him? Did I speak of that other Jew, his brother, who may have resembled him—the Crucified, whose Cross has conquered the world? Did I affirm that the stumbling block to his faith was the cornerstone of mine, and that the conformity between the Cross and the suffering of men was in my eyes the key to that impenetrable mystery whereon the faith of his childhood had perished? . . . We do not know the worth of one single drop of blood, one single tear. All is grace. If the Eternal is the Eternal, the last word for each one of us belongs to Him. This is what I should have told this Jewish child. But I could only embrace him, weeping.[42]

[41] Ibid., p. 640.
[42] Wiesel, *Night*, pp. x–xi.

The Holocaust as Understood by Edith Stein

A vivid contrast to Elie Wiesel's response is provided by that of another Jewish (later Catholic) theologian, St. Edith Stein. As a brilliantly profound German philosopher, as an expert on St. John of the Cross and his theology of suffering, as a Carmelite nun and as a victim of Auschwitz, Edith Stein was in a unique position to understand the meaning of the Holocaust. More importantly, the illumination of our intellects to understand God's ways comes from the light of the Holy Spirit, which becomes more available as personal sanctity and prayer increase. Edith Stein stood out as unique in both her sanctity and her recollection in prayer, even as a Carmelite nun, and even (and especially) as a prisoner en route to certain death at Auschwitz.[43]

From the beginning of the Nazi takeover of Germany in 1933, she saw what was happening to the Jews in the light of the Cross. During a holy hour at the Carmelite convent in Cologne, she had the following illumination:

> I spoke with the Savior to tell him that I realized it was his Cross that was now being laid upon the Jewish people, that the few who understood this had the responsibility of carrying it in the name of all, and that I myself was willing to do this, if he would only show me how. I left the service with the inner conviction that I had been heard, but uncertain as ever as to what "carrying the Cross" would mean for me.[44]

---

[43] See the many personal reminiscences, of both Jews and Christians who met her, in *Never Forget: Christian and Jewish Perspectives on Edith Stein*, Waltraud Herbstrith, ed. (Washington, D.C.: ICS Publications, 1998).

[44] Waltraud Herbstrith, *Edith Stein* (San Francisco: Ignatius Press, 1992), p. 119.

She also saw a special relationship between what was happening to the Jewish people and their rejection of Jesus. On the day that she found out about the synagogue burnings she made the following comment (later printed in the monthly of the Benedictine abbey in Beuron, where Abbot Walzer was her spiritual director):

> This is the shadow of the cross that falls upon my people! Oh, if they would only realize! That is the fulfillment of the curse which my people have called down upon themselves![45]

Beyond the meaning that the Holocaust had for all Jews, she saw a special role for herself. By being both Jewish and Catholic, she identified fully both with the Jews by blood and with the Church by faith and thus was able in a unique way to bring the suffering of the Jews to the Cross of Christ. She felt it was particularly important for the few victims of the sacrifice who were aware of its meaning to carry this awareness for all:

> I understood the Cross as the destiny of God's people, which was beginning to be apparent at the time (1933). I felt that those who understood the Cross of Christ should take it upon themselves on everybody's behalf.... Beneath the Cross I understood the destiny of God's people.[46]

In this role she compared herself to Queen Esther, who also offered her life before the king to save her (the Jewish) people:

[45] Original quote taken from Benedictine monthly *Erbe und Auftrag*, published by the Archabbey of Beuron, cited by Herbstrith, *Never Forget*, p. 111.

[46] *Program for St. Edith Stein's Canonization* (Vatican, Oct. 11, 1998), p. 30 (retranslation).

I firmly believe that the Lord has accepted my life as an offering for all. It's important for me to keep Queen Esther in mind and remember how she was separated from her people just so that she could intercede for them before the king. I myself certainly am a poor and insignificant little Esther, but I take comfort from the fact that the King who has chosen me is infinitely kind and merciful.[47]

Out of this awareness she made an offering of herself to God in her final testament, written in 1939:

I joyfully accept in advance the death God has appointed for me, in perfect submission to his most holy will. May the Lord accept my life and death for the honor and glory of his name, for the needs of his holy Church—especially for the preservation, sanctification, and final perfecting of our holy Order, and in particular for the Carmels of Cologne and Echt—for the Jewish people, that the Lord may be received by his own and his Kingdom come in glory, for the deliverance of Germany and peace throughout the world, and finally, for all my relatives living and dead and all whom God has given me; may none of them be lost.[48]

This final testament was echoed in her last words, said to her sister Rosa[49] as they were led from their convent by the SS guards to be taken to Auschwitz, "Come, let us go for our people".[50]

Her intention, that "the Lord may be received by his own", was repeated by Pope John Paul II during his canonization Mass for the new saint:

[47] Herbstrith, *Edith Stein*, p. 162.

[48] Ibid., pp. 168–69.

[49] Rosa was living at the convent and acting as "Sister Portress", but was not formally accepted into the community due to the political situation.

[50] Herbstrith, *Edith Stein*, p. 180.

God of our fathers, you led the holy Martyr Teresa Benedicta of the Cross, Edith Stein, to a knowledge of your
crucified Son and called her to follow his example in death.
By her prayers, bring all to recognize their Savior in the
Crucified Christ and through him, to arrive at the vision
of your glory.[51]

Edith Stein's understanding of her own fate, as well as of the
Holocaust, was based on her knowledge of *The Science of the
Cross* (the title of her last book, written immediately prior
to her arrest and deportation to Auschwitz). When she was
seeking to enter the Carmelite Convent in Cologne she told
the prioress that one of her reasons was "[h]uman activities
cannot help us, but only the suffering of Christ. It is my
desire to share in it." [52] Many of her writings reflect on the
redemptive value of suffering, of the Cross:

By assuming human nature, Christ became capable of suffering and dying. His divine nature, which He has had
from eternity, gave infinite value and a redeeming power
to His suffering and death. Christ's suffering and death
continues in His mystical Body and in each one of His
members. Everyone has to suffer and die. And if he is a
living member of the Body of Christ, then his death and
suffering acquires redemptive power through the divine
nature of the Head. In the light of the mystery of redemption, [this] is the ultimate raison d'etre. Those who are
joined to Christ, therefore, will unflinchingly persevere
even in the dark night of subjectively feeling remote from
and abandoned by God. . . . The way of the Son of God is

[51] *Canonization of Blessed Theresa Benedicta of the Cross Edith Stein* (Canonization booklet, Vatican, Oct. 11, 1998), p. 131. Theresa Benedicta of the
Cross was the name Edith Stein took when she entered religious life.

[52] *The Hebrew Catholic*, Assoc. of Hebrew Catholics, Ypsilanti, Mich., no. 70,
May–June and Sept–Oct 1998, p. 18.

to get to the resurrection through suffering and the cross. Getting to resurrection glory with the Son of Man, through suffering and death, is also the way for each one of us and for all mankind.[53]

She wrote to a fellow Carmelite:

One can only gain a *scientia crucis* (knowledge of the cross) if one has thoroughly experienced the cross. I have been convinced of this from the first moment onwards and have said with all my heart: '*Ave, Crux, Spes Unica*' ('Hail, Cross, our only hope').[54]

Pope John Paul II, in his canonization homily, praised her understanding of the Cross:

The Cross of Christ! Ever blossoming, the tree the Cross continues to bear new fruits of salvation. This is why believers look with confidence to the Cross, drawing from its mystery of love the courage and strength to walk faithfully in the footsteps of the crucified and risen Christ.... Edith Stein is an eloquent example of this.... I am able solemnly to present this eminent daughter of Israel and faithful daughter of the Church as a saint to the whole world. Let us give glory to God for what he has accomplished in Edith Stein.

Through the experience of the Cross, Edith Stein was able to open the way to a new encounter with the God of Abraham, Isaac and Jacob, the Father of our Lord Jesus Christ. Faith and the Cross proved inseparable to her. Having matured in the school of the Cross, she found the roots to which the tree of her own life was attached. She understood that it was very important for her to "be a

[53] Ibid., p. 22.
[54] Ibid., p. 19.

daughter of the chosen people and to belong to Christ
not only spiritually, but also through her blood. . . ."

May the new saint be an example to us in our commitment to serve freedom, in our search for the truth.
May her witness constantly strengthen the bridge of mutual understanding between Jews and Christians.

St. Theresa Benedicta of the Cross, pray for us! Amen.[55]

To fully elaborate the meaning that St. Edith Stein saw in
the Holocaust would require sharing in the depth of her understanding, which is impossible. However, it is clear that
she saw in it an aspect of expiatory suffering, expiating for
the Jews' rejection of Christ. She saw in it a redemptive value
for the redemption of the whole world. She saw a specific
link between her sacrifice and the special grace needed to
bring about the conversion of the Jews. In that light, it may
not be irrelevant that she perished with a train transport composed entirely of baptized Jews.[56]

All of these aspects are very consonant with the idea that
the Holocaust is related to the Second Coming—to the return of Christ in glory. Grace is always "purchased" by suffering. Suffering and sacrifice is the coin that we here on
earth have to offer up to God and receive grace in return.
The greatest grace possible is the grace of Redemption, of
salvation. The first coming of the Messiah was purchased by
the prayers and the sufferings of twenty centuries of Jews,
climaxing in the particularly odious and offensive "slaughter
of the innocents" under Herod. We know that the Jews had
a unique and central role to play in salvation in bringing
about the first coming; is it possible, as St. Paul intimates in
Romans, that they also have a central role to play in the Second

[55] Ibid., p. 26.
[56] Herbstrith, *Edith Stein*, p. 187.

Figure 5-1: Edith Stein as a young woman

Coming? And if so, and if suffering is the coin that brings heaven to earth, could the special, particular, and extreme suffering that was imposed on them in the Holocaust be part of that role? There is a symmetry in the idea that the final return of the Messiah, the Second Coming, would be preceded once again by a slaughter of the innocents, centered on the Jews.[57]

Another way to think of this is to consider the curse laid on Adam and Eve, and on all mankind, as a result of the sin in the Garden of Eden (Genesis 3:16): "[I]n pain you shall bring forth children". As a result of original sin, birth must always be preceded by pain. Natural, individual birth is preceded by natural, individual pain—one of the most acute pains that naturally occurs. The Second Coming is the "birth" of the New Jerusalem (Revelation 21:1–2):

> Then I saw a new heaven and a new earth; for the first heaven and the first earth had passed away, and the sea was no more. And I saw the holy city, new Jerusalem, coming down out of heaven from God, prepared as a bride adorned for her husband.

Just as the birth of an individual is preceded by acute suffering, so was the birth of the first coming (in the slaughter of the innocents), and so must be the birth of the Second Coming, the "New Jerusalem". The Jewish people were called on to bear a disproportionate share of the suffering that preceded the first coming; perhaps they are also called upon to

---

[57] When the Second Coming will occur has been the subject of speculation throughout the two thousand years of the Church, most of it wrong. Here and throughout this book any speculations on the timing of the Second Coming should not be mistaken for Church teaching.

bear a disproportionate share of the pains of giving birth to the Second Coming.

The special grace of conversion, too, is always associated with suffering. Edith Stein offered her life, in part, for the grace of conversion for the Jewish people. St. Paul makes clear that the Second Coming will be preceded by the large-scale conversion of the Jews (in Romans 11); the sacrifice of Edith Stein, and through her act of oblation, the sacrifice of the other Jews, too, might be associated with the grace for that very special period of conversion that will prepare the way for the Second Coming.

Even without considering the spiritual aspects, even in a worldly sense there is a deep relationship between the formation of the State of Israel and the Holocaust. It is hard to imagine how the new state would have come into existence were it not for the tragedy. And the return of the Jews to Israel, and the reestablishment of their nation there, is consistently seen in the Old Testament as immediately preceding the coming of the Messiah in glory—an event that in the Christian understanding is in fact the Second Coming.

This possibility that the Holocaust is a harbinger of the Second Coming is given additional weight by private revelations[58] granted to another recently canonized saint, St. Faustina of Poland. In revelations received by St. Faustina during the period 1936–1938, Jesus implied that the Second Coming was not far off:

---

[58] Although the Church does not attest to the veracity of private revelations, as the *Catechism of the Catholic Church* states: "Guided by the magisterium of the Church, the *sensus fidelium* knows how to discern and welcome in these revelations whatever constitutes an authentic call of Christ or his saints to the Church" (no. 67).

You will prepare the world for My final coming.[59]

You have to ... prepare the world for the Second Coming of Him who will come, not as a merciful Savior, but as a just Judge. Oh, how terrible is that day. Determined is the day of justice, the day of divine wrath. The angels tremble before it. Speak to souls about this great mercy while it is still the time for mercy. [words of the Blessed Virgin Mary to St. Faustina][60]

Speak to the world about My mercy; let all mankind recognize my unfathomable mercy. It is a sign for the end times; after it will come the day of justice. While there is still time, let them have recourse to the fount of My mercy.[61]

Jesus also said that Poland would play a key role in preparing the way for it:

From her [Poland] will come forth the spark that will prepare the world for My final coming.[62]

The "spark" to which Jesus here refers is often thought to be the current Holy Father, Pope John Paul II, or perhaps the revelation of Divine Mercy itself. Yet is it not possible that, in another way, the spark could be the suffering and sacrifice of Auschwitz—the offering of the Holocaust—purchasing the grace of the Second Coming?

[59] Sister M. Faustina Kowalska, *Divine Mercy in My Soul: The Diary of Sister M. Faustina Kowalska* (Stockbridge, Mass.: Marian Press 1987), p. 190, no. 429.
[60] Ibid., p. 264, no. 635.
[61] Ibid., p. 333, no. 848.
[62] Ibid., p. 612, no. 1732.

"Holocaust" or "Shoah"?

As mentioned, the term "holocaust" was first applied by Elie Wiesel to the Nazi extermination of Europe's Jews. When he did so, he was making explicit reference to Abraham's willingness to sacrifice Isaac, recounted in Genesis. According to Wiesel:

> Take the word "Holocaust." I am among the first, if not the first to use it in that context. By accident. I was working on an essay, a biblical commentary, and I wrote about the sacrifice, the binding of Isaac, by his father Abraham. In the Bible, there is a Hebrew word "*ola*", which means burned offering. I thought the word "holocaust" was good: fire and so on. . . . The word had so many implications that I felt it was good.[63]

Yet now the term has fallen into disfavor among the Jews. As Dr. Ernst Ehrlich, the European director of the Jewish organization B'nai Brith, wrote:

> Holocaust or Shoah? A discussion is taking place with good reason over which of these two terms should be applied to the mass murder of the Jews. Apparently Elie Wiesel first introduced the expression "Holocaust" (Hebrew "*ola*", i.e., burnt offering) into our usage, but he later moved away from it and now uses the term "Shoah". This word appears in Isaiah 47:11 and means "disaster".
>
> Genesis 22, the story of how Isaac is not sacrificed, is the most emphatic polemic against any form of human sacrifice: God does not want it, cannot want it!

---

[63] Elie Wiesel, interview June 29, 1996, Sun Valley, Idaho, on American Academy of Achievement website www.achievement.org.

[Connecting] this mass murder with the Biblical expression for "sacrifice" . . . exonerate[s] people of that time
from their responsibility.

By the way, it is characteristic that in the passage from
Isaiah from which the word "shoah" is taken, the concept
of disaster as expiation is rejected (Isaiah 47:11). . . .

At long last, one ought to stop attributing to the murdered Jews religious concepts that are not in accord with
Judaism. That way does not honor their memory, but tries
instead to introduce a creeping missionary theology, as if
this horrible murder might have had meaning after all,
and what's more, a meaning derived from Christian
theology.[64]

It is worth considering this quote in some detail, because it
contains a number of current fallacies. The assertion that Genesis 22 is a polemic against any form of human sacrifice is
contradicted by the fact that rather than being condemned,
Abraham's willingness to sacrifice Isaac was portrayed as the
purest virtue on Abraham's part, entirely pleasing to God—so
much so that it merited an eternal blessing for his seed. Although God intervened and saved Isaac, at no time is it suggested in the biblical account that there was in any way
anything wrong in what Abraham did.[65] And at least during
the Middle Ages, Judaism saw Abraham's near sacrifice of
Isaac as having a universal salvific value strongly reminiscent
of the Christian understanding of Christ's sacrifice, as is
reflected in one of the foremost Rabbinic writings of the

---

[64] Ernst Ludwig Ehrlich, "The Jews Did Not Want to Bring Burnt Offerings", first published in *Christ in der Gegenwart* 1988, cited in Herbstrith, *Never
Forget*, pp. 129, 130.
[65] Several other Old Testament passages, notably Leviticus 27:28–29 and
Judges 11:30–40, also fall short of unequivocally condemning human sacrifice.

thirteenth century, the *Torat Habayit*.[66] The question posed was: "How can the sins of the Jewish people be taken away, since the means given in the law of Moses require Temple sacrifices, which became impossible since the destruction of the Temple in A.D. 70?" The response given by Solomon ben Abraham Adret[67], one of the greatest Rabbinic authorities of the Middle Ages, was that since the prescribed ritual means no longer existed "for pushing away of the *Tuma* [spiritual impurity] ... in the divine presence of our Lord on Mount Moriah, Isaac our forefather was bound to be offered as an unblemished offering and to atone for all our sins".[68]

Nevertheless it is not surprising that Dr. Ehrlich asserts that God never wants human sacrifice in any form, not even in the form of accepting a martyrdom imposed on one by others. For the parting of the ways between Judaism and Christianity came about precisely around this issue—whether Jesus could, in fact, have been the Messiah, given that He ended up as that sort of a "human sacrifice". The entire theology of Christianity revolves around the role of sacrifice. Pre-Jesus Judaism (that is, the Judaism described in the Old Testament and observed until the destruction of the Temple) revolved around sacrifice, around animal sacrifice, performed by the ritual priesthood in the Temple. Animal sacrifice, the shedding of blood, was necessary in every instance to atone for sin—for individual sin and for corporate sin on the part of the Jewish people as a whole. In a symbolic way human sacrifice, too, was represented in the animal sacrifice to be presented in the Temple upon the birth of a first-born son (Numbers 18:15–16). That sacrifice was in fact a ransom

[66] Rabbi Solomon ben Abraham Adret, *Torat Habayit*.
[67] He was born 1235 in Barcelona and died 1310.
[68] Adret, *Torat Habayit*.

paid to "buy back" the son. As Pope John Paul II described the presentation of the infant Jesus in the Temple, "[Jesus] submitted to the destiny of every first-born male child of his people: according to the Law of the Lord he had to be 'ransomed' with a sacrifice, 40 days after his birth (cf. Ex 13,2.12; Lv 12, 1–8)".[69]

The Letter to the Hebrews expounds on the role that blood sacrifice played in Judaism, and the way that the "human" sacrifice of Jesus fulfilled it (Hebrews 9:1–26, condensed):

Now even the first covenant had regulations for worship and an earthly sanctuary. Behind the second curtain stood a tent called the Holy of Holies, . . . into [which] only the high priest goes, and he but once a year, and not without taking blood which he offers for himself and for the errors of the people. . . .

But when Christ appeared as a high priest of the good things that have come, then through the greater and more perfect tent (not made with hands, that is, not of this creation) he entered once for all into the Holy Place, taking not the blood of goats and calves but his own blood, thus securing an eternal redemption. For if the sprinkling of defiled persons with the blood of goats and bulls and with the ashes of a heifer sanctifies for the purification of the flesh, how much more shall the blood of Christ, who through the eternal Spirit offered himself without blemish to God, purify your conscience from dead works to

---

[69] Homily from Vigil Mass for the Feast of the Presentation, February 1, 2003, in *L'Osservatore Romano*, English ed., Feb. 5, 2003, p. 1, commenting on Luke 2:22–23: "And when the time came for their purification according to the law of Moses, they brought him [Jesus] up to Jerusalem to present him to the Lord (as it is written in the law of the Lord, 'Every male that opens the womb shall be called holy to the Lord') and to offer a sacrifice according to what is said in the law of the Lord, 'a pair of turtledoves, or two young pigeons'."

serve the living God. Therefore he is the mediator of a new covenant, so that those who are called may receive the promised eternal inheritance, since a death has occurred which redeems them from the transgressions under the first covenant. . . .

[E]ven the first covenant was not ratified without blood. For when every commandment of the law had been declared by Moses to all the people, he took the blood of calves and goats, with water and scarlet wool and hyssop, and sprinkled both the book itself and all the people, saying, "This is the blood of the covenant which God commanded you." And in the same way he sprinkled with the blood both the tent and all the vessels used in worship. Indeed, under the law almost everything is purified with blood, and without the shedding of blood there is no forgiveness of sins. Thus it was necessary for the copies of the heavenly things to be purified with these rites, but the heavenly things themselves with better sacrifices than these. For Christ has entered, not into a sanctuary made with hands, a copy of the true one, but into heaven itself, now to appear in the presence of God on our behalf. Nor was it to offer himself repeatedly, as the high priest enters the Holy Place yearly with blood not his own; for then he would have had to suffer repeatedly since the foundation of the world. But as it is, he has appeared once for all at the end of the age to put away sin by the sacrifice of himself . . . we have been sanctified through the offering of the body of Jesus Christ once for all.

Whoever the author of the Letter to the Hebrews was (the traditional attribution to St. Paul has been heavily contested), he was certainly a well-trained and knowledgeable "Temple" Jew, writing to other Jews of his day. Therefore the theology that he presents, that "without the shedding of blood there is no forgiveness of sins", must be an accurate

JUDAISM AND THE HOLOCAUST 175

portrayal of the Jewish theology of its day. The extension from the blood sacrifice of animals to that of Jesus is, of course, a "Christian" one, but one that lies at the very heart of Christian theology from its very beginnings in Judaism.

Dr. Ehrlich also asserts that connecting this mass murder with the biblical expression for "sacrifice" exonerates people of that time from their responsibility. Yet in the Gospel account of Jesus' death it is clear that although His death was a willing sacrifice:

> [Jesus said] "Behold, we are going up to Jerusalem; and the Son of man will be delivered to the chief priests and the scribes, and they will condemn him to death . . . and kill him; and after three days he will rise" (Mark 10:33–34).

It in no way lessened the guilt of those responsible for His death:

> "For the Son of man goes as it is written of him, but woe to that man by whom the Son of man is betrayed! It would have been better for that man if he had not been born" (Mark 14:21).

In fact, this is the only case in the New Testament in which Jesus identifies someone as damned, for that is the only circumstance under which, in the long run, it would be better for him not to have been born.

Dr. Ehrlich claims that the passage in Isaiah from which the word "*shoah*" is taken rejects the concept of disaster as expiation. Let us look at the passage (the word "*shoah*", "disaster", appears in verse 11), and see if this is so (Isaiah 47:1–3,6–11,15):

> ¹ Come down and sit in the dust, O virgin daughter of Babylon; sit on the ground without a throne, O daughter

of the Chaldeans! For you shall no more be called tender and delicate.

² Take the millstones and grind meal, put off your veil, strip off your robe, uncover your legs, pass through the rivers.

³ Your nakedness shall be uncovered, and your shame shall be seen. I will take vengeance, and I will spare no man. . . .

⁶ I was angry with my people . . . I gave them into your hand, you showed them no mercy. . . .

⁷ You said, "I shall be mistress for ever," so that you did not lay these things to heart or remember their end.

⁸ Now therefore hear this, you lover of pleasures, who sit securely, who say in your heart, "I am, and there is no one besides me; I shall not sit as a widow or know the loss of children":

⁹ These two things shall come to you in a moment, in one day; the loss of children and widowhood shall come upon you in full measure, in spite of your many sorceries and the great power of your enchantments.

¹⁰ You felt secure in your wickedness, you said, "No one sees me"; your wisdom and your knowledge led you astray, and you said in your heart, "I am, and there is no one besides me."

¹¹ But evil shall come upon you, for which you cannot atone; disaster [Hebrew: "*shoah*"] shall fall upon you, which you will not be able to expiate; and ruin shall come on you suddenly, of which you know nothing. . . .

¹⁵ [T]here is no one to save you.

Contemporary Jews have chosen the word "*shoah*" rather than "holocaust" to move away from the idea that the Holocaust was a deliberate act of God, either a sacrifice that He wanted or, even more unthinkably, a punishment visited upon the Jewish people. However, in so doing, instead of identifying the Jewish victims with Isaac, one of the three great founding saints and patriarchs of Judaism (remember God Himself is identified in Judaism as the "God of Abraham, of Isaac and of Jacob"), who because of his very chosenness was to be sacrificed, they are identified with the emblem of all that is most displeasing to God in the Old Testament, with the infamous "whore of Babylon". For, according to Dr. Ehrlich, the term "*shoah*" is drawn from this story of God's vengeful judgment and punishment on the whore of Babylon for her wantonness (v. 3), her merciless cruelty (v. 6), her arrogant pride (vv. 7–8, 10), and her sorcery (v. 9). The reason there is no atonement in the "*shoah*" that overtakes her is not that suffering cannot atone for sin, but rather that the culprit here is beyond redemption! This hardly seems to be doing a service to the memory of the victims of the tragedy.

Finally, let us return to the last paragraph in the quote from Dr. Ehrlich:

> [S]top attributing to the murdered Jews religious concepts that are not in accord with Judaism ... as if this horrible murder might have had meaning after all, and what's more, a meaning derived from Christian theology.

If the Holocaust did have a role in Divine Providence, that role is not dependent on "religious concepts" being "attribut[ed] to the murdered Jews". God is not dependent on our understanding for something to have meaning in His eyes; even less is the meaning that He finds in something dependent on the meaning that we attribute to it. It is the role of theology, whether Christian or Jewish, to understand God, not to define Him as though He does not exist outside of our interpretation of Him. If "Christian theology" finds a meaning in the Holocaust that "Jewish theology" does not, that is because it has a different understanding about how God works through human events, about the role of suffering and death, about the economy of salvation and the unfolding of salvation history, and about who Jesus was, not because the source of the meaning itself comes from the theology. The meaning can come only from God; theology contributes only the ability to understand that meaning.

CHAPTER SIX

Ideological Foundations of Nazism

In order to understand the relationship between the Holocaust and God's plan for salvation, it is necessary to understand the spiritual forces lying behind the Holocaust—the ideological foundations of the Nazi movement.

Eugenics

There is a facile temptation to think of Nazi anti-Semitism as an expression of Christianity and Christian theology—"applied Christianity", if you will. Yet even a cursory examination of Nazi writings and policies shows that this is far from the truth—on the contrary, the campaign to exterminate the Jews grew out of the worldview of secular materialism, of evolution and the exaltation of the natural over the supernatural, and was in fact an extreme expression of "applied Darwinism".[1]

In the past, there have been many persecutions of the Jews in Christian countries. These persecutions fell into one of three categories. Some were mob actions, inflamed expressions of blood lust and fury. Tragically, many of these were incited by pseudo-Christian exhortations to avenge the death

---

[1] That is, an application of the principles of Darwinism to the social sphere.

of Christ or by related blood libels against the Jews (most particularly accusing them of the human sacrifice of Christian children). The pogroms and the rampaging mobs of the Crusades fall into this category. However, the Holocaust does not. The slaughter of the Holocaust was not produced by momentary mob hysteria, but was a calculated, "rational", long-term campaign plotted by sober, if deranged, minds.

The second category consists of campaigns to produce a Christian society and a Christian state free from the "immoral" (because un-Christian) influence of the Jews. The expulsion of the Jews from Spain in 1492 falls into this category. These persecutions were predicated on the idea that Jews were deficient in virtue because they lacked the grace that is available only through baptism and the other sacraments. Baptized—that is, converted—Jews were always welcome and exempt from the persecution. The Inquisition was related to this second category of anti-Jewish campaigns. In order to avoid the forced expulsion from Spain, a large number of Jewish families had pretended to convert to Christianity, while continuing to practice the Jewish religion in secret. It was these "crypto"-Jews, known as Marranos, who were targets of the Inquisition, not as Jews—for the Inquisition always acknowledged that it had no authority at all over non-Christians—but as heretical, or false, Christians. As a fight against heresy and sacrilege within the Catholic Church, the Inquisition pursued only Christians. The Marranos, by participating in the sacraments and pretending to be Christian, fell into the purview of the Inquisition. They were unfortunately also heretics because of their Jewish beliefs and committed sacrilege whenever they participated in the sacraments. This brought the wrath of the Inquisition down upon them. Yet it was not based on their being Jewish, but on their being false Catholics.

The third category of persecutions of the Jews flowing out of Christianity is represented by laws and actions that were aimed at getting Jews to convert to Christianity. These campaigns were rooted in Christian theology as understood at the time and motivated by goodwill.[2] Since, as it was believed at the time, there was no possibility of heaven for the unbaptized, it was thought an act of charity to the Jews to do everything possible to bring them to convert to Christianity and so save them from damnation. These persecutions, aimed at the conversion of Jews, bear no relationship to a campaign to eradicate the Jewish race from the earth because of their race. Not only were Christians of Jewish origin spared during these persecutions, but they were even the expressed goal of it.

With this background one can see the very different character of the Nazi persecution of the Jews. Rather than being aimed at "saving" the Jews by bringing about their conversion, or "protecting" Christian culture or morals from the lack of virtue of the unbaptized, its sole aim was the eradication of the race as a race, the freeing of the world from the "taint" of Jewish blood.

The issue was not the religion of the Jew; it was the racial identity. It was not the apostasy of Judaism that was to be wiped out, but the Jewish race (or "gene pool"). Being baptized was not an escape; in fact, being born and raised Christian, by parents who had already converted to Christianity, did not make the slightest difference to being marked for extermination—the only issue was being of "Jewish blood". The campaign to exterminate the Jews was a eugenics program, done to free the world of the "scourge" of the

---

[2] Recent Catholic teaching makes clear that it is always wrong to use coercion to bring about conversion (see Vatican II's *Dignitatis Humanae*, Dec. 7, 1965).

Jewish race. The undesirable characteristics of the Jews were intrinsic; it was not their Jewish faith, or their refusal of Christianity, that made them offensive, but simply their race. Germany and the world was to be purified of the pollution of Jewish blood as part of the campaign to improve the human race and create a nation of "supermen" through selective breeding. It was applied Darwinism, not applied Christianity. Hitler himself expressed his ideas in the terms of Darwinism:

> Whoever, ignores or despises the laws of race ... places an obstacle in the victorious path of the superior race and, by so doing, he interferes with a prerequisite condition for all human progress.[3]

In a 1934 conversation with two Protestant bishops, Hitler emphasized that the problem with the Jews was one of race and not religion:

> The church must get used to the doctrine of blood and race. Just as the Catholic church could not change the fact that the earth goes round the sun, so the church could not do away with the irrefutable facts which are given in blood and race. Unless they recognize that, developments will simply pass them by.[4]

When Hitler came to power in 1933, many in the eugenics movement viewed it as a triumph for their science. In June, Hitler set up the Expert Committee on Questions of Population and Racial Policy and on its recommendation enacted, on July 14, 1933, a law requiring compulsory sterilization for those who

[3] Quoted in Nora Levin, *The Holocaust* (New York: Schocken Books, 1973), p. 41.

[4] Klaus Scholder, *A Requiem for Hitler* (Philadelphia: Trinity Press International, 1989), pp. 174–75, citing H. A. Oberman, *Wurseln des Antisemitismus*, Berlin, 1981.

carried hereditary conditions or diseases, including feeble-mindedness, schizophrenia, alcoholism, and epilepsy. Under this law German doctors sterilized nearly 400,000 people. The "Law for the Protection of German Blood and German Honor" enacted two years later, which prohibited marriage between Germans and Jews, was more eugenics, this time to protect the German blood from contamination from "subhuman" Jews (in the words of the Reich). In 1939, Hitler set up an advisory committee to institute a program to euthanize disabled children, saying, "If Germany were to get a million children a year, and was to remove 700,000 to 800,000 of weakest of them, the final result might even be an increase in strength." Later that year all state governments received the order: "Children up to the age of three who are retarded or deformed must be registered by midwives or physicians, and a questionnaire must be completed describing their disability." On the questionnaire the child's case was assessed and a "plus" or "minus" placed to indicate whether the child was to be allowed to live or be killed. Clinics were set up throughout Germany to euthanize the children by injection, oral drugs, or by the cessation of feeding. The program eventually included children up to twelve years old. The committee also initiated a program, carried out by the "T4" group (named after its headquarters at 4 Tiergarten Strasse), which "euthanized" between 70,000 and 100,000 inmates of German mental institutions. At the Nuremberg trial, the total number of euthanasia victims was estimated at 275,000.[5]

[5] Sources for this paragraph include, Hans-Heinrich Wilhelm, "The Euthanasia Program", *The Encyclopedia of the Holocaust* (New York: Macmillan, 1990), 2:451–54; Levin, *The Holocaust*, p. 302; Robert J. Lifton, *The Nazi Doctors: Medical Killing and the Psychology of Genocide* (London: Papermac, 1986), p. 142; and Stephen B. Saetz, "Eugenics and the Third Reich" in *The Eugenics Bulletin*, Winter 1985.

Eugenics was central to Hitler's philosophy. In *Mein Kampf*, Hitler attributes all of the ills of a nation to its failure to impose eugenics:

> Whether we consider questions of general justice or cankers of economic life, symptoms of cultural decline or processes of political degeneration, questions of faulty schooling or the bad influence exerted on grown-ups by the press, etc., everywhere and always it is fundamentally the disregard of the racial needs of ones own people or failure to see a foreign racial menace.[6]

The Nazi campaign to eradicate the Jews was a massive eugenics program, a diabolical attempt to apply Darwinian principles to society. As such, its ideological support came not from the proponents of Christianity, but from the proponents of eugenics, i.e., of "planned parenthood".

For the great proponent of eugenics in the English-speaking world was none other than Margaret Sanger, the foundress of "Planned Parenthood". She was unabashed in her atheism as well as her promotion of eugenics. Below the masthead of her magazine, *Woman Rebel*, ran the slogan "No Gods, No Masters".

It is not difficult to see the similarities between her politics and those of the Third Reich. The following is from *Blessed Are the Barren*:[7]

> At a March 1925 international birth control gathering held in New York City, a speaker warned of the menace posed

---

[6] Adolf Hitler, *Mein Kampf*, trans. Ralph Manheim (Boston: Houghton Mifflin, 1974), p. 297.

[7] Robert Marshall and Charles Donovan, *Blessed Are the Barren: The Social Policy of Planned Parenthood* (San Francisco: Ignatius Press, 1991), pp. 1–2.

by the "black" and "yellow" peril. The man was not a National Socialist (Nazi) or a leader of the Ku Klux Klan. The speaker was Dr. S. Adolphus Knopf, a member of Margaret Sanger's American Birth Control League (ABCL), which along with other groups eventually became known as Planned Parenthood. Another doctor at this conference lamented that preventive medicine was saving the lives of "worthless unfits," and he seriously suggested that euthanasia be used to "dispose of some of our utterly hopeless dependents," but noted that this could not happen until the public changed its "prejudices" on the subject. . . .

Elsewhere Sanger spoke of her plan for sterilizing those she designated as "unfit" as the "salvation of American civilization". And she also spoke of those who were irresponsible and reckless", among whom she included those "whose religious scruples prevent their exercising control over their numbers". She further contended that "there is no doubt in the minds of all thinking people that the procreation of this group should be stopped". Whether this was to be accomplished "voluntarily" does not appear to have been a serious policy impediment.

That many Americans of African origin constituted a segment the Sangerites considered as "unfit" can be denied only with great difficulty and in the face of policies that affirm this assumption. At one point Sanger expressed a fear that Negroes might think birth control a clever extermination project, but that selected black ministers could dispose of that idea.

Sanger's other colleagues included avowed and sophisticated racists. One, Lothrop Stoddard, was a Harvard graduate and the author of *The Rising Tide of Color against White World Supremacy*. Stoddard was something of a Nazi enthusiast who described the eugenic practices of the Third Reich as "scientific" and "humanitarian". And Dr. Harry

Laughlin, another Sanger associate and board member of her group, described Slavic and Italian immigrants as "even inferior to our native Negro population not long released from slavery". Laughlin also spoke of purifying America's human "breeding stock" and purging America's "bad strains". These "strains" included the "shiftless, ignorant, and worthless class of antisocial whites of the South".

Laughlin apparently was the inspiration for the Nazi compulsory sterilization law passed in 1933. Under its provisions, nearly two million people were forcibly sterilized from 1933 to 1945.[8]

A number of individuals had high profiles in both Margaret Sanger's and the Third Reich's eugenics campaigns. Lothrop Stoddard, mentioned above, in his 1920 book *The Rising Tide of Color against White World Supremacy* depicted a slowly increasing white race being overwhelmed by more rapidly increasing "colored" races. This was apparently so consonant with Sanger's views that she appointed him to the board of the Birth Control League, the forerunner of Planned Parenthood. In a later book, he noted that the Nazis succeeded in increasing "both the size and the quality of the population", with a "drastic curb of the defective elements . . . weeding out the worst strains in the Germanic stock in a scientific and truly humanitarian way".[9] Hitler met Stoddard and was so favorably impressed that he had Stoddard's writings given great prominence in Nazi school textbooks; so much so that Goebbels, the Reich minister for propaganda, jealously complained.

Another contributor to Sanger's *Birth Control Review* with deep ties to the Third Reich was Ernst Rudin. He was the

[8] Ibid., p. 135.
[9] Lothrop Stoddard, *Into the Darkness: Nazi Germany Today* (New York: Duell, Sloan, and Pierce, 1940), pp. 190–91.

director of the foremost German eugenics research institute, the Kaiser Wilhelm Institute for Genealogy in Munich. When Reich Interior Minister Wilhelm Frick established the Expert Committee on Questions of Population and Racial Policy on June 2, 1933, he included Rudin. This was the committee that recommended the law on forced sterilization enacted July 14, 1933. In an address to the German Society for Race-Hygiene, Rudin said,

> The significance of Rassenhygiene [Race-Hygiene] did not become evident to all aware Germans until the political activity of Adolf Hitler and only through his work has our 30 year long dream of translating Rassenhygiene into action finally become a reality.... We can hardly express our efforts more plainly or appropriately than in the words of the Fuhrer: "Whoever is not physically or mentally fit must not pass on his defects to his children. The state must take care that only the fit produce children." [10]

Rudin echoed this in Margaret Sanger's *Birth Control Review*: "The danger to the community of the unsegregated feeble-minded woman is more evident. [They] should be prevented from procreation. In my view we should act without delay." [11]

Another board member and associate of Margaret Sanger's who approved of concentration camps and forced sterilization was Dr. Harry Laughlin, a supervisor of the Eugenics Record Office in Cold Spring Harbor, New York. In Sanger's *Birth Control Review*, he wrote:

[10] William H. Tucker, *The Science and Politics of Racial Research* (Urbana, Ill.: Univ. of Illinois Press, 1994), p. 121.

[11] *Birth Control Review*, vol. 17, no. 4 (April 1933), pp. 102–4.

If it is agreed that certain individuals are so degenerate in their hereditary properties that offspring procreated by them would, in high probability, rank as defective or degenerate persons . . . then it would seem to be the duty of organized society to prevent their reproduction. If such prevention is accomplished by institutional segregation [i.e., prisons or concentration camps] . . . then sexual sterilization is not necessary. If, however, the degenerate individual is physiologically able to reproduce, and is not restrained from doing so by effective segregation, then the surest way to prevent reproduction would seem to be to destroy the physiological capacity to reproduce. This has been done in many cases.[12]

In the future the several states may well look toward the establishment of a still higher biological standard for the legalization of parenthood. Race betterment, whether in plants, animals, or man, is never achieved with our radical elimination from parenthood of the strains which show hereditary degeneracy. . . . Segregation and eugenical sterilization are sound and legal instruments for preventing reproduction by the most defective strains.[13]

It is obvious that the "improvement" of the race through eugenics was a primary focus of Sanger's efforts. Among the titles of articles published by her were "Some Moral Aspects of Eugenics" (June 1920), "The Eugenic Conscience" (February 1921), "The Purpose of Eugenics" (December 1924), "Birth Control and Positive Eugenics" (July 1925), and "Birth Control: The True Eugenics". In her view, eugenics was the ultimate goal of birth control: "Birth Control is thus the

---

[12] Harry H. Laughlin, "Legal Status of Eugenical Sterilization", *Birth Control Review*, vol. 12, no. 3 (March 1928), p. 78.

[13] Harry H. Laughlin, "Eugenical Aspects of Legal Sterilization", *Birth Control Review*, vol. 17, no. 4 (April 1933), p. 87.

entering wedge for the Eugenic educator . . . the unbalance between the birth rate of the 'unfit' and the 'fit' admittedly the greatest present menace to civilization. . . . The most urgent problem today is how to limit and discourage the overfertility of the mentally and physically defective" (*Birth Control Review* October 1921);[14] and, "Birth Control . . . is really the greatest and most truly eugenic method . . . the most constructive and necessary of the means to racial health." [15] This was in fact explicitly the purpose stated for the New York State Planned Parenthood in their bylaws: "to develop and organize on sound eugenic, social and medical principles, interest in and knowledge of birth control".[16]

Her plans for a national eugenics program consisted of the same elements found in that of the Third Reich—forced sterilization and concentration camps (which she referred to euphemistically as "separation" or "segregation"). Consider the following points from her "Plan for Peace", published in her *Birth Control Review* (April 1932, pp. 107–8):

> d. to apply a stern and rigid policy of sterilization and segregation to that grade of population whose progeny is tainted, or whose inheritance is such that objectionable traits may be transmitted to offspring . . .
>
> f. to give certain dysgenic [i.e., genetically undesirable] groups in our population their choice of segregation or sterilization.
>
> g. to apportion farm lands and homesteads for these segregated persons where they would be taught to work under competent instructors for the period of their entire lives.

[14] Marshall and Donovan, *Blessed Are the Barren*, pp. 8–9.

[15] Margaret Sanger, *The Pivot of Civilization* (New York: Brentano's Press, 1922), p. 189.

[16] Marshall and Donovan, *Blessed Are the Barren*, p. 25

[W]ith five million mental and moral degenerates segre-
gated . . . we could then turn our attention to the basic needs
for international peace.

This debased philosophy was, of course, diametrically opposed to the values of Christianity and, realizing this, Sanger
saw the Christian churches, and the Catholic Church in particular, as her worst enemies. Consider the following quotes
from her *Birth Control Review*:

> The Catholic Church is the bigoted, relentless enemy
> of birth control. . . .This [birth control] movement
> threatens its hold upon the poor and the ignorant, and
> probably only the existence of restraining laws prevents it
> from applying the thumb-screw and the rack to all those
> who believe in [a] woman's right to practice voluntary
> motherhood.[17]

> The fight for Birth Control becomes increasingly a
> fight against the usurpations of the Roman Catholic
> Church.[18]

> Our only real enemy is the [Catholic] church.[19]

> I . . . look forward to seeing humanity free some day of
> the tyranny of priests no less than of capitalists.[20]

---

[17] *Birth Control Review*, vol. 2, no. 6 (June 1918), p. 16, editorial comment.
[18] "The World We Live In", *Birth Control Review*, vol. 8, no. 4 (April 1924),
p. 99.
[19] "Sir W. Arbuthnot Lane, M.D., on Birth Control", *Birth Control Review*,
vol. 8, no. 4 (April 1924), p. 115.
[20] Walter Adolphe Roberts, "Birth Control and the Revolution", *Birth Control Review*, vol. 1, no. 6 (June 1917), p. 7.

The contrast between Sanger's philosophy and Christianity is also apparent in her views on charity and helping the poor:

> Organized charity itself is . . . the surest sign that our civilization has bred, is breeding and is perpetuating constantly increasing numbers of defectives, delinquents and dependents. . . . [Nothing is] more insidiously injurious than . . . to supply gratis medical and nursing facilities to slum mothers."[21]

Associating the Holocaust with a Christian ethic is exactly backwards. The extermination of the Jews by the Third Reich did not flow out of Christianity, but out of a philosophy directly opposed to Christianity and all that it stands for, one introduced by Darwinism and epitomized in our country by Planned Parenthood and Margaret Sanger. The Holocaust owed nothing to the principles of "Christianity"; it owed everything to the principles of Margaret Sanger and "Planned Parenthood".

Preparing the Way for Nazism

In looking back on the development of the ideas and social movements that paved the way for Nazism, one can only be struck by the breadth and depth of the foundations that were laid to enable its later success. It appears as though a patient master planner had carefully mapped out a program including intellectual, social, and spiritual dimensions that would span most of a century before coming to fruition in the "Final Solution". Let us look more closely at this campaign.

[21] Sanger, *Pivot of Civilization*, pp. 108, 114.

Intellectual

The Nazi campaign to exterminate the Jews was, as discussed, a program of planned eugenics. Eugenics assumes a population with desirable traits to be strengthened and a population with undesirable ("dysgenic") traits to be eliminated. The Nazis, of course, were intent on improving the "Aryan race" by weeding out the dysgenic Jews, as well as other non-Aryan populations. Where did this belief in the intrinsic superiority of the "Aryan race" and inferiority of the Jews come from?

From an intellectual perspective, the social theories that underlay Nazism can be traced back to the Second Reich. In the words of Jewish historian Nora Levin, it was then that

> there developed in Germany a new religion, a cult of race based on . . . the elevation of theories of blood and soil to final "truths." Germany had just won a decisive victory over the French. Bismarck's "blood and iron" policies had created a powerful, even dominant nation. A strident economic and political nationalism erupted. In this new age, it was argued, the national state must be the power-state whose highest duty was to increase its power and safeguard itself against . . . every trace of national weakness. In the atmosphere of this period, called by one historian "the seed-time of totalitarian nationalism," many Germans succumbed to the cult of race. The myth of a "master race" destined to conquer the world and subdue lesser "races" gripped many Germans. Influential scholars and writers were carried away by a rampant social Darwinism. . . . [I]t seemed obvious that the Germans must belong to a superior race. . . . German nationalism and imperialism thus became impregnated with ideas of German racial superiority. (Levin, *The Holocaust*, pp. 11–12.)

The philosophical foundations of this theory had been laid by French aristocrat Count Joseph Arthur de Gobineau, in his 1854 *Essay on the Inequality of the Human Races*. Then, toward the end of the century, Gobineau's philosophy was further developed by Houston Chamberlain, who, although an Englishman, was strongly attracted to the "glory" of German militarism and spent most of his life in Germany and Austria, eventually marrying the daughter of German composer Richard Wagner and settling in Beyreuth. In 1899 Chamberlain finished his major work, *The Foundations of the Nineteenth Century*,[22] in which he laid out the racial theories that would make him "the idolized prophet of the Nazi party".[23] According to him the Nordic race and, in particular, the Germans were the master race and the creators of everything good in the world, while the Jews were a "negative" race, a "bastard" breed, deserving of nothing but contempt and denial from the superior Aryans. The world would be saved when the Aryan race lay claim to its destiny to rule humanity, a cause to which every German should totally dedicate himself. The then emperor of Germany, Wilhelm II, enthusiastically embraced Chamberlain's theories, which were to become the base upon which the Nazis built their racial myth. The book became a huge bestseller, selling out eight printings in its first ten years, and had a profound influence on Hitler. Gobineau and Chamberlain had paved the way for the intellectual acceptance of the Nazi theories to come.

[22] H. S. Chamberlain, *Foundations of the Nineteenth Century*, trans. John Lees (London: John Lane, 1910).
[23] Levin, *The Holocaust*, p. 13.

Social

During this same period following the Prussian-Austrian war of 1866, the German-speaking parts of central and eastern Europe were swept by what became known as the *völkisch* movement. This movement had its roots in a mass of small, highly nationalistic German-chauvinist social clubs that sprang up to foster German culture in the Austrian empire following the war. These were a reaction to the national and legal changes of the period. Democratization and the inclusion of a number of non-German peoples into the empire led to fears that the German culture would be submerged under the Slav and Latin influence—the Germans constituted only about 35% of the population in the new, democratic Austria. In response, some of the Germans in Austria wished to make German-Austria a province of the German Reich. This tension was heightened by a tug-of-war of authority between the Catholic Church and secular government, marked by the Vatican's decrees, in 1870, asserting the primacy of the authority of the Pope over loyalty to the state, the subsequent passing of the anti-Catholic "Falk Laws" in May 1873, and their relaxation and the restoration of Catholics' rights in 1887 as a result of the Pope's negotiations. The *völkisch* groups were formed with the intention of raising national consciousness among Germans, foster German culture and identity, and defend German interests. They studied German history, literature, and mythology; pursued activities such as choral singing, gymnastics, and mountain sports with *völkisch* ritual; and worked for a virulent nationalism. The movement was steeped in race mysticism, pseudo-biology/science, romantic yearning for a mythical past Germanic rural life, and anti-Semitism. Its literature portrayed history as a primeval battle between the pastoral blond Nordic hero and the urban parasitic Jew. The later Nazi concept of *Blut und Boden* ("blood and soil") found its origins in the *völkisch* view of a pastoral Germanic past. By 1900 there were more than 300 *völkisch* clubs, involving probably between 100,000 and 150,000 people.

In *Mein Kampf* Hitler wrote: "[T]he basic ideas of the National-Socialist movement are völkisch and the völkisch ideas are National-Socialist." By 1939, many of the *völkisch* groups were absorbed into the NSDAP (Nazional-socialistische Deutsche Arbeiterpartei), most members having already joined the Nazi Party.

Spiritual

Even such bizarre beliefs as these had to have "spiritual" principles to rest on, and ultimately those were provided by occultists and occultism. From the outset, this pseudo-science of racial superiority was deeply intertwined with occultism and occult "religion". This was not as strange in the culture of the time as it appears to us today. During the nineteenth century, there was frequent confusion between science and spiritualism, and spiritualistic practices were often seen as "scientific" investigation into spiritual phenomena. Such confusion abounded in such areas as magnetism, skull shape ("phrenology"), hypnosis, agriculture and nutrition (e.g., "biodynamics"), and electricity. "Race-science" was just another one of these pseudo-sciences. Most of the leading theorists of the racial superiority of the German race were also actively involved in occultism.

Before explicitly addressing the occultism that underlay the Nazi movement, it would be useful to step back and consider the larger context. Thus far we have been examining the role of the Jews and Judaism in the "economy of salvation". God created the world and mankind with the intent that men, to the greatest extent possible consistent with man's free will and God's justice, "be saved"—that is, end up enjoying eternal life in beatitude with God. All of creation and all of Divine Providence are ordered to this end, and the pattern of that order may be called the "economy of salvation". We have seen a number of aspects of that economy of salvation so far—the way that God chooses one or a few individuals to represent all of humanity, the way that God uses man's willingness to sacrifice and his suffering to bring grace for the salvation of others, and so forth.

In a parallel way one can consider that there is also an "economy of perdition". An intelligent agent lies behind the campaign to lead as many souls to perdition as possible, and he too has standard methods with which he operates and an economy of forces that he exploits to try to bring about the loss of as many souls as possible, as well as as much human misery and sin as possible. This agent was given the name "Satan" in the Old Testament, which is simply the Hebrew for "adversary", since he is the adversary of man's salvation. It was he who incited David to commit his greatest offense against God, in punishment for which 70,000 Israelites died (1 Chronicles 21:1–2,7,14):

> Satan stood up against Israel, and incited David to num-
> ber Israel. So David said to Joab and the commanders of
> the army, "Go, number Israel, from Beersheba to Dan,
> and bring me a report, that I may know their number."
> ... But God was displeased with this thing, and he smote
> Israel.... So the LORD sent a pestilence upon Israel; and
> there fell seventy thousand men of Israel.

It was also he who induced God to test Job's fidelity with a series of severe trials (Job 1:7–11):

The LORD said to Satan, "Whence have you come?" Satan answered the LORD, "From going to and fro on the earth, and from walking up and down on it." And the LORD said to Satan, "Have you considered my servant Job, that there is none like him on the earth, a blameless and upright man, who fears God and turns away from evil?" Then Satan answered the LORD, "Does Job fear God for nought? Hast thou not put a hedge about him and his house and all that he has, on every side? Thou hast blessed the work of his hands, and his possessions have increased in the land. But put forth thy hand now, and touch all that he has, and he will curse thee to thy face."

The fundamental situation is succinctly summarized by St. Paul: "For we are not contending against flesh and blood, but against the principalities, against the powers, against the world rulers of this present darkness, against the spiritual hosts of wickedness in the heavenly places" (Ephesians 6:12).

In examining the ideological roots of Nazism the "economy of perdition" can be observed at close hand. The adversary draws men into sin by appealing to their vices—pride, desire for power, lust, and so forth. He draws them deeper and deeper toward him and away from God by drawing them more and more deeply into sin—in this case, sins against chastity, sexual perversions, sadism, and murder. His power over them as individuals increases as they become more and more debauched in sin; their ability to reason and even their basic sanity dissolves away as his influence over their minds increases. Their morality spirals downward, leading both to greater and greater cruelty and sadism and also to greater and greater sexual degeneracy. They abandon anything resembling true religion, replacing it with idolatry, occultism, or outright Satanism. As they become involved with the occult, their thinking drifts further and further away from what we would think of as a sane worldview, and over time once-rational individuals become willing to accept the most bizarre ideas as facts. All of this we see in the development of the Nazis. Again, in the words of St. Paul:

> [T]hey became futile in their thinking and their senseless minds were darkened. Claiming to be wise, they became fools, and exchanged the glory of the immortal God for images resembling mortal man or birds or animals or reptiles. Therefore God gave them up in the lusts of their hearts to impurity, to the dishonoring of their bodies among themselves, because they exchanged the truth about God for a lie and worshiped and served the creature rather than the Creator. . . .
>
> For this reason God gave them up to dishonorable passions. Their women exchanged natural relations for unnatural, and the men likewise gave up natural relations with women and were consumed with passion for one another, men committing shameless acts with men and receiving in their own persons the due penalty for their error. (Romans 1:21–27)

A huge portal was opened up to hell, and a four-lane highway on which eighteen-wheelers carrying a demonic import/export traffic sped back and forth—in one direction, the Nazis feeding the forces of hell with their cruelty, their murder, their occult rites, worship and practices, their idolatry; in the other direction, hell feeding them with power, excitement, inspiration, lust, and success in their malevolent undertakings. For just as God gives spiritual consolations and the fruits of the Holy Spirit to those who serve Him—"love, joy, peace, patience, kindness, goodness, faithfulness, gentleness, self-control" (Galatians 5:22–23)—the evil one rewards his servants with demonic counterfeits of these—lust, excitement, power, passion, an iron will, and so forth. And as the Holy Spirit allows His followers to share in the charismatic gifts for the common good—gifts such as "wisdom, knowledge, healing, prophecy", and so forth (1 Corinthians 12)—the evil spirit has counterfeits of these too that he gives to his servants—occult abilities and powers, clairvoyance, the ability to overpower the will of others, extraordinary strength, Machiavellian cleverness, and so forth. It is this exchange that we will now examine. It is the explanation for the central role that occultism, sadism, sexual perversion, and murder played in the story of the Third Reich.

One should always, however, remember in viewing history as the interaction between the "economy of salvation" and the "economy of perdition", that the economy of perdition itself is a part of God's mysterious providence and is encompassed by the economy of salvation. God does not will evil; yet, mysteriously, the "adversary" of man's salvation himself was created by God and is sustained in existence entirely by God's sovereign will to serve His purpose, which is goodness itself. Although at times evil may appear to gain the upper hand, absolutely everything that God allows to happen "works together for good for those who love God, who are called according to his purpose" (Romans 8:28).

Theosophy

The discussion on which we are about to embark is of necessity somewhat lengthy, since it covers the development of occult racist theory over the course of some fifty years, culminating in the neo-pagan pseudo-religion of the Nazis. Each link in this chain exhibits a virulent hatred of Jews and Judaism and a complete adoption of a pagan, gnostic, "New Age" type religion. Each enthusiastically embraces a morality of unbridled and perverted sexual license. Each has total contempt for the dignity, freedom, or sanctity of the individual. Not surprisingly, since all of these philosophies and values are antithetical to Christianity, they all also exhibit nothing but contempt for Christianity, Christians, and Christian morality, and look forward to the demise of Christianity.

The first link in this chain was Madame Blavatsky with her version of occultism known as "Theosophy". Blavatsky was born in Russia of German parents in 1831. At sixteen, she married a much older man, but after a few weeks she left him and spent the next twenty years traveling the world, spending time in Turkey, Egypt, Greece, Europe, North and South America, India, and Tibet. She claimed to have received the occult doctrines that became the basis of Theosophy during seven years she spent in Tibet studying under Hindu "Mahatmas" (Masters). In 1888, she published some of these doctrines in *The Secret Doctrine*, from which the following passages are extracted:[24]

> The human Races are born one from the other, grow, develop, become old, and die. Their sub-races and nations follow the same rule.
>
> Since the beginning of the Atlantean Race[25] many million years have passed, yet we find the last of the Atlanteans, still mixed up with the Aryan element, 11,000 years ago. This shows the enormous overlapping of one race over the race which succeeds it. Occult philosophy teaches that even now, under our very eyes, the new Race and Races are preparing to be formed.

[24] Helena P. Blavatsky, *The Secret Doctrine*, Theosophical University Press electronic version, ISBN 1-55700-124-3. Originally published in 2 vols., 1888.

[25] The myth is that long ago there was an island in the Atlantic named Atlantis, which was home to a very advanced civilization and which later sank into the ocean and disappeared.

[I]n about 25,000 years the Sixth Root-Race will have appeared on the stage of our Round, as they increase, and their numbers become with every age greater, one day they will awake to find themselves in a majority. It is the present men who will then begin to be regarded as exceptional mongrels, until these die out in their turn. . . .

There will be no more Americans when the Sixth Race commences . . . to sow the seeds for a forthcoming, grander, and far more glorious Race than any of those we know of at present. The Cycles of Matter will be succeeded by Cycles of Spirituality and a fully developed mind. On the law of parallel history and races, the majority of the future mankind will be composed of glorious Adepts. Humanity is the child of cyclic Destiny. . . . Thus will mankind, race after race, perform its appointed cycle-pilgrimage . . . each year after the other dropping one sub-race, but only to beget another higher race on the ascending cycle; while a series of other less favoured groups—the failures of nature—will, like some individual men, vanish from the human family without even leaving a trace behind.[26]

During her lifetime, thousands of (otherwise) intelligent, educated people accepted her bizarre pseudo-science as authoritative, as many still do today.[27] Her race-theory, further developed by later "ariosophists",[28] held that Aryans are a superior race, descended from priests of Atlantis who escaped before it sank into the sea, who then migrated to India, where they became the Hindu Aryans, the Brahmins.

[26] Blavatskyk, *Secret Doctrine*, vol. 2, pp. 444–46.

[27] Many of her followers today are probably unaware of the more overtly racist aspects of her teachings.

[28] The ariosophists were an offshoot of the Theosophical Society with a particular interest in "Aryan" race theory ("Aryan" + "theosophy" = "ariosophy").

This superior race degenerated with the dilution of its pure blood by intermarriage with baser races, but can be restored to its former, super-human splendor and powers by careful selected breeding to restore the bloodlines to their former purity.

Blavatsky's pseudo-science incorporated her undisguised contempt for Jews and Judaism:

> [T]he "Semitic" languages are the bastard descendants of the first phonetic corruptions of the eldest children of the early Sanskrit.... The Semites, especially the Arabs, are later Aryans—degenerate in spirituality and perfected in materiality. To these belong all the Jews and the Arabs. The former are a tribe descended from the Tchandalas of India, the outcasts, many of them ex-Brahmins, who sought refuge in Chaldea, in Scinde, and Aria (Iran), and were truly born from their father A-bram (No Brahmin) some 8,000 years B.C. [29]

> [T]he Semite interpretations [about God] emanated from, and were pre-eminently those of a small tribe, thus marking its national features and the idiosyncratic defects that characterize many of the Jews to this day—gross realism, selfishness, and sensuality. [30]

The Jews' inferiority is contrasted to the Aryan superiority:

> With the Hindu Aryan—the most metaphysical and spiritual people on earth—religion has ever been, in his words, "an everlasting lode-star, that beams the brighter in the heavens the darker here on earth grows the night around him." [For] the Israelites—"religion is a wise prudential feeling grounded on *mere calculation*"—and it was so from

[29] Ibid., vol. 2, p. 200.
[30] Ibid., vol. 2, p. 470.

its beginnings. Having burdened themselves with it, Christian nations feel bound to defend and *poetise* it, at the expense of all other religions. . . . The Aryan Hindu belongs to the oldest races now on earth; the Semite Hebrew to the latest. One is nearly one million years old; the other is a small sub-race some 8,000 years old and no more.

[T]here was a day when the Israelites had beliefs as pure as the Aryans have. But now Judaism, built *solely* on Phallic worship, has become one of the latest creeds in Asia, and theologically a religion of hate and malice toward everyone and everything outside themselves. Philo Judaeus shows what was the genuine Hebrew faith. The sacred Writings, he says, prescribe what we ought to do . . . commanding us to hate the heathen and their laws and institutions. . . . [I]t is with the Talmudic Jews that the grand symbols of nature were the most profaned . . . and by them applied to conceal the most terrestrial and grossly sexual mysteries, wherein both Deity and religion were degraded[31] (italics in original).

According to Blavatsky, the God of Judaism—Jehovah—is no more than a phallic symbol, invented by the Jews "in the know" to dupe the ignorant mass of Jews (the typical gnostic distinction between the knowers and the ignorami):

For how could those who invented the stupendous scheme now known as the Bible, or their successors who knew, as all Kabalists do, that it was so invented for a popular blind—how could they, we ask, feel reverence for such a phallic symbol . . . as Jehovah is shown most undeniably to be in the Kabalistic works? How could anyone worthy of the name of a philosopher, and knowing the real *secret* meaning of their "pillar of Jacob," their *Bethel*, oil-anointed

[31] Ibid., vol. 2, pp. 470–71.

phalli, and their "Brazen Serpent," worship such a gross
symbol, and minister unto it, seeing in it their
"Covenant"—the Lord Himself! ... We know from the
Jewish records that the Ark contained a table of stone ...
that stone was phallic, and yet identical with the sacred
name *Jehovah*[32] (italics in original).

The swastika figured prominently in Blavatsky's Theosophy,
appearing on the seal of the society, on her personal emblem, and on the cover of *The Secret Doctrine*.[33] It then became a dominant symbol for all of the other occult groups
that follow in this discussion, before finally being adopted by
the Nazis.

Tragically, Madame Blavatsky's Theosophy is still with us
today, both in its original form and in the enormous influence it has had throughout the New Age movement. Her
influence is universally acknowledged by writers both inside
and outside the movement, as the following quotes from recent publications demonstrate:

> Theosophy occupies a central place in the history of new
> spiritual movements, for the writings of Blavatsky and some
> of her followers have had a great influence outside of her
> organization. . . . The importance of Theosophy in mod-
> ern history should not be underestimated.[34]

> Madame Blavatsky . . . stands out as the fountainhead of
> modern occult thought, and was either the originator

[32] Ibid., vol. 2, p. 473.

[33] Madame Blavatsky considered the swastika to be the emblem of the Aryan
"root" race. In reality, it is found in cultures throughout the world, with various meanings. The word itself comes from Sanskrit and means, roughly, "good
fortune".

[34] Robert S. Ellwood and Harry B. Partin, *Religious and Spiritual Groups in
Modern America* (Englewood Cliffs, N.J.: Prentice Hall, 1988), pp. 63, 79–80.

and/or popularizer of many of the ideas and terms which have a century later been assembled within the New Age Movement. The Theosophical Society, which she co-founded, has been the major advocate of occult philosophy in the West and the single most important avenue of Eastern teaching to the West.[35]

Madame Blavatsky may be credited with having set the style for modern occult literature.[36]

Guido List—Armenen and Wotanism

It was Guido List (1848–1919),[37] an Austrian mystic, who developed Blavatsky's Theosophy into the direct occult precursor of Nazism. He blended Theosophy with his own "revelations", with the occult use of the old Germanic runes and other occult practices, and with his version of "ancient" Germanic paganism, and came up with an occult sect that he called the Armenen Order ("*Armenenschaft*"), which worshipped the Norse god Wotan. He claimed that the religion and its practices had been revealed to him in visions. Relying on the use of pagan rites that involved the shedding of blood and reportedly incorporating degenerate sexual practices, it was in fact a form of satanism in Teutonic guise. List developed an elaborate occult science of the meaning and use of runes, including the double-sig rune, later adopted as the emblem of the SS (the double "lightning-bolts"), and the swastika, which he called the "holy secret of constant

[35] J. Gordon Melton, Jerome Clark, and Aidan A. Kelly, eds., *New Age Almanac* (Detroit, Mich.: Gale Research, 1991), p. 16.

[36] Theodore Roszak, *The Unfinished Animal: The Aquarian Frontier and the Evolution of Consciousness* (New York: Harper and Row, 1975), p. 125.

[37] List added an aristocratic "von" to his name around 1903.

regeneration". He taught that the Aryans were the race of upward spiritual evolution, and that in the future only Aryans would be citizens and there would be strict laws to maintain the purity of the blood. Aryans would "be relieved of all wage-labor and demeaning tasks, in order to rule as an exalted elite over the slave castes of non-Aryan peoples".[38] According to List the Wotanist religion had flourished for millennia until Christianity had been imposed by force by the wicked Charlemagne, the "slaughterer of the Saxons". To List the imposition of Christianity was a vicious assault in which "the Vicar of God ... induced stupidity and ruled over a shamefully demoralized people that was almost ignorant of its nationality."[39] The conventional history of German people was the result of a Christian conspiracy to obliterate all knowledge of their glorious Wotanist past.

List's "ancient Teutonic" Wotanism was a gnostic nature-worship with many elements familiar from current New Age sects. It stressed the mystical union of man with the universe, as well as his ability to obtain occult powers. The universe is in a ceaseless repetitive process of birth–death–rebirth; Nature contains an immanent God; all things are an emanation of a primal spiritual force; Man is an integral part of this unified cosmos and must therefore live in accord with Nature. He followed the teachings of Theosophy on the evolution of the root-races and the origin of the superior races from the now-sunken Atlantis.

Despite the absurdity of List's claims, he had such great support in the higher echelons of Austrian society that when

[38] Nicholas Goodrich-Clarke, *The Occult Roots of Nazism* (New York: New York University Press, 1985, 1992), p. 64.

[39] Guido List, *Deutsch-Mythologisched Landshaftsbilder*, 2d ed., 1913, 2:438, cited in Goodrich-Clarke, *Occult Roots of Nazism*, p. 69.

he was censured for improperly adding an aristocratic "von" to his name, Austria's Minister for Culture and Education sprang to his defense and demanded an apology in parliament. When the List Society was founded in 1905 to promulgate his ideas, among the fifty initial supporters were the mayor of Vienna, editors of a number of popular newspapers and magazines, and the founder of a theater, as well as other prominent citizens. With the support offered by the society, List continued to publish his occult and pseudo-historical "research" and gained an international reputation. His work was taken up in academic institutions and by other authors. Early in his adult life Hitler was a follower of List and probably even a formal member of his occult *Armenenschaft*, judging by the fact that one of the books confiscated from Hitler's personal library after the war was inscribed by another *Armenenschaft* member "To Adolf Hitler, my dear Armenen-brother".[40]

List died in 1919 but his teachings survived—in his writings, in his disciples, in the organizations he left behind and their offshoots, and, tragically, in the fulfillment of his most disturbing prophecy in which he had predicted the emergence of a benevolent, dictatorial messianic figure who would emerge to save the Germans from the social problems of the day. The ideal German world, as it existed before it was "undermined by a conspiracy of inferior, non-Germanic peoples, the Church, the capitalists, the Jews,"[41] would be

restored by a new aristocracy under a God-sent savior who would fulfill the religious and political expectations of the

[40] Goodrich-Clarke, *Occult Roots of Nazism*, p. 199. The book was inscribed by Dr. Babette Steininger, an early Nazi Party member.
[41] Ibid., p. 87.

oppressed. . . . An ostensibly superhuman individual would end all human factions and confusion with the establishment of an eternal order. . . . From his calculations based on "cosmic and astrological laws", List . . . favored the year 1932 as the time when a divine force would possess the collective unconsciousness of the German people [and] usher in the new age. Order, national revenge, and fervor would then transform modern pluralist society into a monolithic, eternal, and incorruptible state. In his anticipation of Nazi Germany, his calculation was only one year out.[42]

Lanz and Ostara

One of List's early disciples was Adolf Lanz (1874–1954), who gave himself the aristocratic name Jorg Lanz von Liebenfels. After six years in a Cistercian monastery, he was expelled in 1899 for "carnal and worldly desires". He then settled in Vienna, where he further developed List's ideas and founded his own occult society styled after a religious order, "The Order of the New Temple", with the aim of reestablishing the purity of the "Aryan" race. He published his ideas in his virulently anti-Semitic occult and erotic journal *Ostara* and in a book entitled *Theozoology or the Lore of the Sodom-Apelings and the Lectron of the Gods.* Lanz claimed that the Jews and the Pygmies were degenerate races that had resulted from interbreeding between the once super-human Aryan race and animals. The Jews were "demonic beast-men [who] oppress us from above, slaughtering without conscience millions of people in murderous wars waged for their

[42] Goodrich-Clarke, *Occult Roots of Nazism*, pp. 87–89.

own personal gain".[43] He taught that the ancient Aryans had extrasensory organs for the transmission and reception of electrical signals, which gave them powers of telepathy and omniscience. These organs had atrophied into the "useless" pituitary and pineal glands of modern man due to cross-breeding of the god-men with the beast-men. The inferior races, particularly the Jews, should be gotten rid of by methods including forced sterilization and castration, deportation, incineration as a sacrifice to God, and enslavement, and the Aryan population enhanced by keeping Aryan brood-mothers in eugenic convents serviced by Aryan stud-males. All of these recommendations were later implemented by the Nazis.

Judaism was not the only religion that attracted Lanz' contempt. In his *Theozoology* he writes that the Passion of Christ was the attempted rape of Christ by Pygmies urged on by the disciples of satanic bestiality cults devoted to interbreeding.

Lanz' journal *Ostara* was sold in a tobacconist's shop at Felberstrasse 18 in Vienna, only a few doors down from Felberstrasse 22, where Hitler lived from November 1908 to August 1909. Hitler was an avid reader of the magazine and even called on Lanz to acquire back copies missing from his files.[44] Lanz wrote to a member of his order, "Hitler is one of our pupils. We will yet be privileged to see that he, together with us, will win, and will be able to establish a movement so powerful that it will shake the world."[45] Lanz later asserted that his Order of the New Templars, which used the

[43] J. Lanz-Lieberfels, *Theozoologie oder die Kunde von den Sodoms-Afflingen und dem Gotter-Elektron* (Vienna, 1905), pp. 26–27, quoted in Goodrich-Clarke, *Occult Roots of Nazism*, p. 96.

[44] Mordecai Lenski, "Who Inspired Hitler to Destroy the Jews?", in *Yad Vashem Bulletin*, no. 14 (March 1964), pp. 49–52.

[45] Ibid.

swastika as its emblem, had been the first manifestation of the Nazi movement. It was during this period, when Hitler was under the influence of Lanz' writings, that his virulent anti-Semitism first emerged. As Hitler relates in *Mein Kampf*:

> I began to see Vienna in a different light. Wherever I went I saw Jews, and the more I saw of them, the sharper I began to distinguish them from other people. Was there any form of filth or profligacy in which [the] Jew did not participate? . . . The scales dropped from my eyes. I gradually began to hate them. This was the time in which the greatest change I was ever to experience took place in me. From a feeble cosmopolite I had turned into a fanatical anti-Semite.[46]

The Thule Society

The history of the Thule Society can be traced back to about 1910, when some virulently anti-Semitic members of the *völkisch* movement started the quasi-Masonic, clandestine *Germanenorden* based on the Germanic pagan tradition. The founders were veterans of a host of anti-Semitic organizations, publications, and political parties, all linked to Guido List and his Ariosophy. According to its own literature, the principal aims of the *Germanenorden* were the monitoring of Jews and their activities, the distribution of anti-Semitic material, and the mutual aid of the brothers in business matters. All members were to be of flawless Germanic descent and preferably have blond hair, light eyes, and pale skin. A recruitment guide referred to specific issues of *Ostara* that discussed racial characteristics; *Armenenschaft*

[46] Extracts from Adolf Hitler, *Mein Kampf* (New York: Reynal and Hitchcock, 1940), pp. 74, 75, 78, 81, 83.

rules and rituals were also explicitly referenced. The swastika figured prominently in their rituals and appeared on the seal of the order.

After the First World War, the *Germanenorden* found itself in a state of disarray. It reformed with the purpose, in part, of assassinating public figures who were seen as enemies of the *völkisch* German people. An early target was Matthias Erzberger, who had signed the armistice, as well as other Jewish and republican "enemies of the German nation". As a result of notoriety from these political activities, the *Germanenorden* changed its name to the Thule Society. Thule was a mythological Northern land from which the Aryans supposedly had come, apparently identified with Atlantis.

In 1918, the Bavarian branch of the Thule Society was taken over by a man born Adam Glauer, the son of a locomotive driver. Glauer had given himself the aristocratic name Baron Rudolf von Sebottendorf while spending nine years in Turkey, where he had been forced to flee after running off with the married mother of the children he had been hired to tutor.[47] In Turkey, he studied Sufi occultism, Islamic alchemy, Rosicrucianism, and Freemasonry. His interest in rune occultism, which he thought was related to Islamic mysticism, led him to the society.

When Jewish socialist Kurt Eisner was installed as premier of Bavaria in 1918 following a bloodless coup, Sebottendorf delivered an impassioned speech to the society that typified the Thule Society's blend of anti-Semitism, Germanic militarism, and paganism—a mixture that became the hallmark of the Third Reich:

---

[47] He claimed to have been adopted by the expatriate Baron Heinrich von Sebottendorf while in Turkey.

Yesterday we experienced the collapse of everything which was familiar, dear and valuable to us. In the place of our princes of Germanic blood rules our deadly enemy: Judah.... A time will come of struggle, the most bitter need, a time of danger.... I am determined to pledge the Thule to this struggle. Our Order is a Germanic Order, loyalty is also Germanic. Our god is Walvater, his rune is the Ar-rune. And the trinity: Wotan, Wili, We is the unity of the trinity. The Ar-rune signifies Aryan.... [We must] fight until the swastika rises victoriously out of the icy darkness.[48]

According to Sebottendorf, the Thule Society played a central role in Hitler's rise to power:

Thule members were the people to whom Hitler first turned, and who first allied themselves with Hitler. The armament of the coming Fuhrer consisted—besides the Thule Society itself—of the *Deutscher Arbeitverein*, founded in the Thule by Brother Karl Harrer at Munich, and the *Deutsch-Sozialistische Partei*, headed there by Hans Georg Grassinger, whose organ was the *Munchener Beobachter*, later the *Völkischer Beobachter*. From these three sources Hitler created the *Nationalsozialistische Arbeiterpartei*.[49]

The *Munchener Beobachter* had been an obscure Munich weekly until Thule Society members bought it and turned it into the official paper of the Nazi party. The Thule Society assembled weapons, trained soldiers, and helped organize the counter-revolution that overthrew the Bavarian socialist government in early 1919.

[48] Goodrich-Clarke, *Occult Roots of Nazism*, p. 145.

[49] Rudolf Sebottendorf, *Bevor Hitler Kam* (Before Hitler came) (Munich: Deufula-Verlag Grassinger, 1933), cited in Goodrich-Clarke, *Occult Roots of Nazism*, p. 146.

The Thule Society's aristocratic nature proved an impediment to its expansion. In order to increase its political influence, it created a working-class sister society called the DAP, or Deutsche Arbeiterpartei (German Worker's Party). In 1919, Hitler gained control of the DAP and renamed it the Nazional-socialistische Deutsche Arbeiterpartei (NSDAP)—more commonly known in its abbreviated form, the "Nazi" Party. Thus the Thule Society was the direct precursor to the Nazi Party. The Nazi flag, a black swastika in a white circle against a red background, was designed by Thule Society member Dr. Friedrich Krohn.

From the Thule Society came many of those who set the direction of the Third Reich, including Dietrich Eckart, Alfred Rosenberg, and Rudolf Hess.[50]

Dietrich Eckart

Dietrich Eckart was another leading member of the Thule Society. He was an occultist and publisher of a virulently anti-Semitic *völkisch* periodical named *Auf gut Deutsch* (In plain German). His articles flowed from the theories of Chamberlain, Lanz, and List. He predicted the imminent coming of a German messiah who would free Germany from the chains of Christianity and inaugurate a new era. Eckart was made editor-in-chief of the *Völkischer Beobachter*, the official Nazi newspaper, and would become very influential in Nazi Germany.

[50] Goodrich-Clarke, *Occult Roots of Nazism*, pp. 149, 221, and D. Sklar, *The Nazis and the Occult* (New York: Dorset Press, 1977), p. 6. Since no official membership lists of the Thule Society have been found, it is unclear whether these men were formal members or simply frequent guests.

Eckart claimed to have "initiated" Hitler into occultism while visiting him in Landsdorf Fortress prison. In occult circles, initiation is the rite by which, from the point of view of the occultist, "higher centers" are opened and he gains extrasensory powers. In reality, it entails the introduction of demonic entities into the individual, entities who then deeply influence him. Eckart wrote a friend shortly before his death in 1923: "Follow Hitler! He will dance, but it will be to my tune. I have initiated him into the Secret Doctrine, opened his centers of vision and given him the means to communicate with the powers. Don't grieve for me, for I have influenced history more than any other German." [51] This claim is given some credibility by the fact that Hitler referred to Eckart on at least one occasion as his "John the Baptizer", and that the very last words in *Mein Kampf* are Hitler's warm dedication of it to "that man, who ... by words and by thoughts and finally by deeds dedicated his life to the awakening ... of our nation: *Dietrich Ekart*." [52] As Hitler's social, as well as occult, mentor, Eckart was also responsible for having introduced him to the moneyed and influential social circles of post-war Munich during the early days of his rise to power and thus had been instrumental in launching Hitler's career.

Alfred Rosenberg

The son of a poor shoemaker, Rosenberg gained his standing in the Thule Society by introducing to it the scurrilous

---

[51] Joseph Carr, *The Twisted Cross* (Shreveport, La: Huntington House, 1985), p. 87.

[52] Hitler, *Mein Kampf* (New York: Reynal and Hitchcock), p. 993. (This dedication is frequently edited out of abridged translations.)

anti-Semitic fabrication known as the *Protocols of the Elders of Zion*, which he had brought with him when he emigrated to Germany from Moscow. He eventually became the official ideologist of the Nazi party and the primary "theologian" of its new religion, as well as editor of the Nazi party paper. He claimed to have been the author of the original program for the Nazi party.

His official positions were summarized in the 1934–1935 "Das Deutsch Fuhrer Lexikon" as follows:

> From 1921 until the present, editor of the Voelkische Beobachter; editor of the "*N.S. Monatshefte*"; 1930, Reichstag deputy and representative of the foreign policy of the movement; since April 1933, leader of the foreign political office of the NSDAP; then designated as Reichsleiter; January 1934, deputized by the Fuhrer for the spiritual and philosophical education of the NSDAP, the German labor front and all related organizations.[53]

As the official spiritual leader of the Nazi movement, Rosenberg was explicit about the rejection of Christianity in favor of Nazism's own new Germanic, nationalist pagan religion. In his 1930 book *Myth of the Twentieth Century* he wrote:

> We now realize that the central supreme values of the Roman and the Protestant Churches, being a negative Christianity, do not respond to our soul, that they hinder the organic powers of the peoples determined by their Nordic race, that they must give way to them, that they will have to be remodeled to conform to a Germanic

[53] Chief of Counsel for Prosecution of Axis Criminality, *Nazi Conspiracy and Aggression—A Collection of Documentary Evidence Prepared by the American and British Prosecuting Staffs for Presentation before the International Military Tribunal at Nurnberg* (Washington, D.C.: U.S. Government Printing Office, 1946), vol. 2, chap. 16, p. 593.

Christendom. Therein lies the meaning of the present religious search.

Today, a new faith is awakening—the Myth of the Blood,
the belief that the divine being of mankind generally is to
be defended with the blood. The faith embodied by the
fullest realization, that the Nordic blood constitutes that
mystery which has supplanted and overwhelmed the old
sacraments.[54]

Racism was at the heart of his view of the new world order:

The essence of the contemporary world revolution lies in
the awakening of the racial types, not in Europe alone but
on the whole planet. This awakening is the organic counter
movement against the last chaotic remnants of liberal economic imperialism . . . once the great world battle is con-
cluded, after the defeat of the present epoch, there will be
a time when the swastika will be woven into the different
banners of the Germanic peoples as the Aryan symbol of
rejuvenation.[55]

Also, with, of course, the need to get rid of the Jews for
once and for all:

For Germany the Jewish Question is only then solved when
the last Jew has left the Greater German space. . . . Since
Germany with its blood and its nationalism has now broken for always this Jewish dictatorship for all Europe and
has seen to it that Europe as a whole will become free
from the Jewish parasitism once more, we may, I believe,
also say for all Europeans: For Europe the Jewish question

---

[54] Alfred Rosenberg, *Myth of the Twentieth Century* (Torrance, Calif.: Noontide Press, 1982), p. 114, cited in *Nazi Conspiracy and Aggression*, p. 595.

[55] Rosenberg, *Myth*, p. 479, cited in *Nazi Conspiracy and Aggression*, p. 594.

is only then solved when the last Jew has left the European continent.[56]

[I]f the Jew were to stifle us, we would never be able to fulfill our mission, which is the salvation of the world, but would, to be frank, succumb to insanity.... Considered in himself the Jew represents nothing else but this blind will for destruction, the insanity of mankind.... To strip the world of its soul, that and nothing else is what Judaism wants. This, however, would be tantamount to the world's destruction.[57]

Rosenberg drew up the program for the "National Reich Church", which included:

— The National Church will clear away from its altars all crucifixes, Bibles and pictures of saints.

— On the altars there must be nothing but *Mein Kampf* and to the left of the altar a sword.

— On the day of its foundation, the Christian Cross must be removed from all churches, cathedrals, and chapels ... and must be superseded by the only unconquerable symbol, the swastika.[58]

A hymn written for the new faith included the stanza:

The time of the Cross has gone now,
The Sun-wheel shall arise,

[56] Speech given March 28, 1941, on the occasion of the opening of the Institute for the Exploration of the Jewish Question, cited in *Nazi Conspiracy and Aggression*, p. 596.

[57] Alfred Rosenberg's "The Earth-Centered Jew Lacks a Soul", quoted in Sklar, *Nazis and the Occult*, p. 148.

[58] William L. Shirer, *The Rise and Fall of The Third Reich* (New York: Ballantine, 1992), pp. 332–33.

And so, with God, we shall be free at last
And give our people their honor back.[59]

The "sun-wheel" is the swastika. Once again, the direct opposition of the Nazis to Christianity and to all things Christian is evident.

Martin Bormann, Hitler's Deputy Fuhrer, worked closely with Rosenberg in his effort to establish the new Nazi religion. In various letters to him, Bormann mentioned the need for Rosenberg's department to abolish religious services in the schools, confiscate religious property, circulate anti-religious material to the soldiers, and close down Christian periodicals and theological faculties. For it was clear to him that the Christian churches stood in the way of Nazism and had to be "conquered"; and as he wrote to Rosenberg: "The churches cannot be conquered by a compromise between National Socialism and Christian teachings, but only through a new ideology whose coming you yourself have announced in your writings." [60]

Himmler, Wiligut, the SS, and the Ahnenerbe

No treatment of occultism in the Third Reich would be complete without discussing Himmler's occultism, his occult mentor Karl Maria Wiligut, the occult underpinnings of the SS, and the special SS branch formed to deal with occult matters, the *Ahnenerbe*.[61]

---

[59] Servando González, *The Riddle of the Swastika: A Study in Symbolism* (Oakland, Calif.: publ. by Servando González), unpaged.

[60] *Nazi Conspiracy and Aggression*, p. 595.

[61] This may be roughly translated as "Ancestral Heritage Society".

Himmler's SS was intrinsically a neo-religious order, incorporating the new mythology of the Third Reich. To qualify, candidates not only had to have proven pure Aryan blood going back three generations, but had to fit the physical Aryan model in height, coloring, and overall looks. Representing the bloodline for reconstructing the Aryan race, they were to reproduce as freely as possible, not only with their own wives but also with additional women. To provide these additional women, Himmler set up the *lebensborn* program, in which young women who exhibited the desired Aryan racial characteristics were recruited for specially set up "hostels" established on confiscated Jewish properties, where they would breed with SS men. It was considered an honor to be selected—60% of the applicants were turned down—and official figures show that the program resulted in about 6,000 illegitimate births.

Initiation into the SS reflected its character as an occult brotherhood, requiring memorization of a formal "catechism", exercises in torturing animals, and a night-time final initiation ceremony. The headquarters of the SS, Himmler's castle at Wewelsburg, housed the SS officer's college and was explicitly set up along occult, neo-religious lines. The emblem of the SS, the two "lightening bolts", was the occult double-sig rune taken from Ariosophy. Officer candidates at the college were given courses on runes and their occult significance.

Himmler believed in reincarnation and karma—his spiritual outlook was primarily based on Hinduism (as is much of the New Age), and he was never without his copy of the *Bhagavad-Gita*, the Hindu scriptures. He believed he was the reincarnation of the tenth-century German king Henry the First, who spoke to him and told him what to do.[62] He

---

[62] Source: the memoirs of Himmler's personal masseur: Felix Kersten, *The Kersten Memoirs 1940–1945* (London: Hutchinson, 1956), pp. 148–53, 296.

had the king's bones exhumed and placed in the crypt of a cathedral, where each year on the anniversary of his death Himmler would hold a midnight ritual. He practiced the now popular New Age technique, positive visualization (e.g., "Visualize World Peace"), in an attempt to force others' wills to his own. He had an institute in Berlin set up to study the potential of harnessing occult sources of power, including black magic, spiritualist mediums, pendulum practitioners, and astrologers, for the war effort. In 1935, Himmler established the *Ahnenerbe* to conduct research into the mythological and occult background of the Third Reich. By the time it was fully developed in 1939, it comprised fifty branches. Its research projects, conducted at a cost estimated to have exceeded the budget spent by the U.S. in developing the atomic bomb, included the following:

— expeditions to Tibet to analyze Tibetan skull structure to establish Aryan ancestry;

— expeditions to South America to study Indian medicines;

— an expedition to find the legendary lost continent of Atlantis, the supposed original home of the Aryan race;

— expeditions to southwest France to search for the Holy Grail in the vicinity of Cathar fortresses;

— gathering information on the Rosicrucian movement;

— researching the supposed occult significance of (among other topics) Gothic towers, the Etonian top-hat, and the Irish harp;

— studying the supposed special properties of "Aryan" horses and "Aryan" bees.

After the war ended, an academic U.S. journal[63] reviewed the astronomical research that had been carried out in Germany during the war. After summarizing the many legitimate research projects, the article continued:

This report would be unbalanced without a reference to the darker side of the picture. One of the symptoms of intellectual deterioration in Nazi Germany was the widespread use of pseudo-scientific theories. Not only was astrology widely practiced, even in Hitler's headquarters, but the theory was popular that the world was a hollow shell, with the human race living on the inside (*Hohlwelt-theorie*). Certain German naval circles believed in the *Hohlwelt-theorie*. They considered it helpful to locate the British fleet, because the curvature of the Earth would not obstruct observation. Accordingly a party of about ten men under the scientific leadership of Dr. Heinz Fischer[64] was sent out from Berlin to the isle of Rugen [in the Arctic] to photograph the British fleet with infrared equipment at an upward angle of some 45 degrees. Other groups, including officers of flag rank, practiced or supported "*Pendelforschung*"; a large map of the Atlantic was spread out horizontally, with a 1-inch toy battleship as test object. A pendulum was swung above the battleship. If the pendulum reacted it proved the presence of a true battleship at that location.[65]

[63] *Popular Astronomy*, published by the Goodsell Observatory of Carleton College, Northfield, Minn.

[64] Dr. Fischer joined the U.S. nuclear weapons program following the war. He complained that in the Third Reich scientists had been continually pulled off promising weapons research for such insane projects.

[65] Gerard P. Kuiper, "German Astronomy during the War", *Popular Astronomy*, vol. 54, no. 6 (June 1946), condensed from pp. 266–68.

As mentioned earlier, Himmler's mentor in his occultism was Karl Maria Wiligut. Wiligut's own occult "gifts" supposedly included ancestral memory, enabling him to "remember" both his own experiences of past lives and also the experiences of others in his ancestral past, thereby enabling him to have "first-hand" knowledge of the culture and esoteric lore of the Third Reich's glorious pagan Teutonic past extending over thousands of years. This made him invaluable to Himmler for research on ancient (actually mythical) Germanic traditions and history, a role he filled as a member of the SS staff from 1933 to 1939, being promoted during that period from SS-*Hauptsturmfuhrer* (captain) to SS-*Brigadefuhrer* (brigadier) on the personal recommendation of Himmler. It was Wiligut who designed the infamous SS "death's-head" ring. Wiligut had a long history in *völkisch* and Ariosophical research, having had a book on Teutonic rune mythology published in 1903 by the same publisher who handled some of List's works. He had been active in occult circles, including Lanz's Order of the New Templars and a quasi-Masonic lodge called the Schlarrafia since the turn of the century.

Wiligut taught that the Bible had been originally written in German, and that Christ was in reality the ancient Germanic god Krist and only later adopted and distorted into the savior known to Christianity. His version of German history went back to 228,000 B.C. and was based on his own supposed "ancestral memory". This "memory" showed him three suns in the sky and an earth populated by giants, dwarves, and other fantastical creatures. He "saw" that he himself came from a family prominent in Germanic political, cultural, and spiritual affairs as early as 78,000 B.C., but whose glorious heritage was later sabotaged by Jews and Freemasons conspiring against the ancient Germanic religion. His involuntary commitment in the Salzburg insane asylum from

1924 to 1927 apparently did not disqualify him from his later role as the spiritual leader of Himmler and the SS. It did however force him to change his name, from Wiligut to Wiesthor, when he joined the SS.

It was on the advice of Wiligut that in November 1933, Himmler took over the seventeenth-century castle of Wewelsburg to be the officer's training college and "order-castle" of the SS. Wiligut had convinced him that the castle would play an important role in the ultimate East-West confrontation to come. Wewelsburg castle was described in Time-Life's book *The SS* :

> In 1934 Himmler selected a moldering cliff top castle in Westphalia to serve as the SS high temple. Known as Wewelsburg, the seventeenth-century fortress was over-hauled at a cost of more than three million dollars, a sizable sum considering that labor was extracted free from concentration camp inmates. The sanctum included a 12,000-volume library of Aryan lore and a cavernous dining hall with an Arthurian round table for Himmler and twelve trusted lieutenants. Reportedly, each knight of Himmler's round table received a coat of arms; at the man's death, his emblem was to be incinerated in the pit of the Supreme Leaders' Hall, and the ashes placed in an urn atop one of twelve pedestals there.[66]

At Wewelsburg Wiligut sought to reestablish what he claimed had been the ancient Germanic religion, introducing a host of religious rituals, including pagan wedding ceremonies for SS men and their brides, pagan baby-naming ceremonies to replace baptism, and so forth. A 1936 memorandum from

---

[66] Editors of Time-Life Books, *The SS*, The Third Reich Series (Alexandria, Va.: Time-Life Books, 1988), p. 46.

Himmler dictated that the new religious festivals to be observed included Hitler's Birthday (April 20), May Day, Summer Solstice, Harvest Feast, The Beer Hall Putsch Anniversary (November 9), and Winter Solstice. Once again the Nazis' utter disdain for and desire to replace Christianity is more than apparent.

Hitler and the New Nazi Religion

We have seen that Nazi ideology consisted of an interweaving of Germanic ultra-nationalism and a neo-Germanic paganism, from its earliest manifestations in the *völkisch* clubs and *wandervogel* groups, through its intellectual development in proto-Nazi eugenics and race-theory, to the movements aimed at political activity culminating in the Nazi party itself. Throughout it was imbued with a fanatical sense of national/racial superiority, and permeated with a revival of a romanticized Teutonic paganism, replete with the revival of "ancient" gods, rites, rituals, and symbols, including the swastika, and imbued with an active occultism coming from Eastern religions via Theosophy.

The same is true of the culture adopted by the Nazis, as shown by its favorite cultural expression, the operas of Wagner. His famous "Ring Trilogy", for instance, is at least on the surface an exaltation of Teutonic paganism. Another of his operas, "Parsifal", although more ambiguous, served the Nazis' purposes equally well. Some see its mixture of magic, occultism, and Christian symbolism to be thinly veiled paganism; others see it as Christianity, expressed in allegory. Whichever Wagner's intent might have been (and his personal comments on the matter are highly contradictory), this very ambiguity perfectly suited the Nazis' plan. For, faced with the task of converting a population who thought of themselves as Christian to Nazi neo-paganism, one of their prime techniques was to co-opt Christian concepts and incorporate them into their new diabolical religion.

The most blatant example of the Nazis' perverse co-option of Christianity is the assigning of the role of Messiah to Hitler. In this blasphemy Hitler takes the place of Christ; the thousand year reign of the Third Reich is the Messianic Era on earth; the Aryan race takes the place of the Jews as the Chosen People; and blood purity takes the place of holiness as the essence of salvation. Hitler alluded to this messianic role when he said: "Humanity accomplishes a step up every 700 years and the ultimate aim is the coming of the sons of God. All created forces will be concentrated in a new species. It will be infinitely superior to modern man", and again when he said: "Those who see in National Socialism, nothing more than a political movement know scarcely anything of it. . . . It is more even than a religion. It is the will to create mankind anew." He explicitly asserted the underlying paganism when he said: "The old beliefs will be brought back to honor again. The whole secret knowledge of nature, of the divine, the demonic. We will wash off the Christian veneer and bring out a religion peculiar to our race."[67]

The promised "thousand year reign" of the Reich was an overt allusion to Christ's thousand year reign, part of the Second Coming, prophesied in the book of Revelation:

---

[67] *Nazis: The Occult Conspiracy*, video no. 621631, produced by the Discovery Channel. This perversion of Christianity, with Hitler as the "messiah", is also described in Himmler's own words, recounted by his masseur, in Felix Kersten, *The Kersten Memoirs 1940–1945*, pp. 152, 296. Hitler gave Himmler the task of preparing the doctrines for this great Germanic religion to be imposed on all Europe (ibid., also Carr, *Twisted Cross*, p. 203).

Then I saw an angel coming down from heaven, holding
in his hand the key of the bottomless pit and a great chain.
And he seized the dragon, that ancient serpent, who is
the Devil and Satan, and bound him for a thousand years,
and threw him into the pit, and shut it and sealed it over
him, that he should deceive the nations no more, till the
thousand years were ended.... Also I saw the souls of
those who had been beheaded for their testimony to Jesus
and for the word of God. ... They came to life, and reigned
with Christ a thousand years.... This is the first resurrection. Blessed and holy is he who shares in the first resurrection! ... [T]hey shall be priests of God and of Christ,
and they shall reign with him a thousand years (Revelation 20:1–6).

Already in 1931, a Protestant pastor in Germany identified
the extreme nationalistic movement of the Nazis as a perverted reflection of messianic prophecy in a lecture entitled
"Political Messiahship": "[E]ven Protestant pastors confuse
the secularized eschatology of the *völkisch* movement with
the legitimate eschatology of the church's proclamation and
enthusiastically fall in with the National Socialist camp." [68]
The cause of Satan's fall was his desire to take the place of
God, whose role he apes among his followers; in parallel
fashion, his earthly representative aped the role of messiah
and claimed his own advent as the "Second Coming".

The 1935 German *Farmer's Almanac* provides an example
of this replacement of Christianity. In it every single Christian feast day was replaced with a pagan celebration, earning
the following protest from the Catholic Bishop of Trier:

---

[68] Scholder, *Requiem for Hitler*, quoting R. Karwehl, "Politisches Messsias-
tum. Zur Auseinandersetzung zwischen Kirche und Nationalsozialismus",
Zwischen den Zeiten, 1931, pp. 542–43.

I am surprised and deeply shocked that the Reich Agricultural Corporation, to which every German farmer, man and woman, must belong, should have offered this Almanac . . . it is a deep insult to every Christian and Catholic feeling. The Saints' Days, the mention of every Christian Feast Day, even Christmas, Easter, and Pentecost, have disappeared. January 6th (The Three Kings) is "The Three Asir Day." February 22 (The Feast of St. Peter's Chair) is the "Feast of Thor's Chair." Ash Wednesday is "Ash Woden's Day." On Maundy Thursday, the feast of the institution of the Blessed Sacrament, there takes place the "consecration of the night-light oil." (!) Easter, the Resurrection of Our Lord, is the "Feast of Ostara" (a German Spring goddess). Ascension Day is "Rescue of Thor's Hammer." . . . Christmas Eve is "The Birthday of Baldur, god of Light, and the Visit of the Infant Yule." [69]

A few years later it was another bishop of Trier, Msgr. Bornewasser, who complained of the Nazis' intent to eliminate the celebration of Christmas. In his New Year's Eve sermon at the close of 1937, he said:

You have heard of the so-called Winter Solstice celebrations. A few years ago I said: "I am not sure whether there lies therein a hidden danger for our youth." Today I am sure. *This artificially stirred-up old Germanic pagan Consecration of Fire is meant as a direct challenge to the highest mystery of our religion, the Incarnation of Jesus Christ on the Holy Night of Bethlehem.* I leave it to you to judge for yourselves. What I am going to read is taken from the periodical *Fuhrerdienst* (The Leader's Task) of the Jungvolk (Junior Section of

[69] Bishop Franz Rudolf, in the "Official Gazette of the Diocese of Trier", February 1, 1935, cited in *The Persecution of the Catholic Church in the Third Reich* (anonymous), originally published 1941, republished by Fort Collins, Colo.: Roger McCaffrey Publishing, p. 355.

the Hitler Youth), 12th Number, December, 1937, page 6:

> At another meeting the Winter Solstice will be celebrated. We have to train our young members in order to enable them to celebrate this Christmas stripped of all the parasitical excrescences which were implanted in the hearts and minds of the German people by the Christian denominations.

What is the meaning of this blasphemous remark? Our young children are told that they have to get rid of all parasitical excrescences implanted in the hearts and minds of the German people by the Christian denominations. What are these? The mystery of the Incarnation of Jesus Christ on the Holy Night. From the hearts of the young, the memory that Christmas is the day of the birth of our Saviour is to be eradicated, and an old Germanic pagan Consecration of Fire is to take its place.

Christian Fathers and Mothers! Now you know the real meaning of the celebration of the Winter Solstice. Up to now it had been concealed behind a mask, but today this mask has been dropped. We know now that all this talk about the German Winter Solstice is in reality directed against the most sublime mystery of Christmas, the Incarnation of Jesus Christ the Son of God.[70]

This is particularly interesting since now in the U.S., there is an attempt to replace Christmas with "winter solstice" or "festival of light" celebrations in many schools and other public settings. One must wonder whether it is not the same spirit at work among us today.

[70] Ibid., pp. 487–88.

It is also interesting that it was the Farmer's *Almanac* (note the word *Farmer's*!) that was the vehicle for this attempt to eradicate Christianity. It calls to mind today's New Age movement, in which the paganization of agriculture is also a recurrent theme. Those interested in new farming techniques, motivated by a reverence for the earth, that can border on, or cross over into, actual worship, are also in the forefront of the movement to replace Christianity with a pagan, "earth mother" religion. Again we must ask if it is the same underlying spirit at work in both cases. The fact that the Reich *Agricultural* Organization was in the foreground of the attempt to eliminate Christianity was evident. One of its leaders succinctly stated: "Hitler is our Savior; it is to him that we must pray." [71]

In saying this, he was merely putting in a nutshell the heart of the Nazi religion. It was a theme constantly repeated by devoted followers of Hitler. When a Nazi journal asked readers what "the Fuhrer meant to them", typical responses included:[72]

"The Fuhrer is the visible personal expression of what in our youth was represented as God."

"I have never felt the Divine Power as near as in the greatness of our Fuhrer."

"What the Fuhrer has given me is not only a political ideology, but also a religion."

[71] Ibid., p. 357.
[72] The following quotes are from *Schwartz Korps*, April 20, 1939, cited in ibid. pp. 482–84.

"How shall I put in words what I feel for my Fuhrer ...
I look up to him now as I prayed to God in my childhood. . . ."

"[The Fuhrer] is the bread of which the soul stands in
need. I would like to say openly that the high teaching of
the Fuhrer is to me a religion, the German religion!"

"Adolf Hitler means the same as the word God means to
a fanatical and orthodox Christian."

"[The Fuhrer's portrait] hangs in my office as well as in
my drawing-room at home. [Every glance at it releases in
me] the feelings that devout people allege they experience in earnest prayer."

The Nazis made no secret of what the future held for Christianity should they have their way. At a meeting of the German Faith Movement in Hanover in 1937, the provincial
leader, when asked, "What is to become of the numerous
churches when the present generation which still clings to
Christianity has died out?" replied:

Churches of artistic and historic value will, of course, be
preserved; they will be used for the solemn festivals of the
German people, but naturally only after removing all Christian symbols. . . . [S]econd and third rate churches, however, will be demolished."[73]

As the devil "apes" God, always providing a distorted, gro-
tesque caricature of God and true religion, so too did the
Nazi religion "ape" the Christianity it sought to supplant.
For instance, it took various Christian symbols and rites
and imbued them with its own perverse, usually occult,

[73] *Reichspost*, April 2, 1937, cited in ibid., p. 484.

significance. Thus, upon the Nazis' triumphant entry into Vienna, Hitler immediately took possession of the Holy Lance, the spearhead thought to have pierced the side of Christ, in the belief that the possession of this Christian relic would magically guarantee success to his schemes of world conquest. The Christian use of sacred relics was aped with the "blood flag", which was a Nazi flag used in the failed "Beer Hall Putsch" of 1923 and stained with the blood of Nazi Storm Troopers killed in the unsuccessful coup. It was considered to be sacred and to be imbued with magical power that was transmitted to new Nazi flags when Hitler touched them to the "blood flag" in a rite which only he could perform.[74]

And in a striking way, the extreme nationalism of the Nazi religion "aped" the role of the Jewish people in Christianity. The Jews had two key roles to play to prepare for the Incarnation—one related to the line of descent that would culminate in the Blessed Virgin Mary and the other related to the land. In the Old Testament, there is a deep mystery to line of descent, or "bloodlines"—one need only think of how the Jews were blessed in perpetuity for having descended from Abraham, of how the priests in Judaism had to be descended from Aaron,[75] and how the Messiah was to come from the line of David. This sense of Mary as the culmination of the most perfect line of descent was beautifully expressed by the Venerable Anne Catherine Emmerich, a Catholic nun, stigmatist, and visionary of the late eighteenth century:

---

[74] *Nazis: The Occult Conspiracy*, video no. 621631, produced by the Discovery Channel.
[75] Exodus 28.

The Blessed Virgin Mary was the one and only pure blossom of the human race, flowering in the fullness of time.
All the children of God from the beginning of time who
have striven after salvation contributed to her coming. . . .
She alone was the pure immaculate flesh and blood of the
whole human race, prepared and purified and ordained
and consecrated through all the generations of her ances-
ters, guided, guarded, and fortified by the Law until she
came forth as the fullness of Grace.[76]

The other role the Jews were to play involved conquering
and defending the Holy Land, the sacred land promised to
them by God, which was to become the home on earth of
God as man. Both of these roles were aped in the Nazis'
religion of *Blut und Boden* ("Blood and Soil"), in which they
dedicated themselves to preserving (or restoring) the purity
of the Germanic bloodlines and protecting the sacred German soil. And as Judaism was to be followed by Christianity,
which would universalize the salvation offered to the Jews
by extending the covenant to all mankind through faith rather
than through blood, so too was the *völkisch* movement to
be followed by the Third Reich, which would universalize
the Aryan "salvation" by exterminating or enslaving all
non-Aryans.

There are many indications that Hitler's relationship to
the satanic was intentional, explicit, and extensive. No less
an authority than the current chief exorcist of Rome, Father
Gabriele Amorth, stated that "certainly Hitler was consecrated to Satan."[77] A book that extensively details Hitler's

---

[76] Ven. Anne Catherine Emmerich, *The Life of the Blessed Virgin Mary* (Rockford, Ill.: TAN Books, 1970), p. 145.

[77] Article by Melinda Henneberger in *The New York Times*, January 1, 2001,
cited in "News Notes", *The Wanderer*, January 17, 2002, p. 3.

explicit involvement in Satanism, written by a respected academic historian,[78] was praised by Rev. Lawrence Gesy of the Vatican Commission on Cults as "a masterpiece of historical research".[79] A final, macabre confirmation was given by Hitler's choice of one of the most significant dates of the year in satanism to commit suicide—April 30, the pagan Feast of Walpurgis Night.[80]

Sexual Degeneracy

Another aspect that highlights the contrast between the Nazi pagan religion and Christianity is its attitude toward human sexuality. Pagan religions, including those mentioned in the Bible as well as Greek and Roman paganism, as well as the neo-Paganism of the New Age, all extol the pursuit of sexual pleasure, especially in its more debased and degrading forms. At the same time, the separation of sexual pleasure from its natural and divinely ordained function has always been strongly condemned by Judaism and Christianity. No concept is more characteristically Christian than that of sexual purity. This is particularly visible in the Catholic Church, which teaches that the absolute epitome of the human race, the most perfect human creature who ever was or ever will be, is the Blessed *Virgin* Mary. The Church has traditionally considered celibacy to be an intrinsically superior

[78] The book is *Masks of Satan* by Dr. Christopher Nugent, Associate Professor of History at the University of Kentucky. Originally published by Sheed and Ward, London, 1983, and republished by Christian Classics, Westminster Md., 1989.

[79] Ibid., p. x.

[80] "The eve of May Day, when the old pagan witch-world was supposed to hold high revelry under its chief . . .", *Dictionary of Phrase and Fable* (London: Cassell, 1900), s.v. Walpurgis Night.

state[81] (although not intended for everyone), and requires it of those especially consecrated to God in religious life or the priesthood. Even in the case of married life, in which celibacy is not appropriate, chastity is still required, as reflected for example in the solemn statement of Pope Pius XI in his 1930 encyclical *Casti Connubii* (which *means* "Chaste Marriage"): "Any use whatsoever of matrimony exercised in such a way that the act is deliberately frustrated in its natural power to generate life is an offense against the law of God and of nature, and those who indulge in such are branded with the guilt of a grave sin."[82]

So it is not surprising that where one finds the antithesis of Christianity, one finds the pursuit of sexual pleasure for its own sake, in increasingly depraved forms. That was certainly the case in all of the streams—intellectual, social, and spiritual—that led up to the Third Reich. Given the distastefulness of the subject only the briefest outline will be given here. We have seen how the intellectual underpinnings

---

[81] For instance, St. Ignatius of Loyola's "Rules for Thinking with the Church": "We must praise highly ... virginity and continency; and matrimony ought not be praised as much as any of these", cited in John Hardon, S.J., *A Treasury of Catholic Wisdom* (San Francisco: Ignatius Press, 1995), p. 404.

[82] The paragraph in its entirety is even more emphatic: "Since, therefore, openly departing from the uninterrupted Christian tradition some recently have judged it possible solemnly to declare another doctrine regarding this question, the Catholic Church, to whom God has entrusted the defense of the integrity and purity of morals, standing erect in the midst of the moral ruin which surrounds her, in order that she may preserve the chastity of the nuptial union from being defiled by this foul stain, raises her voice in token of her divine ambassadorship and through Our mouth proclaims anew: any use whatsoever of matrimony exercised in such a way that the act is deliberately frustrated in its natural power to generate life is an offense against the law of God and of nature, and those who indulge in such are branded with the guilt of a grave sin", *Casti Connubii*, no. 56.

of the Third Reich were intimately linked to the eugenics and birth control movement, which existed to separate sexual pleasure from procreation. The movement's champion, Margaret Sanger, was an outspoken proponent of promiscuity, "the joys of the flesh", and open marriage.[83] Central to the *völkisch* revival were the *wandervogel* hiking and camping clubs for boys that later evolved into the Hitler Youth. Not only was homosexuality rampant in these groups, but the movement itself was also "an effort to revive the Greek ideal of pedagogic pederasty. . . . [It] was pederast at its roots."[84]

The founders and leaders of the movement (Karl Fisher, Hans Blüher, Wilhelm Jansen, etc.) were open both about their own homosexuality and about its appropriateness among the members. Already in 1912, Hans Blüher, who was also the "theoretician" of the organization of homosexuals known as the *Gemeinschaft der Eigenen* (Community of the Elite), wrote a book extolling the role of pederasty in the movement, *The German Wandervogel Movement as an Erotic Phenomenon*. This open embrace of homosexuality continued in the Hitler Youth to such an extent that a prominent German newspaper, the *Rheinische Zeitung*, warned parents to "protect your sons from 'physical preparation' [i.e., initiation into homosexuality] in the organization".[85] The leader of the Hitler Youth organization, Baldur von Schirach, "was arrested by the police for perverse sexual practices and liberated on the intervention of Hitler, who soon afterward made him

---

[83] See Marshall and Donovan, *Blessed Are the Barren*, pp. 6–7.

[84] Parker Rossman, *Sexual Experience between Men and Boys* (New York: Association Press, 1976), p. 103.

[85] Quoted in Scott Lively and Kevin Abrams, *The Pink Swastika: Homosexuality and the Nazi Party* (Keiser, Ore.: Founders, 1995), p. 39.

leader of the Hitler Youth".[86] In 1934, the Gestapo reported over forty cases of pederasty in a single troop of the Hitler Youth. These pederastic relationships between the boys and the group leaders became in fact the prototype for the "Fuhrer principle"; as one former *Wandervogel* member wrote: "We little suspected then what power we had in our hands. We played with the fire that had set a world in flames, and it made our hearts hot.... It was in our ranks that the word Fuhrer originated, with its meaning of blind obedience and devotion."[87] The Nazis' "Sieg Heil" salute originated in the *Wandervogel* groups.

The Storm Troopers fared no better. They were the successors of the *Rossbachbund*, created by the homosexual Gerhard Rossbach as a predominantly homosexual unit of the *Freikorps*, the independent inactive military reserve units that roamed Germany following its defeat in the First World War. Ernst Roehm, the later leader of 2,500,000 Storm Troopers, was a notorious and open homosexual, whose brash homosexual displays in public resulted in open scandals requiring public defenses by Hitler.[88] Weimar defense force official Helmut Klotz described Roehm as "one of the most notorious pederasts walking about on this earth".[89] A contemporary historian, very sympathetic to homosexuals,

[86] Samuel Igra, *Germany's National Vice* (London: Quality Press, 1945), quoted in ibid., p. 40.

[87] E. Y. Hartshorne, *German Youth and the Nazi Dream of Victory* (New York: Farrar and Reinhart, 1941), p. 12.

[88] For instance, Hitler publicly defended Roehm's "right" to his homosexual activities in an official statement on February 3, 1931, and in a leaflet distributed April 6, 1932. See Hans Peter Bleuel, *Strength through Joy: Sex and Society in Nazi Germany* (London: Secker and Warburg, 1973), pp. 97–99.

[89] Helmut Klotz, *The Berlin Diaries: May 30, 1932–January 30, 1933* (New York: William Morrow, 1934), p. 131.

writes, "Roehm's gay fun and games were certainly no secret; his amorous forays into gay bars and gay Turkish baths were riotous. Whatever anti-homosexual sentiments may have been expressed by straight Nazis were more than offset by the reality of highly visible, spectacular, gay-loving Roehm."[90] The openly homosexual German magazine Der Eigene wrote in 1930, "Men such as Captain Roehm are, to our knowledge, no rarity at all in the National Socialist Party. It rather teems there with homosexuals of all kinds.... [T]he joy of man in man ... [is] the highest virtue of the Teutons, [it] blossoms around their campfires and is cultivated and fostered by them in a way done in no other male union that is reared on party politics."[91] Pulitzer prize-winning American reporter H.R. Knickerbocker, who lived in Berlin for much of the 20s and 30s, wrote that "[Roehm's] chiefs ... were almost without exception homosexuals. Indeed, unless a Storm Troop officer were homosexual he had no chance of advancement."[92] The former Chancellor, General Kurt von Schleicher, himself the originator of the Freikorps, referred to the Roehm's Storm Troopers and the early Nazis as "filthy boy streetwalkers!"[93]

Hitler, too, was without doubt a sexual pervert. His homosexuality has been hotly debated for the past fifty

[90] Frank Rector, The Nazi Extermination of Homosexuals (New York: Stein and Day, 1981), p. 51.

[91] Harry Osterhuis and Hubert Kennedy, eds., Homosexuality and Male Bonding in Pre-Nazi Germany: Original transcripts from Der Eigene (New York: Harrington Park Press, 1991), pp. 236–37.

[92] H.R. Knickerbocker, Is Tomorrow Hitler's? (New York: Reynal and Hitchcock, 1941), p. 55.

[93] Rector, Nazi Extermination of Homosexuals, p. 64.

years, but the evidence in favor is compelling. Samuel Igra, a Jewish historian who escaped from Germany in 1939, cites police reports that show that Hitler worked as a homosexual prostitute in Vienna from 1907 to 1912 and in Munich from 1912 to 1914.[94] These police documents are also mentioned in an OSS report on Hitler prepared during the war,[95] and copies of them reportedly ended up in the possession of Benito Mussolini,[96] who referred to Hitler as "that horrible sexual degenerate".[97] The same OSS report also claimed that German military records show that Hitler was court-martialed for "pederastic practices".[98] The OSS also had interviews with two young men who claimed that they had been Hitler's homosexual partners.[99] There is evidence of other sexual perversions as well. Hitler's coprophilia (gaining sexual satisfaction by being defecated or urinated on) and masochism are detailed in the same OSS report,[100] and of the four women with whom Hitler is known to have had affairs, one was his own teenaged niece and another was the thirteen-year-old daughter

---

[94] Igra, *Germany's National Vice*, pp. 66–67, cited in Scott Lively, *The Poisoned Stream* (Salem, Ore.: Lively Communications, 1997), p. 37. Also, Desmond Seward, *Napoleon and Hitler* (London: Harrap, 1988) "[T]he files of the Viennese police station list him as a homosexual", p. 299.

[95] The OSS, Office of Strategic Services, was the predecessor to the CIA. The report was written for the use of Allied command by Boston psychologist Dr. William Langer and later published as William Langer, *The Mind of Adolf Hitler* (New York: Basic Books, 1972), see pp. 124–25, 128–29.

[96] Rector, *Nazi Extermination of Homosexuals*, p. 57.

[97] Seward, *Napoleon and Hitler*, p. 148.

[98] Langer, *Mind of Adolf Hitler*, pp. 128–29.

[99] Ibid., p. 178.

[100] Ibid., p. 138.

of a friend. (All four later attempted suicide; two succeeded.[101])

The concentration camps themselves were not free from the scourge of deviant sexuality, as evidenced in a number of survivors' accounts. Elie Wiesel, in *Night*, writes, "The head of our tent was a German. He was so fat he could hardly move. Like the leader of the camp he loved children. . . . [T]here was a considerable traffic in children among homosexuals here, I later learned."[102] According to survivors of the Treblinka concentration camp, one particularly brutal guard, Max Bielas, "had a harem of little Jewish boys. He liked them young, no older than seventeen. . . . Bielas sought in Treblinka only the satisfaction of his homosexual instincts."[103]

The occult groups that led up to Nazism suffered from the same vices. Whether Madame Blavatsky was actively a lesbian is a matter of some dispute; there is some cause for suspicion, including the endearments she used with her successor, Annie Besant, addressing her in one letter as "My Darling Penelope" and signing it "Your . . . female Ulysses". In any case, her second in command for the Theosophical Society in England, Charles Leadbeater, was in continual legal trouble for his pederasty. Lanz, the publisher of *Ostara*, was expelled from his monastery for "carnal desires"; some believe that to be a reference to homosexuality. A profound misogyny was reflected in his writings: "[T]he soul of the woman has something pre-human, something demonic . . .

---

[101] Langer, *Mind of Adolf Hitler*, pp. 96–99, and Otto Stasser, *The Gangsters around Hitler*, cited in Lively, *The Poisoned Stream*, pp. 50–51, 84. Although the coroner's verdict for the niece was suicide—she was found dead in Hitler's apartment, shot by his revolver—there has also been speculation that she was shot by Hitler (Langer, *Mind of Adolf Hitler*, p. 97).

[102] Elie Wiesel, *Night* (New York: Hill and Wang, 1960), p. 55.

[103] Jean-François Steiner, *Treblinka* (New York: Signet, 1968), pp. 117–18.

about it." He also asserted that "75% of all unmarried girls were fornicators [and] 95% of all married women were adulteresses".[104]

The role that sexual perversion and debauchery played in Nazism and the movements leading up to it provides yet more evidence of the deeply anti-Christian impulse behind it.[105]

The Reaction of the Rest of the World

While the active campaign to exterminate the Jews came from Germany and the Nazis, the rest of the civilized world did less than one might expect to try to save the victims. Out of the country that represented the apex of Western culture, from which the best of the world's great music, philosophy, and science had come, arose a concerted effort to wipe the Jews off the face of the earth. And from the rest of the civilized world came a deafening silence.

The lack of response by the rest of the West is typified by the 1938 Evian conference. Ten days after Germany's invasion of Austria, Roosevelt called an international conference in Evian, France, to try to find countries that might be willing

---

[104] James M. Rhodes, *The Hitler Movement* (Stanford, Calif.: Hoover Institution Press, 1980), p. 108.

[105] The Nazi persecution of homosexuals that did exist does not contradict the thesis of this section. Reasons for that persecution included the need to respond to public outrage at the overt homosexuality among the Nazis, internal Nazi power struggles, and as a pretext for getting rid of individuals. An excellent analysis that explains the apparent contradiction was given by the prominent German homosexual activist Hans Bluher, who as a leader of the homosexual movement in Germany during the period leading up to the Third Reich, was in an excellent position to know (Hans Bluher, *Die Rede des Aristophanes* [Hamburg: Kala-Verlag, 1966], quoted in Lothar Machtan, *The Hidden Hitler* [New York: Basic Books, 2001], pp. 242–43). A similar analysis appears in Lively and Abrams, *The Pink Swastika*.

to accept Jewish refugees from the Nazis. Since the ascension of Hitler to power in 1933, the campaigns and intentions of the Third Reich toward the Jews were well known throughout the West. For instance, already on April 22, 1933, a *New York Times* correspondent wrote a first-hand description of Dachau. On September 6, 1933, the *New York Times* wrote, "Aryanism is now the keystone of Nazi policy . . . and of all the Nazi tendencies it is the most warmly defended by the Germans. Its corollary is persecution even to extermination—the word is the Nazis own—of the non-Aryans, if that can be established without too much world disturbance." [106] An eyewitness account from a boy (non–Jewish) released from the Oranienburg concentration camp was published on October 6, 1933, in the *New York Times*.[107] During 1933, other eyewitnesses of the horrors of the concentration camps reported their experiences in the United States and British press, as well as in the British House of Commons. When the *New York Times* covered the 1936 Nazi party congress, it reported that one of the speakers stressed that extermination was, in the last analysis, the only real solution to the Jewish problem: "If the final solution were to be reached one must go the bloody path. To secure the safety of the whole world they [the Jews] must be exterminated." [108]

What the Nazi invasion of Vienna in 1938 meant for Austria's Jews was also well documented in the *New York Times* of March 20, 1938:

The death carts of the Anatomical Institution are busy daily collecting the bodies of those [Jews] poisoned by

[106] Arthur Morse, *While 6 Million Died* (New York: Ace Books, 1968), p. 130.
[107] Ibid., p. 132.
[108] *New York Times*, September 16, 1936, quoted in ibid., p. 159.

their own hands.... Death seems to them the kindest
gift.... Truckloads of pale faced citizens [are] being hur-
ried through the streets to vanish through the great gates
of the central prison—for many of them the first stage of
the journey to the concentration camp.[109]

During this period, the Third Reich was keeping a close eye
on the reaction of the rest of the world to their campaign
against the Jews, to see how far they could go without pro-
voking a response. The United States did not even boycott
the Berlin Olympic Games of 1936, despite the fact that by
that time the anti-Semitic Nuremberg Laws had been passed
and Jews in Germany were barred from any employment in
government, the arts, the professions, or even manual crafts
and deprived of their citizenship. They were even banned
from the very town where the 1936 Winter Olympics were
being held (Garmisch-Partenkirchen), as well as many others.

The lack of response from the rest of the world did not
escape the Nazis. A month after assuming office, Hitler was
referring sarcastically to the United States refusal to allow
Jewish refugees into the United States when he said: "Through
its immigration law America has inhibited the unwelcome
influx of such races as it has been unable to tolerate in its
midst. Nor is America now ready to open its doors to Jews
fleeing from Germany." [110]

Just five days after *Kristalnacht*—when every synagogue in
Germany was burned, every Jewish establishment vandal-
ized and looted, 25,000 Jews taken to concentration camps,
and the Jewish community fined one billion marks for the
damage—Roosevelt was asked at a White House press

[109] Ibid., pp. 164–65.
[110] *New York Times*, April 6, 1933 quoted in ibid., p. 121.

conference: "Would you recommend a relaxation of our immigration restrictions so that the Jewish refugees could be received in this country?" His reply: "That is not in contemplation. We have the quota system." [111]

Hitler explicitly offered to send Germany's unwanted Jews to any country that was willing to receive them, knowing however that none was:

> "I can only hope and expect that the other world, which has such deep sympathy for these criminals, will at least be generous enough to convert this sympathy into practical aid. We, on our part, are ready to put all these criminals at the disposal of these countries, for all I care, even on luxury ships." [112]

Ironically, this prophecy was tragically fulfilled, when on May 13, 1939, Jewish refugees numbering 734 who had been approved as immigrants to the United States left Bremen on the German luxury ship *St. Louis*. Since their quota numbers would only "come up" in several months they were headed for Cuba to wait until their numbers came up. However, the temporary landing certificates for Cuba that they had obtained prior to departure were rescinded before they arrived, and they were refused permission to land. They appealed to the United States to be allowed to arrive early, in anticipation of the already approved visas, but the United States government staunchly refused. The refugees were forced to return to Europe, where most died in concentration camps.

The fate of the *St. Louis* was the natural outcome of the Evian conference. On the eve of the conference, Roosevelt

[111] *New York Times*, November 15, 1938, quoted in ibid., p. 124.
[112] Hitler's speech at Konigsberg, *New York Times*, March 27, 1938, quoted in ibid., p. 167.

reassured the American people that the United States would not increase or revise its immigration quotas. The *Völkischer Beobachter* newspaper had jibed: "We cannot take seriously President Roosevelt's appeal to the nations of the world as long as the United States maintains racial quotas for immigrants." [113] Apparently none of the participants at the conference took the appeal seriously, either. Australia, hardly suffering from excess population, responded: "As we have no real racial problem, we are not desirous of importing one." [114] The Peruvian delegation sarcastically responded that the United States has given Peru an example to follow in the "caution and wisdom" [115] followed in its own immigration policies. Argentina pointed out that it had already accepted about as many of the refugees as the United States (that is, a few thousand) and so could not be expected to take any more. And so on for 32 of the 34 participants. The only exceptions were tiny Denmark and Holland.

The United States ended up not even filling its miniscule quota of a few thousand European Jews a year. Prospective immigrants were blocked with such impossible requirements for a Jew fleeing Nazi Germany as having to obtain a police certificate testifying to good character for the previous five years and two certified copies of all personal public records kept by the authorities. British-controlled Palestine was also unwilling to provide them a refuge. Even when fleeing Jews managed to reach it, the British authorities refused them entry, in one notorious case forcing a sinking ship crowded with refugees back to sea,

[113] Ibid., p. 169.
[114] Ibid., p. 174.
[115] Ibid.

resulting in the drowning deaths of 697 out of the 699 Jews on board within sight of shore.[116]

One of the more poignant aspects of reading the testimonies of survivors of the concentration camps, or of the ghetto exterminations, is their pathetic hope and certainty that if only the Allies were informed of what was being done to the Jews, they would immediately respond with bombers overhead. Heroic efforts, often at the cost of lives, were made by resistance-fighting Jews to get the word to Allied authorities. The truth never occurred to them—that the authorities had been getting reliable reports for months and years, often first-hand from Jews who had made miraculous escapes, and had decided to do nothing in response.

Diabolical Motivations Behind the Holocaust

One cannot read very much about the Holocaust without being struck, over and over again, by the indications of diabolical inspiration for what happened. It appears in the extraordinary cruelty of the Nazis, in the philosophy of their leaders, in their explicit hatred of God and of religion, in their determination to wipe out Christianity as well as Judaism, in their open embrace of paganism and occultism, in their sexual perversity, and in their satanic, cultic practices. It in no way diminishes the responsibility or guilt of the perpetrators to suggest that they were directly inspired, and at times possessed, by demonic forces. This raises the question of *why* the attack on the Jews of the Holocaust was so important to the adversary of man's salvation.

---

[116] The *Struma*, sunk February 24, 1941, recounted in ibid., p. 250.

One hypothesis is that it might, in part, have been an attempt to forestall the Second Coming. Obviously the first coming of the Messiah came through the Jews, and the New Testament also implies—most notably in Romans 11—that the Jews will have a role to play in the Second Coming. If so, then the eradication of the race might have been an attempt to prevent the Second Coming. It may seem paradoxical that the adversary should try to prevent the Second Coming— since it is going to happen as a certain fact, why should the adversary "hope", or try, to prevent it? The full answer lies within the mystery of iniquity, but that it is the case we know from the *Catechism of the Catholic Church*:

> Though already present in his Church, Christ's reign is nevertheless yet to be fulfilled "with power and great glory" by the king's return to earth (Lk 21:27; cf. Mt 25:31). This reign is still under attack by the evil powers, even though they have been defeated definitively by Christ's Passover (cf. 2 Thess 2:7).[117]

If the adversary's primary motivation behind the Holocaust was to prevent the Second Coming of Christ by exterminating all of the Jews, there was still a secondary way he could succeed even if some Jews survived. That would be by stopping the conversion of the Jews that must precede Christ's return. As the *Catechism* states, "The glorious Messiah's coming is suspended at every moment of history until his recognition by 'all Israel' (Rom 11:20–26; cf. Mt 23:39)."[118] And the Holocaust has certainly had a tremendous deterring effect on conversion of Jews to Christianity. On the part of Jews there is a natural tendency to think of the Nazis as

[117] *Catechism of the Catholic Church*, no. 671.
[118] Ibid., no. 674.

Christians, which increases the sense that many Jews have that Christianity is the enemy and results in an almost insurmountable emotional barrier against conversion. A Jew who does convert is often thought of as having gone over to the side "of the enemy", even at times "to the Nazis". On the side of Christianity, a sense of collective guilt for the crimes of the Holocaust have caused many Christian denominations, and even the Catholic Church,[119] to curtail or eliminate entirely any efforts to evangelize Jews. Any Christian missionary efforts that remain are often met with the challenge "How can you, after the Holocaust...?" Individual Jews who convert, as well as Christian evangelization efforts toward Jews, whether coming from Jewish converts or Gentile Christians, are sometimes accused of "trying to finish Hitler's work", or even of being "worse than Hitler", because Hitler, at least, was overt in his attempt to destroy the Jews, whereas they are doing it covertly. If the adversary's "fall-back" plan was to rely on the Holocaust to impede the ability of Jews to recognize the claims of Christianity, in that he has, at least in part, succeeded.

The adversary may have also had a more immediate motivation—sheer, raw hatred of the Jews, as God's "Chosen People". His fundamental hatred is against God; his attacks against man are an indirect way of "getting at" God, since God loves man so deeply. Given God's special love for the Jews, it is logical that the adversary should have a special hatred and vindictiveness toward them, a special eagerness to hurt them. God's particular love for the Jews is well

---

[119] For instance, in the Bishops' Committee on Ecumenical and Interreligious Affairs of the United States Conference of Catholic Bishops 2002 document *Reflections on Covenant and Mission*.

documented in the Old Testament, where they are described as the "chosen people", the "apple of God's eye":

> For you are a people holy to the LORD your God; the LORD your God has chosen you to be a people for his own possession, out of all the peoples that are on the face of the earth (Deuteronomy 7:6).

> For the LORD's portion is his people, Jacob his allotted heritage. He found him in a desert land, and in the howling waste of the wilderness; he encircled him, he cared for him, he kept him as the apple of his eye (Deuteronomy 32:9–10).

> For thus said the LORD of hosts ... he who touches you touches the apple of [my] eye (Zechariah 2:8).

The adversary's special hatred against the Jews is further inflamed by the fact that Christ was a Jew. As Cardinal Lustiger has pointed out, the fundamental root of anti-Semitism on a spiritual level is hatred of Christ. Thus the motivating fury behind the Holocaust was an almost pure outpouring of hell's hatred of God and hatred of Christ.

In the Holocaust this hatred was expressed in three ways—trying to eliminate Jews and Judaism, causing the Jews as much suffering, pain, anguish, and humiliation as humanly (or, more precisely, diabolically) possible, and finally by trying (one hopes unsuccessfully) to "damn" as many Jews as possible. For the concentration camps were not only designed to torture and kill the Jews, but they were also designed to dehumanize them, to wear down their moral resistance, and to cause them to act in ways that would offend God—either by rebelling against Him or by committing suicide (which was a frequent occurrence at Auschwitz, primarily by throwing oneself against the electrified fence)

or by succumbing to the instinct of self-preservation and acting out of pure selfishness with no regard for others. For the
adversary wished not only to see the Jews suffer and die, but
worse, to be damned.

The Witness of Cardinal Jean-Marie Lustiger

Earlier we discussed the witness of the Lemann brothers as
paragons of the "faithful remnant", as Jews who embraced
the Jewish Messiah and His Church with "all [their] heart,
and with all [their]soul, and with all [their] might" (Deuteronomy 6:5). Another, more recent such witness is the current Archbishop of Paris, Cardinal Jean-Marie Lustiger, who
was born and raised Jewish in France under the Nazi occu-
pation. In his book-length interview, *Choosing God—Chosen
by God*,[120] he touches on many of the themes addressed in
this book. The following citations illustrate some of Lustiger's thoughts:

On Nazism as anti-Christian paganism:

As a child of thirteen, Lustiger spent the summer of 1937
in Germany living with a Christian family. He relates his
relationship with another boy, a "Hitler Youth" (*Hitler-
jugend*), who did not know that Lustiger was Jewish:

> [He told me about] Saint John's day, the summer solstice,
> the Aryan traditions of the Germans.... [I]t was clear to
> me that Nazism ... was the resurgence of the "pagan"
> and "goyim" idolatries.[121]

---

[120] Jean-Louis Missika and Dominique Wolton, *Choosing God—Chosen by
God* (San Francisco: Ignatius Press, 1991).
[121] Ibid., p. 35.

Hitler's anti-Semitism had its roots in the anti-Semitism of the Enlightenment and not in a Christian anti-Semitism. . . . [It was a] refusal of the Jews' divine election, a hate for their religious singularity.[122] [T]he Jews, as figures of election, caused jealousy and catalyzed on themselves the Nazis' negation of man and God.[123]

I mention in passing that Nazism perverted the notion of a chosen people in order to create a diabolical messianism of their own. It was not subjected to God, but on the contrary looked to the coming of the Superman and thus to the annihilation of the rest of humanity. Nazism identified "election" with domination and unconscionable privilege.[124]

On the continuing role of the Jews:
Cardinal Lustiger clearly believes that Judaism and Jewish identity maintain their unique importance until the Second Coming:

Yes, Israel has its raison-d'etre until the coming of the heavenly Kingdom. . . . The Jews, the Jewish people, exist because God has chosen them. They have no other reason for existing, not even national sentiment. . . . The existence of the chosen people concerns God's plan for humanity: if Israel exists, it is because God has chosen this people for the purpose of saving all mankind.[125]

[I]t is God who has favored Israel. God brought it into existence for the salvation of all humanity, for the coming of the reign, and, according to the promise, it is in Israel

---

[122] Ibid., p. 71.
[123] Ibid., p. 76.
[124] Ibid., pp. 78–79.
[125] Ibid., p. 78.

that the Messiah, suffering, has already appeared. Until the Messiah's coming in glory, the Jew remains, and he remains a Jew, whether he is Christian or not. . . .[126] Israel is a guarantee of the Parousia's coming.[127]

In an address given to the European Jewish Congress in January 2002, Lustiger said the Pope wants Christians to delve more deeply into the mystery of Jewish election:

> The Pope asks Christians to discover the Jewish people by looking at them, not just in the Bible, but also in the history of the last two millennia ... to understand the reason, for all people, why the Jewish people were chosen. Mistaking or renouncing this election would deprive of all its meaning the history of salvation which founds the Christian faith, and perhaps all human history as well. . . .
>   For Christians, how enriching it will be to accept the election of Israel as a fundamental datum of human history, and consequently to consider their own vocation in this light![128]

Pope John Paul II has also taught that God's covenant with the Jews has a continuing meaning in the plan of salvation:

> [T]he Church of Christ discovers her "bond" with Judaism by "searching into her own mystery"(cf. *Nostra Aetate*, no. 4.) ... [I]t is not lawful to say that the Jews are

---

[126] Ibid., p. 79.

[127] Ibid., p. 82. The Parousia is Christ's Second Coming in glory.

[128] Address by Cardinal Lustiger to the European Jewish Congress, Paris, January 28–29, 2002, in *L'Osservatore Romano*, English edition, March 13, 2002, p. 9.

repudiated . . . the Jews are beloved of God, who has called them with an irrevocable calling.[129]

On the diabolical roots and goal of Nazism:
Lustiger sees Nazism as explicitly diabolical:

These men [the Nazis] are only weak creatures, puppets, immersed in an absolute evil that surpasses them. They are victims of their own ignominy. You may demonstrate that a particular person is a sadist, but you will have given only a limited explanation. You may show that this sadist controlled the levers of an immensely powerful machine that brought about an appalling death for his victims, but you are still faced with someone insignificant, who does not suffice to explain what happened. That "pathetic man" is only a contemptible man, and it is normal that he should seem insignificant because the face hidden behind his is Satan's. It is the face of evil in our world, of evil's power, which is so vast as to be unimaginable for the human mind. Those men we see are only the servile actors. . . . Yes, they are individuals who should unquestionably be held responsible for crimes committed, but the evil that surged up in them infinitely surpassed them.[130]

It was not a war "like the others." I felt that we had been plunged into an infernal abyss. . . . At the heart of the opponents' ideology was the persecution of the chosen people, the Jewish people, because they are a Messianic people. When as a child I spent time in Nazi Germany, I had understood: Nazism's aim was more than Promethean; it was Satanic. . . . This utterly overwhelming conflict can

---

[129] Pope John Paul II's address on his visit to the synagogue of Rome, April 13, 1986, reprinted in *John Paul II On Jews and Judaism 1979–1986* (Washington, D.C.: U.S. Catholic Conference, 1987), p. 82.

[130] Missika and Wolton, *Choosing God*, p. 96.

be understood only within the mystery of the suffering Messiah and the redemption with the struggle it implies.[131]

Of course theological speculations by a Cardinal do not constitute official Church teaching. Yet it is interesting to see that this mature and authoritative Catholic theologian and Cardinal, who has first-hand experience of Nazism and the Holocaust, also sees Nazism as overtly pagan, anti-Christian, and even satanic; a diabolical counterfeit of Jewish and Christian messianism directly inspired by hell.

[131] Ibid., p. 108.

CHAPTER SEVEN

Anti-Semitism After the Holocaust

The Nazi campaign to exterminate the Jews ended with the fall of the Third Reich and the Allied liberation of Europe. If it had been a local phenomenon—a characteristic of the German people, an artificial passion created by their leaders for political purposes, or an expression of their social or economic problems—then the end of Nazism in Germany would have been the end of the orchestrated campaign against the Jews. Yet, unfortunately, that was not the case. During the Third Reich itself, the Nazi campaign had received enthusiastic support from a number of Arab leaders who allied themselves with the effort, and upon the fall of the Reich those leaders continued to pursue actively the campaign against the Jews in the Arab world. The Nazi campaign appears not as an isolated instance of genocidal anti-Semitism, but rather as one emergence of a larger, continuing campaign that predated it and continues after it and is now centered in the Arab world.[1]

In considering this genocidal anti-Semitism, whether in Nazi Germany or in the Arab world, one does well to remember the words of St. Paul: "[W]e are not contending

---

[1] "Arab anti-Semitism" is, literally speaking, oxymoronic in that Arabs are also Semites; nonetheless the word "anti-Semitism" will be used here with its common meaning of antipathy toward Jews.

against flesh and blood, but against the principalities, against the powers, against the world rulers of this present darkness, against the spiritual hosts of wickedness in the heavenly places" (Ephesians 6:12). At times these powers are able to gain inordinate sway over entire populations. Whenever such wholesale evil emerges (not necessarily, of course, directed against the Jews), it can be traced to the practice of "diabolical religion"—religious or occult practices that, whether the participants are aware of it or not, serve not God but the "rulers of this present darkness", thus increasing their power and influence.

Nazism in the Arab World

Arab support of Hitler predated his 1933 ascendancy to power, and news of his victory was welcomed with great enthusiasm in the Arab world.[2] Among the first congratulatory telegrams he received were several from Arab capitals. Parties styled after the Nazis soon formed throughout the Arab world. One was Syria's Social Nationalist Party, whose leader, Anton Sa'ada, called himself the "Fuhrer of Syria". The party's banner featured a swastika on a black-and-white background. Sami al-Joundi, one of the founders of the ruling Syrian Ba'ath Party, recalls: "We were racists. We admired the Nazis. We were immersed in reading Nazi literature and books. . . . We were the first who thought of a translation of *Mein Kampf*. Anyone who lived in Damascus at that time was witness to

---

[2] The best scholarly study of the historical link between the Arab countries and Nazism is Roger Faligot and Remi Kauffer, *Le Croissant et la Croix Gammee* (Paris: Albin Michel, 1990), which provided much of the background information in this section.

the Arab inclination toward Nazism."[3] The regard was mutual—Hitler, on his end, said, "The Arab liberation movement is our natural ally".[4]

Egypt's "Young Egypt" party, founded in October 1933 and home to later Egyptian president Gamal Nasser, emulated the Nazis in their adoption of storm troopers, torch processions, and Nazi slogans including "One folk, One party, One leader". They also emulated the Nazis in calling for boycotts of all Jewish businesses and in physical attacks on Jews.[5]

A number of Arab leaders had worked closely with Hitler in his campaign to exterminate the Jews and continued the fight against the Jews in the Arab world even after the end of the war.[6] A prime example is the Grand Mufti of Jerusalem, Hajj Amin al-Husseini.[7]

As the leader of the Arabs in Palestine during the 1930s he called a *jihad* to annihilate the Jews of Palestine. In his own

---

[3] Paul Longgrear and Raymond McNemar, International Christian Embassy, Jerusalem (www.cdn-friends-icej.ca); background on the Syria/Nazi connection in Fouad Ajami, "Two Faces, One Terror", in *Wall Street Journal*, Nov. 11, 2002; David Brooks, "Saddam's Brain", in *The Weekly Standard*, Nov. 11, 2002; Sarah Honig, "Fiendish Hypocrisy I", in *Jerusalem Post*, March 29, 2001. After the war Damascus welcomed many escaped Nazi war criminals; see for instance Gitta Sereny, *Into That Darkness: From Mercy Killing to Mass Murder* (London: Andre Deutsch, 1974), and Faligot and Kauffer, *Croissant et la Croix Gammee*.

[4] Faligot and Kauffer, *Croissant*, frontispiece.

[5] Longgrear and McNemar, International Christian Embassy, Jerusalem (www.cdn-friends-icej.ca).

[6] Joan Peters, *From Time Immemorial* (Chicago: JKAP Publications, 2002), pp. 360–65.

[7] Unless otherwise noted, facts on Husseini from Peters, *From Time Immemorial*, pp. 360–65; Sarah Honig series "Fiendish Hypocrisy", in *Jerusalem Post*, March 29 and April 6, 2001, based on documentation from Eichmann trial; and *Encyclopedia of the Holocaust*, ed. Gutman (New York: Macmillan, 1990), pp. 703–6.

Figure 7-1: Grand Mufti al-Husseini with Hitler, 1941 (source: Yad Vashem Holocaust Museum, Jerusalem)

words: "I declare a holy war, my Moslem brothers! Murder the Jews! Murder them all!" [8] He incited anti-Jewish riots that caused the death of hundreds of Jewish settlers, including in the Jerusalem Riots of 1929 and 1936–1939,[9] and the Hebron Riot of 1929, in which the Jews of Hebron were

---

[8] Leonard J. Davis and M. Decter eds., *Myths and Facts 1982: A Concise Record of the Arab Israeli Conflict* (Washington, D.C.: Near East Report, 1982, p. 199).

[9] Nations Associates of New York, *The Arab Higher Committee, Its Origins, Personnel and Purposes, The Documentary Record Submitted to The United Nations,* May 1947, p. 5.

Figure 7-2: Mufti inspecting Moslem SS Troops in Bosnia, Nov. 1943 (source: Yad Vashem Holocaust Museum, Jerusalem). Extensive photographic documentation of the activities of Muslim Nazi troops and of collaboration between Arab and Nazi leaders during the war has been preserved, some of which is available on the Internet. The interested reader is referred to the Simon Wiesenthal Center in Los Angeles (www.wiesenthal.com), the Netherlands Institute for War Documentation in Amsterdam (www.oorlogsdoc.knaw.nl), and the Yad Vashem Holocaust Museum in Jerusalem (www.yadvashem.org.il).

attacked and scores massacred.[10] An early supporter of Hitler, he sent emissaries to Berlin in December 1937 and in May 1939 suggesting collaboration. Adolf Eichmann intended to meet him during his 1937 trip to Palestine and failed only because the British limited his stay to 48 hours. Later, during his stay in Berlin, Husseini became a friend and frequent visitor to Eichmann. When the war broke out Husseini moved to Iraq, where he supported a pro-Nazi coup in 1941 orchestrated by Hitler.[11] The coup failed, and he had to flee Iraq. Husseini found a warm welcome in Berlin. Shortly after his arrival there he gave a speech in which he called the Jews "the most fierce enemies of the Muslims" and an "ever corruptive element" in the world. Received as a personal guest of Hitler, he was put up in a mansion known as the "*Islamische Zentralinstitut*", which had been a Jewish Hebrew school before its confiscation, and he was given a princely salary, reportedly over $20,000 a month, which came from assets stolen from Jews by the SS prior to their execution.

SS chief Heinrich Himmler took Husseini under his wing, taking him on tours to Auschwitz, where Husseini urged the guards to greater diligence in running the gas chambers. Himmler financed a Muslim clerical academy in Dresden for Husseini to train graduates who would introduce Nazi rule in Muslim lands. In return Husseini recruited Bosnian and other Muslim volunteers for the SS, who wore special uniforms with a Nazi-adorned fez as headgear. Twenty

[10] "[D]eliberate religious inflammation, for which the Mufti and his party bear the sole responsibility, actually led to the riots of 1929" (James William Parkes, *A History of Palestine from 135 A.D. to Modern Times* [New York: Oxford University Press, 1949], p. 315). Also Faligot and Kauffer, *Croissant et la Croix Gammee*, p. 51.

[11] Bernard Wasserstein, *Britain and the Jews of Europe 1939–1945* (New York: Oxford University Press, 1979), p. 79.

thousand of them formed a special SS unit in Croatia known as the "*Hanjar*", meaning "sword", where they fought against partisans in Bosnia, massacring civilians (including 90% of Bosnia's Jews), burning countless Serbian churches and villages, and controlling the area.

Husseini frequently gave speeches on Berlin radio, in which he exhorted the Nazis in their common cause. In one he said, "Kill the Jews—Kill them with your hands, kill them with your teeth! This is well pleasing to Allah!" [12] He gave similar speeches to his Arab brethren, such as the one in which he said, "Arise, o sons of Arabia, fight for your sacred rights. Slaughter Jews wherever you find them. Their spilled blood pleases Allah, our history and religion. That will save our honor." [13]

The condition that the Mufti had set on his support was permission to exterminate the entire Jewish population of Palestine following Hitler's victory. He tried to persuade the Germans to extend the extermination policy to North Africa and Palestine and even made plans for the construction of a death camp outside Nablus to implement the Final Solution for the region. In his memoirs Husseini wrote:

> Our fundamental condition for cooperating with Germany was a free hand to eradicate every last Jew from Palestine and the Arab world. I asked Hitler for an explicit undertaking to allow us to solve the Jewish problem in a manner befitting our national and racial aspirations and according to the scientific methods innovated by Germany in the handling of its Jews. The answer I got was: "The Jews are yours." [14]

[12] Honig, "Fiendish Hypocrisy", April 6, 2001.
[13] Ibid.
[14] Nations Associates, *The Arab Higher Committee, Its Origins, Personnel and Purposes, The Documentary Record Submitted to the United Nations*, May 1947.

Although he was unsuccessful in his efforts to persuade the Nazis to bomb Tel Aviv and to parachute agents into Palestine to poison Tel Aviv's wells, other efforts of his to increase the number of Jews killed were more successful. He successfully lobbied against a plan Hitler was considering in 1943 that would have allowed Jews to leave Hungary, with the result that 400,000 Hungarian Jews were exterminated.[15] He intervened against a deal Eichmann was about to make with the British government that would have exchanged 5,000 Jewish children for German POW's. His violent protest to Himmler against a Red Cross attempt in late 1942 to trade German prisoners for 10,000 Jewish children sent from Poland to the Theresienstadt camp resulted in the exchange being cancelled and the children's deaths.

After the war, Husseini was wanted for war crimes, but escaped to asylum in Egypt. Hungary's attempts to extradite him were blocked, and he lived out his life as a hero in the Arab world. His passing in 1974 was widely mourned by the masses. Today he is venerated as a hero by the PLO. Under his tutelage, several of his younger relatives rose to prominence in the Arab world, including his "nephew", Abd al-Rahman abd al-Bauf Arafat al-Qud al-Husseini, more commonly known as Yassar Arafat.[16] In a public speech in

[15] Ibid.

[16] Al-Husseini was a distant, not direct, uncle of Arafat. The Mufti became the seventeen-year-old Arafat's mentor when he returned from Berlin to Cairo in 1946, where Arafat and his family were living. The blood relationship is at times denied, given how politically charged the situation is, but it has been established beyond doubt. Reliable sources include an interview conducted by Danny Rubenstein for the Israeli newspaper *Haaretz* in November 1996 with a brother and sister of Arafat (source: personal correspondance with David Bedein, Bureau Chief, Israel Resource News Agency, Jerusalem), and an authorized, sympathetic biography of Arafat based on extensive interviews with Arafat and members of his immediate family (Alan Hart, *Arafat* [London:

1985, Arafat declared it an honor to follow in his footsteps, and in 2002 Arafat, in an interview, referred to him as "our hero".[17]

Another protégé of Husseini is his grandson, Sheikh Ekrima Sabri, who is currently the Mufti of the Temple Mount in Jerusalem. Just one day before receiving Pope John Paul II as a guest, he revealed his Nazi sympathies in an interview in which he said: "The figure of 6 million Jews killed during the Holocaust is exaggerated. . . . It was a lot less. It's not my fault if Hitler hated the Jews. Anyway, they hate them just about everywhere." [18] A younger cousin of Husseini's, Faisal Husseini, was the PLO's top figure in Jerusalem and was considered a possible successor to Arafat, until his death in 2001.[19]

Another participant in the 1941 pro-Nazi coup in Iraq, which sent Husseini to Berlin, was Khayrallah Tulfah. He was jailed for four years for his participation, where he wrote a book entitled *Three Whom God Should Not Have Created—Iranians, Jews, and Flies*. In 1947, his ten-year-old nephew was sent to live with him in his house. The main room was dominated by a large portrait of an idolized Adolf Hitler. This nephew was none other than Saddam Hussein, the former leader of Iraq. Hussein made his uncle the mayor of Baghdad and had his book republished by the Iraqi Ministry of

Sidgewick and Jackson, 1994], pp. 45–46). Also Howard M. Sachar, *A History Of Israel* [New York: Knopf, 1976], p. 682: "Arafat's actual name was Abd al-Rahman abd al-Bauf Arafat al-Qud al-Husseini. He shortened it to obscure his kinship with the notorious Nazi and ex-Mufti of Jerusalem, Haj Muhammed Amin al-Husseini."

[17] Palestinian daily *Al Quds*, August 2, 2002.

[18] International Christian Embassy, Jerusalem (www.cdn-friends-icej.ca).

[19] CNN.com, Time Magazine, June 01, 2001 (www.time.com/time/world/article/0,8599,128775,00.html).

Education. Then-President George Bush identified the similarity between the Iraqi and the Nazi leader; on October 15, 1990, he said of Saddam Hussein, "We're dealing with Hitler revisited." Hussein himself, according to a former mistress, would look at himself in the mirror and say, "I am Saddam Hussein. Heil Hitler!" [20] Some of his actions, too, had eerie similarities with those of Hitler. In a purge strongly reminiscent of Hitler's "Night of the Long Knives", on July 22, 1979, Hussein had about 450 high-ranking military officers, government ministers, Revolutionary Command members, and labor leaders rounded up and killed to ensure his power. And like the Nazis, he used poison gas to exterminate many of his own countrymen, perhaps as many as 100,000 Iraqi Kurds. [21]

Among the officers leading the 1952 revolution in Egypt was a member of Young Egypt named Gamal Abdul Nasser, who two years later became the leader of the country. His Egypt became home to dozens of high-profile Nazi war criminals. [22] One was SS General Oskar Dirlewanger, who as leader of the uniquely vicious Dirlewanger brigade helped to crush the Warsaw ghetto uprising and exterminate the Ukraine's large Jewish population. In Egypt, he became Nasser's personal bodyguard and close friend. [23] Another was Johannes

[20] From an interview with the purported mistress, Parisoula Lampsos, with ABC News, abcnews.go.com/sections/primetime/DailyNews/iraq_saddam_mistress020908.html.

[21] ABC News biography of Saddam Hussein, www.abcnews.go.com/reference/bios/shussein.html.

[22] The source for the fugitive Nazis mentioned in this paragraph is, unless otherwise noted, Faligot and Kauffer, *Croissant et la Croix Gammee.*

[23] Dirlewanger was notorious for his sadism. He had also been imprisoned for pedophilia in 1934. See French MacLean, *The Cruel Hunters* (Atglen, Pa.: Schiffer, 1998), and Richard Rhodes, *Masters of Death* (New York: Knopf, 2002).

von Leers, Goebbel's right-hand man in his propaganda ministry who was put in charge of anti-Semitic propaganda for Egypt's Ministry of Information in 1955. Another alumnus of Goebbel's information ministry, Hans Appler, also joined Egypt's Ministry of Information. Among the dozens of others were Franz Bartel, who after learning about getting information as aide to the Gestapo chief in charge of interrogation at Auschwitz, joined Egypt's Ministry of Information;[24] Hans Becher, who applied what he learned with the Gestapo in Vienna as a police instructor in Alexandria, Egypt; SS *Untersturmfuhrer*[25] Wilhelm Boerner, a guard at the Mauthausen concentration camp who later trained the Palestine Liberation Front for the Egyptian Ministry of the Interior; SS *Obergruppenfuhrer*[26] Friedrich Buble, who became the director of Egyptian government's Department of Public Relations; Joachim Daemling, head of the Gestapo in Dusseldorf, who used his Gestapo expertise as advisor to the Egyptian prison system; Dr. Hans Eisele, the "doctor" at Buchenwald who experimented on and killed at least 300 "patients"[27] (and was reputed to have made lampshades out of human flesh) and who went on to establish a flourishing medical practice in Cairo;[28] SS *Hauptsturmfuhrer*[29] Heim Heribert, doctor at Mauthausen concentration camp who became a

[24] Affidavit of Rudolf Hoess, April 5, 1946, at Nurnberg, Germany, www.nizkor.org/ftp.cgi/imt/ nca/nca-06/nca-06-3868-ps.

[25] I.e., Second Lieutenant.

[26] I.e., Lieutenant General.

[27] For this he was sentenced to death *in absentia* by the Dachau war crimes tribunal. Source: Prof. Dr. C. F. Ruter and Dr. D. W. de Mildt, *Nazi Crimes on Trial: German Trials Concerning National Socialist Homicidal Crimes*, University of Amsterdam Institute of Criminal Law, www1.jur.uva.nl/junsv/.

[28] Where he died a natural death in Cairo on May 3, 1967 (*Egyptian Mail*, January 28, 1995).

[29] I.e., Captain.

doctor for the Egyptian police; SS *Sturmbannfuhrer*[30] Seipel, whose work with the Gestapo in Paris qualified him to provide security for the Ministry of the Interior in Cairo; and on and on and on. The infamous Alois Brunner, private secretary to Adolf Eichmann and responsible for the deportation and death of over 100,000 Jews, initially escaped to Egypt, but moved on to Damascus, where he became a close friend and senior advisor to the Syrian government. (As recently as 1989, Syria vehemently refused a French request for his extradition.[31]) When Brunner arrived in Damascus, he joined an already established community of escaped Nazi war criminals that included Franz Stangl, the former commandant of the infamous Treblinka extermination camp.[32]

Nassar's successor as president of Egypt was Anwar Sadat, who is often called a moderate. Yet shortly after the war,

---

[30] I.e., Major.

[31] Brunner was responsible for the deportation to death camps of 47,000 Jews from Austria, 43,000 Jews from Greece, and 25,000 Jews from France, and was sentenced to death *in abstentia* for his war crimes in 1954. Syria has consistently refused numerous extradition requests, for which it was condemned by the European Parliament 1991. In a 1987 interview Brunner said his one regret was that he hadn't killed more Jews. Sources: Simon Wiesenthal Center (www.wiesenthal.com), Macedonian Press Agency (www.mpa.gr), Siège Social Réseau Intermedia (www.diplomatiejudiciaire.com), and Georg Hafner and Esther Schapira, *Die Akte Alois Brunner* (Frankfurt/New York: Campus Verlag, 2000), Faligot and Kauffer, *Croissant et la Croix Gammee*, pp. 17–18.

[32] Stangl was finally extradited to West Germany in 1967 to face trial. He was sentenced to life imprisonment and died in prison on June 28, 1971. Treblinka was, if possible, particularly horrible even for a Nazi death camp; virtually all of the up to 20,000 Jews who arrived each day were immediately put to death—suffocated with diesel fumes, shot, or simply forced into the huge ever-burning pits of corpses. Stangl's career as a Nazi mass murderer had begun with the "T4" group, organized to "euthanize" mental patients. See Sereny, *Into That Darkness*, and Samuel Willenberg, *Revolt in Treblinka* (Warsaw: Jewish Historical Institute, 2000).

believing that Hitler was still alive, this "moderate" wrote
Hitler the following letter:

> My dear Hitler,
>
> I congratulate you from the bottom of my heart. Even if
> you appear to have been defeated, in reality you are the
> victor. You succeeded in creating dissensions between
> Churchill, the old man, and his allies, the Sons of Satan.
> Germany will win because her existence is necessary to
> preserve the world balance. Germany will be reborn in
> spite of the Western and Eastern powers. There will be
> no peace unless Germany once again becomes what she
> was.[33]

As a government minister in 1953 Sadat wrote: "[Hitler] was
wronged and slandered, for he did no more to the Jews than
... the European people who slaughtered the Jews before
him. . . . [He was trying to] save the world from this malig-
nant evil." [34]

Sadat's close confidant Anis Mansour, editor of the Egyptian paper *October*, wrote: "The World is now aware of the
fact that Hitler was right, and that the cremation ovens were
the appropriate means of punishing [the Jews]." [35]

The popularity of Nazism in the Arab world has never
ceased. In 1999, Hitler's *Mein Kampf* ranked sixth on the bestseller list among Palestinian Arabs.[36] Luis Al-Haj, translator
of the Arabic edition, writes glowingly in the preface about
Hitler:

---

[33] *Al Musawwar*, no. 1510, September 18, 1953, cited in D. F. Green, ed.,
Arab Theologians on Jews and Israel (Geneva: Éditions de l'avenir, 1976), p. 87.

[34] Ibid.

[35] Jan Willem van der Hoeven, Director of the International Christian Zionist Center (www.cdn-friends-icej.ca).

[36] Agence France Presse, September 8, 1999.

Adolf Hitler is one of the few great men ... a man of ideology who bequeathed an ideological heritage whose decay is inconceivable. [His] National Socialism did not die with the death of its herald. Rather, its seeds multiplied under each star.... Hitler's opinions and theories on nationalism, regimes, and ethnicity ... are not yet outmoded.[37]

The Holocaust is routinely denied by governments throughout the Arab world. Consider the following quotes from the official Egyptian government press. Egypt is considered one of the more "moderate" Arab states:

[E]ven if the ovens at Buchenwald and Auschwitz were working day and night, it would have taken dozens of years to kill six million people, and not just the three years which the Nazis had (*Al-Akhbar*, July 14, 1998).[38]

Israelis have built their state upon a collection of myths with no truthful basis ... [i.e.,] the myth of the extermination of the Jews in ovens by the Nazis in World War II (*Al-Akhbar*, July 24, 1998).[39]

[T]he Jews invented the myth of mass extermination and the fabrication that 6 million Jews were put to death in Nazi ovens ... the Holocaust is an Israeli myth (*Al-Akhbar*, Sept. 25, 1998).[40]

The American Secretary of State ... stood in front of the memorial of the false Holocaust of the Jews in WWII (*Al-Akhbar*, Mar. 7, 2001).

[37] Middle East Media Research Institute, Washington, D.C., www.memri.org.
[38] Israel Government Press Office, www.pmo.gov.il.
[39] Ibid.
[40] Ibid.

There are no findings to indicate the existence of mass graves, because the size of the ovens makes it impossible for many Jews to have been killed there. According to the lists presented by the Soviets to the Germans, no more than 70,000 Jews were registered as having been at Auschwitz (*Al-Ahram*, Feb. 2, 1998).[41]

Sometimes the Holocaust denial is coupled with a pronounced sympathy for Hitler, as in this article from the Egyptian government daily *Al-Akhbar* of May 27, 2001 (condensed):

Hitler's executioners took [his rights] away from him and attributed to him crimes that he did not commit.... All of Hitler's crimes and infractions were forgotten by the world, except for one crime that was exaggerated and blown completely out of proportion, thanks to the insistence of world Zionism to continue to stoke the fire, the false Holocaust, whose numbers and scope they have exaggerated until it has reached the level of the merciless destruction of six million Jews.

The first dubious fact is the number of six million Jews who were burnt in the gas chamber. Even if we cross off one zero from the six million and are left with a tenth of this number, it would still seem exaggerated and would have to be investigated....

Did Hitler attack the Jews or did their crime deserve even more? The Zionists were a fifth column in Germany, and they betrayed the country that hosted them.

This had to be exposed, Hitler discovered that the Zionists were spies for the Allied Powers. Inevitably, he was enraged and took revenge on them for this great betrayal. Germany should [not be paying] compensations for false crimes that have no proof except for false and misleading claims.[42]

According to the Arab media, it was the Jews themselves who planned the Holocaust:

> Always remember who the Jews are . . . and their corruption in the world . . . they are cursed . . . what has come to be called "the Holocaust", that is the slaughter of the Jews by Nazism . . . was planned by the Jews' leaders, and was part of their policy. . . . They are cursed with the curse of Allah in this world and in the hereafter. — Sermon by religious leader Sheikh Ibrahim Madhi, broadcast on Palestinian Authority (P.A.) television on September 21, 2001.[43]

> And has history, now in the prime of its potency, clarified that the victims of the Holocaust were themselves those who created it . . . the Jews actively participated in directing European feelings against them . . . — official Palestinian Authority daily, *Al-Hayat Al-Jadida*, Apr. 13, 2001.[44]

As for Hitler, there is nothing but congratulations:

> Thanks to Hitler, [of] blessed memory, who on behalf of the Palestinians revenged in advance against the most vile criminals on the face of the earth. Although we do have a complaint against him for his revenge on them was not enough. — Egyptian government daily *Al-Akhbar*, Apr. 18, 2001.[45]

[42] Middle East Media Research Institute, www.memri.org.

[43] Ibid.

[44] Ibid.

[45] Ibid. Significantly, just two months after this column appeared its author, Ahmed Ragab, received the Egyptian Press League's top award (source: May 31, 2001, press release from the Anti-Defamation League, 823 U.N. Plaza, New York City, NY).

People all over the world have come to realize that Hitler
was right, since Jews . . . are bloodsuckers . . . , interested
in destroying the whole world which has . . . expelled them
and despised them for centuries . . . and burnt them in
Hitler's crematoria . . . one million . . . six millions. Would
that he had finished it! — Egyptian government daily *Al-
Akhbar,* Aug. 19, 1973.[46]

There is also the hope that what he began others might
complete:

One of the reasons for [the recognition of the State of
Israel] was the desire of the people in the East and West to
get rid of as many as possible of the representatives of that
human error known as "the Jews", to concentrate them
in one place, so that it would be easier to strike them at
the right moment. We cannot help but see before us the
figure of that great man Hitler, may Allah have mercy on
him, who was the wisest of those who confronted this
problem, and who, out of compassion for humanity, tried
to exterminate every Jew. — Dr. Yahya al-Rakhaw, in *Al-
Ahrar,* the organ of Egypt's Liberal Party, July 19, 1982
(condensed).[47]

Curiously, the Arab identification with the Nazis is so strong
that at times Arab leaders accuse the Allies' attack on Germany as being in reality an attack on Islam, as in the following sermon, which was preached at the mosque on the Temple
Mount in Jerusalem on November 2, 2001, and broadcast on
the "Voice of Palestine" radio. (It is worth remembering that
the mosque's Mufti is Husseini's grandson.):

[46] Ibid.

[47] Jan Willem van der Hoeven, Director International Christian Zionist
Center (www.cdn-friends-icej.ca).

The attack on our Islamic allies seems to be a repetition of the First World War, reminding us of the cooperation between the heretics to bring down the German nation, which was destroyed by the heretic nations, thus giving those heretic and imperialistic nations the freedom to invade our Arab Muslim homelands. These heretic nations are once again attacking, like dogs, Muslim Afghanistan, and are fighting Islam everywhere. . . . When the English and the French fought the Nazis, were they then also fighting terror or were they fighting Islam? . . . We urge all Muslims to unite in a war against the Crusaders, and that Allah will bring vengeance upon them.[48]

Official Arab Anti-Semitism

The anti-Semitic slanders that permeate much of the press in the Arab world are often indistinguishable from those of the Third Reich. Persistent themes that had been previously used by the Nazis include the intrinsic inferiority of the Jews as a race, the degenerate nature of the Jews as a source of moral corruption and sexual degeneracy, the "blood libel" that the blood of non-Jewish children is a necessary ingredient in Passover matzos, that there is a worldwide Jewish conspiracy to take over the world, that the wars of the world are started by Jews for profit, and that the Jews are behind any and all acts of mass violence (including the 2001 World Trade Center attack).

These slanders have not abated despite the fact that a key provision of the Camp David accords was that "[t]he Parties shall seek to foster mutual understanding and tolerance and will accordingly abstain from hostile propaganda against each

[48] Middle East Media Research Institute, www.memri.org.

other" (Article 5 (3) of Annex III). Some typical recent examples follow, most from the government-sponsored Arab press in the "moderate" Arab countries:

> Certainly this cursed yarmulke [the skull-cap required by Jewish religious law] causes whoever wears it to lose his righteousness, to forget justice, and to free himself of any wisdom or logic — March 7, 2001 Egyptian government-sponsored daily *Al-Akhbar*, written by Editor-in-Chief.[49]

> Has there been any change at all in the personality of the fanatic Jew, as it has come to be known and described in the literature and heritage of most of the nations of the world? ... [I]s there any difference between Netanyahu's traits ... and those of the money-lender from the play "The Merchant of Venice"? — Egyptian daily *Al-Ahram* Dec. 8, 1998.[50]

> Anyone who studies the Jewish heritage cannot help but feel that all conspiracies against religions and generally all destructive upheavals and the undermining of values and basic principles—all are the result of this heritage. Jewish guidance directs every axe of destruction. Satan worship is a part of Judaism ... as is the goal of destroying the monotheistic religions — Egyptian weekly *October*, Oct. 4, 1998.

> There is a great Jewish plot to gain control of the world — Egyptian daily *Al-Ahram*, May 13, 1998.[51]

> *Allah* commands the Muslims to fight the friends of Satan wherever they may be found. And among Satan's friends—indeed, his best friends in our age—are the Jews — Shaykh

---

[49] Israel National News archives, www.israelnn.com/archive.php.
[50] Israel Government Press Office, www.pmo.gov.il.
[51] Ibid.

Abd-al-Halim Mahmud, rector of Al-Azhar University, Cairo, Egypt.[52]

Jews are liars, corrupt, jealous, crafty, treacherous, stupid, despicable, coward, and low-life. They violate agreements and contracts and cause all evil in the world.... The Jews are a mortal danger threatening the world, a lethal plague that dismantles and destroys it. They are a hateful Satan. The Jewish message is hatred and jealousy, lies and deception, vilification, duplicity and ruinous — Syrian author Dr. Salah Khalidi.[53]

The Jews have been behind all of the wars and their goal was corruption and destruction. This is their means of getting rich quick after wars — Egyptian daily *Al-Ahram* Nov. 14, 1998.[54]

Israel was behind the attack at Luxor [a terrorist attack on tourists in Egypt] in order to sow division in the Egyptian nation — Egyptian daily *Al-Akhbar*, June 16, 1998.[55]

The Israelis have repeatedly proved their disregard and disrespect of the heavenly religions. They have desecrated the al-Aqsa Mosque and killed worshippers inside the court. And they dug out Christian cemeteries and spread the bodies of the dead in an abhorrent manner on the surface of the soil. This indicates their racist ideology and practices — official Syrian paper *Tishrin*, May 2001.[56]

---

[52] Shaykh Abd-al-Halim Mahmud, *Jihad and Victory* (Cairo, 1979), p. 150, cited in Yossef Bodansky, *Islamic Anti-Semitism As a Political Instrument* (Houston, Tx.: Freeman Center for Strategic Studies, 1999), p. 84. Bodansky is a former director of the Congressional Task Force on Terrorism and Unconventional Warfare.

[53] Dr. Salah Khalidi, *The Jewish Mentality Based on the Qu'ran* (Damascus, 1987), cited in ibid., p. 84.

[54] Israel Government Press Office, www.pmo.gov.il.

[55] Ibid.

[56] Israel National News archives, www.israelnn.com/archive.php.

Riyad Az'noun, who holds the P.A.'s [Palestinian Authority's] health portfolio, told reporters that both the U.S.
and Israel were using the area as a testing ground for new
weaponry, including non specified poisonous gases ...
[and] missiles laced with diluted uranium — Reuters News
Agency, Mar. 23, 2001.[57]

A reliable source at the Arab League provided details of
the report circulated by the League to its member states
warning of imported blood units contaminated with the
AIDS virus, hepatitis and bilharzias. . . . Israel treated the
blood units before they were sent to Arab and Third World
nations. . . . The question is: Is Israel waging chemical and
biological warfare against the Arab states and Islam?
— Egyptian weekly *Roz Al-Yusuf*, Aug. 24, 1998, article
titled "Senior Arab League Official Tells U.S.: The Story
of Israeli Blood Tainted with AIDS."[58]

Our brother, the Colonel Mu'ammar Al-Qadhafi, the
leader of the Libyan revolution, revealed that two years
ago Libyan children in the city of Benghazi suffered from
the most abominable crime in the history of mankind,
when foreign nurses injected them with the AIDS virus,
while pretending to immunize them. . . . Qadhafi added
that there are those who think that the CIA or the Israeli
Mossad were behind this crime. . . . Qadhafi added that
this act . . . reveals the ugly face of those who introduced
the AIDS virus to Africa to exhaust its strength and de-
plete its resources with the intention of gaining control
over Africa — Egyptian government daily *Al-Ahram*, week
of Apr. 25, 2001.[59]

[57] Israel National News archives, www.israelnn.com/archive.php.
[58] Israel Government Press Office, www.pmo.gov.il.
[59] Israel National News archives, www.israelnn.com/archive.php.

Israeli planes and helicopters have dropped poisoned sweets in the West Bank in order to kill children who would pick and eat them — official Iranian news agency IRNA, May 2001.[60]

Some of the calumnies against the Israelis are so outrageous that they would be humorous if they were not intended in all seriousness to incite murderous hatred. A front-page story in the Palestinian Authority (P.A.) newspaper *Al-Hayat Al-Jadida* in early August 2001 reported that the Israeli army is using armed female strippers in their war against Arab youth. When rock-throwing incidents begin, the male Israeli soldiers run for cover while a female soldier begins to perform a striptease on top of a barricade, distracting the youth, until she pulls a pistol out of her underwear and begins shooting. One can't help wondering if the intention of the report is to encourage teen-aged boys to take part in rock-throwing. The Israeli government was also accused of sending radio-controlled rabid dogs into the occupied territory to bite Arab children.[61]

The United States is not exempt from being targeted by such delusional accusations inspired to stir up hatred. The editor of the mainstream Egyptian newspaper *Al-Ahram* reported in early November 2001 that in Afghanistan the United States is intentionally making its airdrops of food in areas full of landmines in order to cause the death of Afghans, and that the food is genetically altered to kill them. In the aftermath of the World Trade Center attack, New York City mayor Rudy Guiliani was falsely quoted in the Saudi newspaper *al-Riyadh* as saying, "What we must do is kill 6,000 innocent [Arab] people."

---

[60] Ibid.
[61] Ibid.

The editorial went on to state authoritatively that he is a homosexual and a Jew. The Palestinian Authority newspaper, *Al-Hayat Al-Jadida*, equally accurately reported that Guiliani "hides his first name so as not to remind the Jewish voters of the infamous Rudolph Hitler [sic]. This is why he prefers to shorten it to Rudy." [62] This blatant disregard for truth in the interests of stirring up hatred against the United States, as well as Israel, is exhibited daily in the Palestinian Authority press. For instance, after Chechnyan rebels took about 700 theatre-goers hostage in a Moscow theater, and many died in the ensuing operation by the Russian police, the same official Palestinian Authority newspaper [63] reported that the CIA had masterminded the terrorist action in retaliation against Russia for its opposition in the UN to the United States policy toward Iraq—and suggested that France would be the next to suffer from such surreptitious attacks by the CIA, because they too opposed the United States policy.

Shortly after the September 11, 2001, attacks on the World Trade Center and the Pentagon, Egyptian Sheik Muhammad al-Gamei'a, Imam of the Islamic Cultural Center and Mosque of New York City, told an Egyptian interviewer, backed by the full authority of his position, that the Jews had planned the terrorist attack themselves and now were secretly killing Muslim children in New York City hospitals:

> Jewish doctors in one of the hospitals poisoned sick Muslim children, who then died ... the Jewish element is as Allah described it when he said "They disseminate corruption in the land." ... You see these people [the Jews] all the time, everywhere, disseminating corruption, heresy,

---

[62] Israel National News, October 26, 2001, www.israelnationalnews.com.
[63] *Al-Hayat Al-Jadidah*, October 29, 2002, cited in Israel National News archives, www.israelnn.com/archive.php.

homosexuality, alcoholism and drugs. [Because of them] there are strip clubs, homosexuals and lesbians everywhere. . . . Before this, they rode on the back of England and on the back of the French empire. After that, they rode on the back of Germany. But Hitler annihilated them because they betrayed him and violated their contract with him . . . only the Jews are capable of planning such an incident [the attacks on the World Trade Center and the Pentagon], because it was planned with great precision of which Osama bin Laden or any other Islamic organization or intelligence apparatus is incapable. . . . [T]his incident urges people to come to know Islam, now that it has been proven to the Americans that they were deceived by the Jews. . . . Allah has foiled the Jews, who set a trap to try to destroy the image of the Muslims.[64]

During the Middle Ages the primary blood libel used to stir up hatred and violence against the Jews was the accusation that they killed Christians for their blood, which was allegedly needed to make Passover matzos. Although this vicious calumny has largely faded from Europe, it is alive and well in the government-sponsored Arab press. On the eve of the Arab summit in Amman in early 2001, the Egyptian government daily printed an article "exposing" the practice:

The Talmud, the second holiest book for the Jews, determines that the "matzahs" of Atonement Day[65] must be kneaded "with blood" from a non-Jew. The preference is for the blood of youths after raping them!! Rabbi Moshe Abu Al-Afiah revealed this during the

---

[64] Israel National News, October 18, 2001, www.israelnationalnews.com.
[65] Matzahs are, of course, used for Passover, *not* the Day of Atonement (*Yom Kippur*).

investigation of the disappearance of Father Toma in the
Jewish quarter of Damascus in 1840. . . . I published some
of the investigation documents which are kept in the files
of Syria's Justice Ministry, in an article that *Al-Akhbar* was
kind enough to publish on October 20, 2000, on the eve
of the emergency summit summoned by Egypt at the
time. . . . I called on the summit to take action so that the
day won't come when big bottles will be filled with Arab
blood. . . . Father Toma entered the Jewish Quarter to at-
tend to a sick man, and ended up slaughtered without a
drop of blood in him! . . . A group of Jews kidnapped him
and his servant. . . . They slaughtered him and collected
his blood in a big bottle which was then left in the house's
cellar . . . [to use] in the dough of the Matzahs for the
celebration of the Atonement Day. . . . I ask myself: was
the purpose of the Al-Aqsa massacres political. . . ? Or
was it for religious purposes, aimed at letting pure Arab
blood for the Jewish holidays? — Dr. Mahmoud Al-Said
Al-Kurdi in *Al-Akhbar*, April 2001.

This was just part of a long running pattern. In 1962, the
Egyptian Ministry of Education published a book entitled
Human Sacrifices in the Talmud as one of a series of official
national books put out by the Egyptian Institute for Publications. The introduction to this reprint of an 1890 work
states that it provides "conclusive evidence . . . that this people permits bloodshed and makes it a religious obligation
laid down by the Talmud".

The Syrian Minister of Defense, Mustafa Tlass, authored
a book on the Damascus blood libel involving Father Toma,
entitled *The Matzos of Zion*. With a typical concern for
accuracy, the back jacket explains, "The book sets forth in
minute detail, and with scientific exactitude, the Jews' blood
ritual, in which they slaughter Christians and Muslims so

they can mix their blood into matzos for Yom Kippur [sic]." [66]

Recently Purim too has been added to the list of Jewish holidays for which Christian or Muslim blood is required. The following ran, a few days before Purim, in a government-sponsored daily newspaper in the "moderate" Arab state Saudi Arabia—not in the Middle Ages, but in 2002:

Special Ingredient for Jewish Holidays Is Human Blood from Non-Jewish Youth

I chose to [speak] about the Jewish holiday of Purim, because it is connected to the month of March. This holiday has some dangerous customs that will, no doubt, horrify you, and I apologize if any reader is harmed because of this.

During this holiday, the Jew must prepare very special pastries, the filling of which is not only costly and rare—it cannot be found at all on the local and international markets.

Unfortunately, this filling cannot be left out, or substituted with any alternative serving the same purpose. For this holiday, the Jewish people must obtain human blood so that their clerics can prepare the holiday pastries. In other words, the practice cannot be carried out as required if human blood is not spilled!!

Before I go into the details, I would like to clarify that the Jews' spilling human blood to prepare pastry for their holidays is a well-established fact, historically and legally, all throughout history. This was one of the main reasons for the persecution and exile that were their lot in Europe and Asia at various times.

---

[66] Israel National News archives, www.israelnationalnews.com.

For this holiday, the victim must be a mature adolescent who is, of course, a non-Jew—that is, a Christian or a Muslim. His blood is taken and dried into granules. The cleric blends these granules into the pastry dough; they can also be saved for the next holiday. In contrast, for the Passover slaughtering, about which I intend to write one of these days, the blood of Christian and Muslim children under the age of 10 must be used, and the cleric can mix the blood [into the dough] before or after dehydration.

The Actions of the Jewish Vampires Cause Them Pleasure

Let us now examine how the victims' blood is spilled. For this, a needle-studded barrel is used; this is a kind of barrel, about the size of the human body, with extremely sharp needles set in it on all sides. [These needles] pierce the victim's body, from the moment he is placed in the barrel.

These needles do the job, and the victim's blood drips from him very slowly. Thus, the victim suffers dreadful torment—torment that affords the Jewish vampires great delight as they carefully monitor every detail of the bloodshedding with pleasure and love that are difficult to comprehend.

After this barbaric display, the Jews take the spilled blood, in the bottle set in the bottom [of the needle-studded barrel], and the Jewish cleric makes his coreligionists completely happy on their holiday when he serves them the pastries in which human blood is mixed— Dr. Umayma Ahmad Al-Jalahma of King Faysal University in the Saudi government daily *Al-Riyadh*, March 10, 2002.[67]

Recently the Arab Radio and Television Network produced a 41-part television series based on *The Protocols of the Elders of*

[67] Middle East Media Research Institute, www.memri.org.

Zion to be broadcast in about 30 Arab countries. According to a report on the series in Egyptian weekly *Roz Al-Youssuf:* "For the first time, the series' writer courageously tackles the 24 Protocols of the Elders of Zion, revealing them and clarifying that they are the central line that still, to this very day, dominates Israel's policy, political aspirations, and racism." [68]

Yet the *Protocols* was already proven to be a fake as early as 1921, when the *London Times* printed identical excerpts from it and an earlier work, which had nothing to do with Jews or Judaism, side by side. That earlier work was an obscure satire of Napoleon III by the Frenchman Maurice Joly entitled *Dialogue in Hell between Machiavelli and Montesquieu.* The author of *Protocols*, an agent of the Russian secret police named Pytor Ivanovich Rachovsky, simply copied much of the text, changing the villians from French royalists to Jews, substituting the "Zion" for "France", and presented it as a true account of a meeting held by Jewish leaders in 1897, in which they developed a plot to take over the world.

The revision of Jewish history

We have seen how the current Arab press has "revised" the history of the Holocaust. Similar historical revision is employed to denigrate further the Jews and especially to portray them as alien interlopers in the land of Israel. In order to manipulate public opinion both within the Arab world and in the world at large, Arab governments deny the history of the Jewish people in Israel:

> Israel [of the Bible] dwelled near Yemen. . . . All these events [of Israel in the Bible] did not happen in Palestine

---

[68] Israel National News archives, www.israelnn.com/archive.php.

— "Palestine: History and Tradition", show on P.A. [Palestinian Authority] television May 26, 1998.[69]

Jerusalem is a Palestinian Arab city, and it has no connection to Israel — Palestinian Authority official Abd al-Rachman on P.A. television May 24, 1998.[70]

The western wall of Al-Haram Al-Sharif is the Buraq Wall, not the Wailing as the Jews allege to justify establishment of their state in Palestine. . . . [The current Moslem mosque on the site] was built 2,000 years before Prophet Solomon and remained so until this day — Arabicnews.com news service Mar. 7, 2001, citing study published by Ain Shams University, Egypt.

It is of particular importance to deny the Jewish connection to Jerusalem. Thus, in an interview on Palestinian television on June 28, 1998, Yassar Arafat stated: "The issue of Jerusalem is . . . a Palestinian, an Islamic and Christian issue", not a Jewish issue at all, since "they [the Jews] consider Hebron to be holier than Jerusalem." He also denied that there had ever been a Jewish Temple on the site: "Until now, all the excavations that have been carried out have failed to prove the location of the Temple. They have not succeeded in giving even one proof as the location of the Temple", and he denied that the Wailing Wall had any historical connection to Jews or Jewish worship.[71] This is, however, contradicted not only by history and archeology, but also by documents written by the Muslim authorities themselves before the current campaign began. For example, in 1930, an English language

[69] Israel Government Press Office, www.pmo.gov.il.
[70] Ibid.
[71] Joseph Farah, "More Myths of the Middle East", World Net Daily, www.WorldNetDaily.com.

tourist guide to the Temple Mount titled *A Brief Guide to al-Haram al-Sharif* was produced by the Supreme Muslim Council, the governing Muslim body in Jerusalem at the time.[72] It reads in part: "The site is one of the oldest in the world. Its sanctity dates from the earliest times. Its identity with the site of Solomon's Temple is beyond dispute. This, too, is the spot, according to universal belief, on which David built there an altar unto the Lord, and offered burnt offerings and peace offerings."[73] Yet in 2001, the Palestinian Authority Mufti Ikrima Sabri flatly asserted: "There is not [even] the smallest indication of the existence of a Jewish temple on this place in the past. In the whole city, there is not even a single stone indicating Jewish history."[74]

In reality it is the Muslim connection to Jerusalem that is in doubt. Islam's claims to Jerusalem depend on the Temple Mount being the site from which Muhammad ascended to heaven in a dream, thus making Jerusalem the third holiest site of Islam. This ascent occurs in the seventeenth Sura in the Koran in a passage entitled "The Night Journey". The passage recounts that in a dream or vision Muhammad was taken by night "from the sacred mosque to the farthest mosque, whose precinct we have blessed, that we might show him our signs". The "farthest mosque" is now considered by the Arab world to be the Mosque of Omar on the Temple Mount. Yet when Muhammad died in A.D. 632 Jerusalem was still a Christian city and had no mosques[75] at all; in fact, up until A.D. 638, when Jerusalem was captured

---

[72] The Supreme Muslim Council was set up by the British government to administer Muslim affairs while Palestine was under the British Mandate.

[73] Etgar Lefkovits, "1930 Moslem Council: Jewish Temple Mount Ties 'Beyond Dispute'", *Jerusalem Post*, January 26, 2001.

[74] Interview in German periodical *Die Welt*, cited in ibid.

[75] Nor other Islamic holy sites that could have justified the term "mosque".

by Khalif Omar, a Christian Church known as Saint Mary of Justinian stood on the site.[76] It was converted into a mosque only around A.D. 711 by Abd El-Wahd, who ruled Jerusalem from 705–715. Thus not only is it certain that Muhammad was never physically present in Jerusalem, but the mosque on the Temple Mount to which he supposedly went during the "Night Journey" was not built until three generations after his death.[77] The Arab world paid little attention to Jerusalem, or to the Temple Mount, whenever they had uncontested possession of it. During the several centuries that the Temple Mount was held by the Muslim Turks, no repairs were done on the Dome of the Rock and the El-Aksa Mosque, as can be seen in photographs taken of them at the time, which show them in a state of disrepair and apparent abandonment, with missing roof tiles and high grass growing though the paving stones.[78] Neither did they receive much attention during the period that the Mount was held by Jordan, from 1948 to 1967.

In contrast to its tenuous connection to Islam, Jerusalem is central to both Judaism and Christianity. The Temple Mount is the site of the only true Temple in Judaism, where the Holy of Holies was and where sacrifice was to be offered, as well as the spot on which Abraham tried to sacrifice Isaac, inaugurating Judaism itself. Jerusalem is absolutely central to

[76] For Muhammad to have ascended to heaven from the claimed site on the Temple Mount, his journey would have had to begin in the crypt of an existing Catholic Church!

[77] See Dr. Manfred R. Lehmann, "The Moslem Claim to Jerusalem is False", *Algemeiner Journal*, August 19, 1994.

[78] Photographs produced by the Bonfils Studio, Beirut, in 1875 and in the possession of Joseph Regenstein Library, University of Chicago. Currently viewable at www.lib.uchicago.edu/e/su/mideast/photo/Jerusalem.html.

Judaism. It is mentioned 871 times in the Old Testament and is one of the most frequent themes in Jewish prayer. It is not mentioned a single time in the Koran.

Peace with Israel

In the Arab press it is all too clear that the purpose of the war of the Islamic states against Israel is not to change the policies or the boundaries of Israel, but to rid the world of it altogether:

> Arab countries have tried every single nationalistic way in attempts to annihilate Israel.... Now the time has come to try Islam as an alternative.... I advise the Palestinian leaders to stop trying to negotiate and instead fight Israel to death by relying upon God, Most Great, the Palestinian people and their arms; as these negotiations cause the struggling nations to lose faith[79] — Ayatollah Khomeni of Iran.

As a member of the Palestinian Authority's legislative council said recently on P.A. television:

> Our struggle is still necessary, we are still at the beginning of the road. Our war with Israel and the Jews has not ended and will not end until the establishment of a Palestinian state on the entire land of Palestine.[80]

Of course, Palestinian television is saturated with hatred of the Jews and a call to violence, as in a recent Friday sermon:

[79] *The Imam Versus Zionism*, Tehran, Ministry of Islamic Guidance, 1984.
[80] Palestinian Television, December 2, 1997, translated in *Palestinian Media Review*, December 2–3, 1997.

[B]lessings to he who shot a bullet into the head of a Jew
... the Jews [are] the enemies of Allah, the cursed nation
in the Koran, whom the Koran describes as monkeys and
pigs.... Allah shall make the Moslem rule over the Jew,
we will blow them up in Hadera, we will blow them up
in Tel-Aviv and in Netanya ... [quoting Mohammed's
words in a Hadith:] "until the Jew will hide behind the
trees and stones and the tree and stone will say 'Moslem,
Servant of Allah, there is a Jew behind me, kill him!'"[81]

Both in school textbooks and on P.A. television there is no
question that the "Palestine" claimed by the Palestinian Arabs
incorporates all of Israel. The maps of "Our Country Palestine" in the official Palestinian textbooks always encompass
all of present-day Israel as well as the "occupied terri-
tories".[82] The map in the graphic that opens and closes the
evening news show on P.A. television does the same.[83] Never,
either explicitly or implicitly, is the right of Israel to exist
acknowledged, no matter how much territory it gives up.
This simply reflects the constitution of the Palestinians, the
Palestine National Charter;[84] the first three articles of
which are

1.   Palestine is the homeland of the Arab Palestinian
     people; it is an integral part of the Arab homeland,

[81] Palestinian Authority broadcast on August 3, 2001, quoted in Israel National News, September 8, 2001, www.israelnationalnews.com.

[82] Itamar Marcus, director of the Center for Monitoring the Impact of Peace,
Report No. P-01-03: The Palestinian Authority School Books, www.edume.org/
reports/1/6.htm.

[83] Israel National News, "News—Arab-Israeli Relations", at www.
israelnn.com/english/newspaper/ondisplay/arab/pa-1d.htm.

[84] The Palestine National Charter can be obtained many places, including
from the Permanent Observer Mission of Palestine to the U.N. (www.
palestine-un.org).

and the Palestinian people are an integral part of
the nation.

2. Palestine, with the boundaries it had during the
    British Mandate,[85] is an indivisible territorial unit.

3. The Palestinian Arab people possess the legal right
    to their homeland and the right to determine their
    destiny after achieving the liberation of their coun-
    try in accordance with their wishes and entirely of
    their own accord and will.

The Indoctrination of Children

A particularly tragic part of the Arab campaign is its use of
children's textbooks to foment hatred of Jews. Following are
some quotes from official textbooks published by the Palestinian Authority Ministry of Education.[86]

> Know, my son, that Palestine is your country, that its pure
> soil is drenched with the blood of Martyrs. Why must we
> fight the Jews and drive them out of our land? . . . Just as
> this sacred soil returned to its owners [in the past] so will
> it return again through your courage and determination
> [the accompanying map in the textbook shows "Pales-
> tine" as including all of Israel] — *Our Arabic Language for
> 5th Grade no. 542*, p. 64–66.

> My brothers! The oppressors [Israel] have overstepped the
> boundary. Therefore Jihad and sacrifice are a duty. . . . Draw
> your sword let us gather for war with red blood and blaz-
> ing fire, Death shall call and the sword shall be crazed

[85] British Mandate Palestine encompassed all of present-day Israel, as well
as Jordan.

[86] Citations from the Center for Monitoring the Impact of Peace, "Palestinian Authority School Text Books", available at www.edume.org.

from much slaughter, Oh Palestine, the youth will redeem your land — Poem in *Reader and Literary Texts for 8th Grade no. 578*, p. 120–22.

In your left hand you carried the Koran, And in your right an Arab sword. Without blood not even one centimeter will be liberated. Therefore go forward crying: "Allah is great" — Poem in *Reader and Literary Texts for 8th Grade no. 578*, p. 131–33.

If the enemy has conquered part of its land and those fighting for it are unable to repel the enemy, then Jihad becomes the individual religious duty of every Muslim man and woman, until the attack is successfully repulsed and the land liberated from conquest and to defend Muslim honor — *Islamic Education for 7th Grade no. 564*, p. 108.

This religion will defeat all other religions and it will be disseminated, by Allah's will, through the Muslim Jihad fighters — *Islamic Education for 7th Grade no. 564*, p. 125.

Lessons to be learned? One must beware of Jews, for they are treacherous and disloyal — *Islamic Education for Ninth Grade no. 589*, p. 79.

Write in your exercise book: An event showing the fanaticism of the Jews in Palestine against Muslims or Christians — *Islamic Education for Ninth Grade no. 589*, p. 182.

The clearest examples of racist belief and racial discrimination in the world are Nazism and Zionism — *The New History of the Arabs and the World*, p. 123.

It is mentioned in the Talmud: "We should cheat them [the non-Jews] and arouse quarrels among them. . . . Non-Jews are pigs who God created in the shape of man in order that they be fit for service for the Jews" — *The New History of the Arabs and the World*, p. 120.

I learn from this lesson: I believe that the Jews are the enemies of the Prophets and the believers — *Islamic Education, Part Two for 4th Grade no. 531*, p. 67.

The Role of Islam

The question must inevitably be raised: What is the relationship between the virulent anti-Semitism of the Arab world and its dominant religion, Islam? The Koran, the sacred scripture of Islam, presents a quite confrontational posture toward those of other religions:

Kill those who join other gods with God wherever you may find them (Koran 9:5–6).

Those who believe fight in the cause of God (Koran 4:76).

I will instill terror into the hearts of the Infidels, strike off their heads then, and strike off from them every fingertip (Koran 8:12).

Oh ye who believe! Fight those of the unbelievers and let them find in you harshness (Koran 9:123).

Humiliate the non-Muslims to such an extent that they surrender and pay tribute (Koran 9:29).

Then when the sacred months are drawn away, slay the idolaters wherever you find them, and take them, and confine them, and lie in wait for them at every place of ambush (Koran 9:5).

Fight those who believe not in Allah and the Last Day and do not forbid what God and His Messenger have forbidden—such men as practice not the religion of truth, being of those who have been given the Book—until they

pay the tribute out of hand and have been humbled (Koran 9:29).

It reserves a particular animosity for the Jews:

> Ignominy shall be their [the Jews] portion wheresoever
> they are found save where they grasp a rope from [i.e.,
> make a covenant with] Allah and a rope from men. They
> have incurred anger from their Lord, and wretchedness is
> laid upon them. That is because they used to disbelieve
> the revelations of Allah, and slew the prophets wrong-
> fully. That is because they were rebellious and used to
> transgress (Koran 3:112).

> Moses came unto you [Jews] with clear proofs of Allah's
> Sovereignty, yet, while he was away, ye chose the calf for
> worship and ye were wrong-doers. . . . Evil is that which
> your belief enjoineth on you . . . to live a thousand years
> would be no means remove him from the doom (Koran
> 2:92–96).

> [Y]our [the Jews'] hearts were hardened and became as
> rocks, or worse than rocks, for hardness . . . such are right-
> ful owners of the Fire; they will abide therein . . . and on
> the Day of Resurrection they will be consigned to the
> most grievous doom (Koran 2:74–85).

> Lo! the riches and the progeny of those ["People of the
> Book"] who disbelieve will not avail them aught against
> Allah; and such are rightful owners of the Fire. They will
> abide therein. . . . Hatred is revealed by (the utterance of)
> their mouths, but that which their breasts hide is greater
> . . . when they go apart they bite their finger-tips at you,
> for rage. Say: Perish in your rage (Koran 3:116–120,
> extracts).

Allah hath cursed them [the Jews] for their disbelief, so they believe not, save a few.... For We bestowed upon the house of Abraham (of old) the Scripture and wisdom, and We bestowed on them a mighty kingdom.... Hell is sufficient for (their) burning. Lo! Those who disbelieve Our revelations, We shall expose them to the Fire. As often as their skins are consumed We shall exchange them for fresh skins that they may taste the torment. Lo! Allah is ever Mighty, Wise (Koran 4:46–56).

During his lifetime Muhammad himself was frequently embroiled in conflicts with the Jews among whom he lived and on a number of occasions oversaw the slaughter of Jewish tribes or individuals who refused to support him. Such murders included the extermination of the Jewish tribes of Banu-N-Nadir in A.D. 626, the Jews of Banu Qurayza in A.D. 627 and of Banu Sa'd in A.D. 628, the Jewish population of Khaybar in A.D. 629, and the killing of Jewish poet Abu 'Afak and Asma bint Marwan in A.D. 623, and of Jewish poet Kaab Ibn Al' Ashraf in A.D. 625.[87] (Poets were the "journalists" of the day.) The definitive biography of Muhammad, written by a follower only a few decades after his death, quotes him as saying, "Kill any Jew that falls into your power".[88] The extermination of the Jews is even, according to Islam, an explicit requirement for the resurrection of the dead:

The Day of Resurrection will not arrive until the Moslems make war against the Jews and kill them, and until a Jew hiding behind a rock and tree, and the rock and tree

---

[87] Different sources give slightly different dates for these events.

[88] Alfred Guillaume, *The Life of Muhammad: A Translation of Ibn Ishaq's Sirat Rasul Allah* (London: Oxford University Press, 1968), p. 369.

will say: "Oh Moslem, oh servant of Allah, there is a Jew
behind me, come and kill him!" [89]

Christians also come in for criticism in the Koran;

> The Jews claim that Ezra is a son of God, and the Chris-
> tians say, "the Messiah is a son of God." . . . May God do
> battle with them! How perverse are they! They have taken
> as lords beside Allah their rabbis and their monks and the
> Messiah son of Mary, when they were bidden to worship
> only One Allah. There is no Allah save Him. . . . Lo! many
> of the (Jewish) rabbis and the (Christian) monks devour
> the wealth of mankind wantonly and debar (men) from
> the way of Allah. They who hoard up gold and silver and
> spend it not in the way of Allah, unto them give tidings
> (O Muhammad) of a painful doom. On the day when it
> will (all) be heated in the fire of hell, and their foreheads
> and their flanks and their backs will be branded therewith
> (Koran 9: 30–36).

> O Ye who believe! Choose not for guardians such of those
> who received the Scripture before you, and of the dis-
> believers, as make a jest and sport of your religion. . . .
> Why do not the rabbis and the priests forbid their evil-
> speaking and their devouring of illicit gain? Verily evil is
> their handiwork. . . . We have cast among them enmity
> and hatred till the Day of Resurrection. . . . Their effort is
> for corruption in the land, and Allah loveth not corrupt-
> ers (Koran 5: 57–64).

> O ye who believe! Take not the Jews and the Christians
> for friends. They are friends one to another. He among

---

[89] *Sahih al-Bukhari*, trans. Dr. Muhammad Muhsin Khan, Hilal Yayinlari,
Ankara, Turkey, vol. 4, p. 110. This Hadith appears in *Muslim's Sahih* as: "The
Hour [the Day of Judgement] will not begin until the Muslims fight the Jews
and kill them" (no. 2922).

you who taketh them for friends is (one) of them. Lo! Allah guideth not wrongdoing folk (Koran 5:51).

The Koran also has harsh words for the "blasphemy" of Christianity:

> Lo! Allah forgiveth not that a partner should be ascribed unto Him [apparent reference to Christianity]. . . . Whoso ascribeth partners to Allah, he hath indeed invented a tremendous sin. See, how they invent lies about Allah! That of itself is flagrant sin. Hast thou not seen those unto whom a portion of the Scripture hath been given, how they believe in idols and false deities (Koran 4:48–51, extracts).

> O People of the Scripture! Do not exaggerate in your religion nor utter aught concerning Allah save the truth. The Messiah, Jesus son of Mary, was only a messenger of Allah. . . . So believe in Allah and His messengers, and say not "Three"—Cease! (it is) better for you!—Allah is only One Allah. Far is it removed from His Transcendent Majesty that He should have a son (Koran 4:171).

In the following passage the Jews are condemned for denying the virgin birth of Jesus, while at the same time His death on the Cross is denied:

> They denied the truth and uttered a monstrous falsehood against Mary. They declared: "We have put to death the Messiah, Jesus son of Mary, the apostle of God." They did not kill him, nor did they crucify him, but they thought they did . . . they knew nothing about him that was not sheer conjecture; they did not slay him for certain. God lifted him up to Him (Koran 4:156–158).

The Koran's commands to "declare war upon those . . . who refuse to acknowledge the true religion" (Koran 9:29) are not just theoretical injunctions. From the very beginning, the Muslims have faithfully put them into practice. Within fifty years of the death of Muhammad, Islam had by force of arms taken over Northern Africa, placing under the state of serfdom and deprivation of rights known as *dhimmitude* all Jews and Christians who did not convert, flee, or be killed. It is barely remembered today that the Arab countries of northern Africa make up most of what was once the original cradle of Christianity. Once they were conquered, Muhammad's followers turned their attention to Europe. As Catholic priest and historian Monsignor Philip Hughes put it:

> In 711 they [the Moors] crossed the straits of Gibraltar and conquered Spain. Nor did they halt, but passed the Pyrenees and overran all the south of France. . . . The whole Mediterranean, from the Rhone westward to Gibraltar and thence east to Alexandria and north again to Antioch, continued to be in their power. The siege of Christendom had begun, and in every generation, for another nine hundred years, there was made upon it, from some quarter of the Mahometan [sic] world, a violent assault.[90]

Christianity's survival in Europe was ensured only by victories of the Christian forces in a few key battles, which repulsed the Muslim invaders. Several of these were attributed to divine intervention, such as the Battle of Lepanto in 1571, which Pope St. Pius V attributed to the miraculous intervention of the Blessed Virgin Mary, and in gratitude for which he instituted the Feast of Our Lady of Victory (later changed to the Feast of the Rosary).

The command in Islam to convert or conquer is still taken literally by some, with deadly consequences, today.

---

[90] Philip Hughes, *A Popular History of the Catholic Church* (New York: Doubleday, 1954), pp. 80–81.

Consider the words of Siddig Ibrahim Siddig Ali, one of the suspects in the 1993 World Trade Center bombing:

> Of course, don't forget God said in the Koran, in times like this, everything is lawful to the Muslim, their money, their women, their honors, everything.... We'll be called sinners in the eyes of God if we don't do something ... [he gives a quote from the Koran] ... infidels must be killed.... [A]nd the Muslim when he dies it is the way to heaven. He becomes a martyr. A Muslim will never go to hell by killing an infidel.[91]

It is natural to think of Islam as closely related to Judaism and Christianity. They all come from the same part of the world and all make reference to the same Old Testament, and they are sometimes called the "three great monotheistic, Abrahamic religions". Yet do all three have the same God? Before considering this, it is important to distinguish the religion itself from its followers. Our enemy is not flesh and blood, but principalities and powers (Ephesians 6:12):

> For we are not contending against flesh and blood, but against the principalities, against the powers, against the world rulers of this present darkness, against the spiritual hosts of wickedness in the heavenly places.

This enemy has one goal—to deprive man of salvation, of eternal happiness—and one of the ways to achieve that is through the propagation of false religion, the primary victims of which are its own adherents. And we know that the enemy's primary ideal would be to take the place of God on His throne—that is the sin for which he was cast out of

---

[91] United Press International news service, August 23, 1993. The almost total absence of condemnation of the actions of Muslim terrorists by Muslim clerics suggests that this literal interpretation is not exceptional.

heaven, "I will not serve". So there is no more attractive scheme to him then to establish a religion in which *he* is worshipped and becomes god to the practitioners. This desire of his to be worshipped was shown when he offered Jesus the entire world (not realizing that it already belonged to him) if only Jesus would worship him (Matthew 4:8–10):

> Again, the devil took him to a very high mountain, and showed him all the kingdoms of the world and the glory of them; and he said to him, "All these I will give you, if you will fall down and worship me." Then Jesus said to him, "Begone, Satan! for it is written, 'You shall worship the Lord your God and him only shall you serve.'"

It is hardly surprising, then, that throughout history the adversary establishes false religions, sects, and cults in which he masquerades as God. Frequently, these cults spring forth from the bosom of real religion; consider the recent instances of David Koresh and his Waco cult, and Jim Jones and his Jonestown cult, both of which pretended to be Christian and made continual reference to the Bible.

Of all the major religions of the world, only Islam arose *after* God's full revelation of Himself to man in His incarnation in the person of Jesus Christ. Thus all of the other major religions are either fully true (Christianity); fully true up to the time of their origin, but lacking the later revelation (Judaism); or based on the incomplete revelations available to mankind before God chose to make Himself truly known. Only Islam's revelation came after Christ, aware of Christianity yet contradicting it. Hence one must ask what the source of the revelation was—was it of human or of supernatural origin? If of supernatural origin, did it come from God or from fallen spirits? It is difficult for a Christian to consider the source of the revelation to be God, given its contradictions with Christian revelation. These contradictions appear in its depiction of heaven, in the role of women, and in the severity of its punishment, in addition to the areas already cited.

Consider the differences between the depiction of heaven in Islam versus that in Judaism and Christianity. Heaven, by definition, entails the greatest state of perfection that God can give man; it represents the ultimate meaning and goal of man's existence. In both Judaism and Christianity, the bliss of heaven comes from the pure joy of being in God's presence; in Islam it comes from base sensual pleasures—food, drink, and sex. Men in heaven are rewarded with 72 beautiful, ever-young virgin "wives" ("*houris*"),[92] which the Koran describes as "bashful and dark-eyed" (Koran 37:48), "as fair as corals and rubies" (Koran 55:58), "loving companions" (Koran 56:37), and "high-bosomed virgins" (Koran 78:33). The *hadith* add the following:

> "A houri is a most beautiful young woman with a transparent body. The marrow of her bones is visible like the interior lines of pearls and rubies. She looks like red wine in a white glass. . . . She is of white color, and free from the routine physical disabilities of an ordinary woman such as menstruation, menopause, urinal and offal discharge, child bearing and the related pollution. . . . A houri is a girl of tender age, having large breasts which are round, and not inclined to dangle." [93]

[92] They also receive 28 "beardless" young boys described as "boys of perpetual freshness; if thou seest them, thou wouldst think them scattered pearls . . . [dressed in]silk and brocade, and embellished with bracelets of silver" (Koran 76:10–25).

[93] *Jame Tirmizi* (Karachi, Pakistan: Muhammad Ali), vol. 2 pp. 35–40, and *Mishka Sharif* (Lahore, Pakistan: Farid), vol. 3 pp. 83–97, trans. in Anwar Shaikh, *Islam: Sex and Violence* (Cardiff, U.K.: Principality Publishers, 1999).

In order to fully enjoy his houris, no matter at what age a man dies when he enters heaven he will have "virility equal to that of 100 men".[94]

The adversary has always used the lures of the flesh to seduce men away from God and into sin; Islam does so in the eschatology of the religion itself. The effect on moral development from teaching that the highest good that God can offer to man is sexual gratification is obvious, as is the kind of a spirit that would present such a picture of heaven as the ultimate meaning of man's existence.

The role of women provides another example of how greatly Islam's moral teachings differ from those of Christianity or Judaism. A man may marry a girl as young as six, although he must wait until she is nine before consummating the marriage. Muhammad, when he was about sixty, married a six-year-old: "The Prophet wrote the marriage contract with Aisha while she was six years old and consummated his marriage with her while she was nine years old."[95] He also taught that women must always be ready to instantly service their husbands' lust: "The prophet of Allah said: When a man calls his wife to satisfy his desire, let her come to him though she is occupied at the oven".[96]

The prophet's own sexual proclivities are also made explicit in the sacred writings. One *hadith* recounts:

Anas bin Malik said "The Prophet used to visit all his wives in a round, during the day and night and they

---

[94] *Jame Tirmzi*, 2:138, trans. in ibid.

[95] *Sahih al-Bukhari*, trans. Dr. Muhammad Muhsin Khan (Ankara, Turkey: Hilal Yayinlari), 7:65.

[96] *Mishkat al-Masabih*, English-Arabic, bk. I, Hadith no. 61, cited in Newton and Rafiqul-Haqq, *Allah, Is He God?*, T.M.F.M.T., 1993, p. 36.

were eleven in number." I asked Anas, "Had the Prophet the strength for it?" Anas replied, "We used to say that the Prophet was given the strength of thirty men." [97]

Beating one's wife is not only allowed but can be a positive duty: "Righteous women are therefore obedient.... And those you fear may be rebellious admonish; banish them to their couches, and beat them" (Koran 4:34).

The severity of punishment, in general, distinguishes Islam from Christianity; for instance, the punishment for any theft valued at over a quarter of a dinar is the amputation of the hand, a penalty still imposed today in countries governed by Islamic law.

Violence is also, of course, endorsed in the central role that *jihad*, or holy war, plays in Islam. Muhammad himself spent much of his life attacking and raiding his "enemies"—at times villages that would not submit to his religion, at times unarmed caravans of valuable goods, at times people who had insulted or offended him. In all these situations, the prophet and the men under him would pillage, loot, plunder, kill, rape, and sell into slavery the hapless victims—behavior that the Koran explicitly endorses: "It is not for any Prophet to have captives until he hath made slaughter in the land. You desire the lure of this world and Allah desires for you the hereafter and Allah is Mighty, Wise.... Now enjoy what you have won as lawful and good" (Koran 8:67–68), as it also endorses extraordinary cruelty in battle as a deterrent for the future: "Those of them with whom you

---

[97] *Sahih al-Bukhari*, 1:165. In this, one cannot help being reminded by this of two more recent "prophets", Charles Manson and David Koresh.

made a treaty and then at every opportunity they break their treaty and they keep not duty to Allah, If you come on them in the war, deal with them so as to strike fear in those who are behind them, so that they may remember" (Koran 8:55–57). One must ask just what spiritual entity lies behind the revelation of Islam.

A Single Campaign

Earlier it was suggested that the Nazi campaign to exterminate the Jews was in fact an attempt, on the part of the enemy of man's salvation, to prevent the Second Coming. Now we see the same campaign, with apparently much of the same inspiration behind it, continuing unabated in the Arab world. In addition we have seen how the religion of Islam itself, from its origin in the days of Muhammad, has been overtly hostile to Jews and to Christianity. Even the fact that this hostility is aimed at Jews as people, but at Christianity as a faith, is of interest. Since the role Jews play in salvation is related more to their racial identity, while that of Christians to their faith, it makes sense that an attempt to prevent the Second Coming would focus on the Jews as a race but on Christianity as a faith. Apparently disparate aspects of Islam— its animosity toward the Jewish people, its attempts to eradicate the Christian faith by force, its internal moral theology and eschatology—become part of a whole if one sees the very source of the inspiration behind the religion as being opposed to salvation through Christ, which began with the Jews and will culminate with the Second Coming.

Explicit consideration of the prophecies related to the Second Coming only serve to strengthen this view. Particular interpretations of the prophecies are necessarily speculative;[98] yet they seem to paint a picture of the time of the Second Coming in which the Jews have regathered in Israel; the Temple has been rebuilt on its original site; and the Antichrist, with origins in Babylon (present-day Iraq), has appeared and initiated a world war centered on Jerusalem. His victory appears certain until prevented by Christ Himself at the Second Coming.

Many aspects of this picture seem to be being fulfilled in our own day. For the first time in two thousand years, Jews have formed a nation in Israel in which dispersed Jews from around the world have regathered. The rebuilding of the Temple in Jerusalem is under discussion, and one can imagine how such an attempt might precipitate a world war. In this scenario the forces of the Antichrist would come from the Muslim world.

The Arab Muslims consider themselves to be the descendents of Abraham's first-born, but illegitimate, son Ishmael. If this should be true, the Arab Muslims would be doing a good job of fulfilling the prophecy of Genesis 16:10–12:

> The angel of the LORD also said to her [Hagar, the mother of Ishmael] "I will so greatly multiply your descendants that they cannot be numbered for multitude ... you are with child and shall bear a son; you shall call his name Ishmael. ... He shall be a wild ass of a man, his hand against every man and every man's hand against him; and he shall dwell over against all his kinsmen."

It certainly seems to be borne out of the fact that in most of the violent conflicts throughout the world—whether in

---

[98] Incorrect speculations on when the Second Coming will take place have been made for the past two thousand years. Those here should not be mistaken as Church teaching.

Africa, the Philippines, former provinces of the U.S.S.R., Bosnia, or the Middle East—one side is fighting in the name of Islam, and thus, at least spiritually, as the sons of Ishmael.

Considering the Muslims as the offspring of Ishmael would result in an interesting symmetry between the roles of Abraham's two sons in salvation history. The sons of Ishmael would then be a kind of mirror image of the Jews—also from the line of Abraham, but through Ishmael, representing Abraham's lack of faith (for he fathered Ishmael when he had ceased to believe in God's promise to give him a child with his wife), rather than through Isaac, who represents Abraham's fidelity to God. Thus if Islam ends up being the force that produces the conflict that culminates in the Second Coming, *both* of Abraham's sons would turn out to have played central roles in the history of the salvation of mankind—Isaac as the father of the Jews from whom Jesus came, and Ishmael as the father of the opposing force that ignites the final war, Armageddon, and brings on the Second Coming.[99]

---

[99] In this scenario the two lines springing from Abraham would turn out to be the archtypical example of the classic Catholic principle "*corruptio optimi pessima*", "the corruption of the best is the worst".

CHAPTER EIGHT

The Jews and the Second Coming

How might the attacks against the Jews, particularly those of the past century, relate to biblical prophecy about the role of the Jews in the Second Coming? For the fact that Christ "will come again in glory, to judge the living and the dead", in the words of the Nicene Creed, is a dogma of the Catholic faith.[1] It is attested to by the words of Jesus Himself, recorded numerous times in the New Testament (Matthew 16:27; Mark 8:38; Luke 9:26; Matthew 24:30; Mark 13:26; Luke 21:27). As described in Matthew 24:30–31:

> [T]hen all the tribes of the earth will mourn, and they will see the Son of man coming on the clouds of heaven with power and great glory; and he will send out his angels with a loud trumpet call, and they will gather his elect from the four winds, from one end of heaven to the other.

Although the fact of the Second Coming is certain, when it will come cannot be known beforehand with certitude:

> "But of that day or that hour no one knows, not even the angels in heaven, nor the Son, but only the Father" (Mark 13:32).

[1] Dogmas are "truths contained in divine Revelation . . . in a form obliging the Christian people to an irrevocable adherence of faith" — *Catechism of the Catholic Church*, no. 88.

So when they [the disciples] had come together, they asked him, "Lord, will you at this time restore the kingdom to Israel?" He [Jesus] said to them, "It is not for you to know times or seasons which the Father has fixed by his own authority" (Acts 1:6–7).

As the *Catechism of the Catholic Church*, no. 673, puts it:

Since the Ascension Christ's coming in glory has been imminent, even though "it is not for you to know times or seasons which the Father has fixed by his own authority" (Acts 1:7; cf. Mk 13:32).

Nonetheless, it will be preceded by certain signs that the wise will be able to discern. In the verses immediately following the description of the Second Coming quoted above, Jesus adds (Matthew 24:32–33):

"From the fig tree learn its lesson: as soon as its branch becomes tender and puts forth its leaves, you know that summer is near. So also, when you see all these things, you know that he is near, at the very gates."

What are these signs? Some we know from the words of Jesus recounted in Matthew 24:

—It will be a time of great upheaval, of both wars between nations and natural disasters (Matthew 24:7): "For nation will rise against nation, and kingdom against kingdom, and there will be famines and earthquakes in various places."

—There will be widespread hostility to Christianity (Matthew 24:9): "Then they will deliver you up to tribulation, and put you to death; and you will be hated by all nations for my name's sake."

— There will be many false prophets (Matthew 24:11, 24): "[M]any false prophets will arise and lead many astray.... For false Christs and false prophets will arise and show great signs and wonders, so as to lead astray, if possible, even the elect."

— The "abomination of desolation" (understood by the Church Fathers to be the Antichrist[2]) will stand in the "holy place" (Matthew 24:15, 31): "Therefore when you see the abomination of desolation, which was spoken of by Daniel the prophet, standing in the holy place ... then will appear the sign of the Son of Man in heaven ... and they will see the Son of Man coming upon the clouds of heaven with great power and majesty." [3]

— The Gospel will have been preached to the whole world (Matthew 24:14): "And this gospel of the kingdom will be preached throughout the whole world, as a testimony to all nations; and then the end will come."

In almost every period since these prophecies were made, there have been those who have thought that these signs were fulfilled in their age and that the Second Coming was imminent. The current age, too, has prompted such speculation, for instance by Pope St. Pius X in 1903:

When all this [the widespread apostasy from God] is considered there is good reason to fear lest this great perversity may be ... perhaps the beginning of those evils which

---

[2] For instance St. Irenaeus, *Irenaeus against Heresies*, book 5 Chap. 25; *Ante-Nicene Fathers*, Roberts and Donaldson, eds. (Peabody, Mass.: Hendricksen, 1995), 1:553–54, and St. Hippolytus, *Treatise on Christ and Antichrist*, nos. 62–63; ibid., 5:218.

[3] Confraternity of Christian Doctrine translation (*The Holy Bible*, Douay and Confraternity Version [New York: P.J. Kenedy and Sons, 1961]).

are reserved for the last days; and that there may be already in the world the "Son of Perdition" of whom the Apostle speaks (II. *Thess.* ii., 3). Such, in truth, is the audacity and the wrath employed everywhere in persecuting religion, in combating the dogmas of the faith, in brazen effort to uproot and destroy all relations between man and the Divinity! [this] is the distinguishing mark of Antichrist. [4]

The discussion that follows is not intended to "prove" that we are in the last days. Many of the prophecies cited have multiple interpretations, and it is certainly speculative to associate them with particular events of our day. Yet some aspects appear to be being fulfilled in our times in unprecedented ways:

—Jerusalem will return again to Jewish hands shortly before the Second Coming (Luke 21:24): "Jerusalem will be trodden down by the Gentiles, until the times of the Gentiles are fulfilled." (A description of the Second Coming then follows in verses 25–28). Jerusalem was in the hands of Gentiles continuously from the fall of the Jewish nation in A.D. 70 until it was recaptured by the modern State of Israel in the 1967 war.

—Sometime before the Second Coming, two-thirds of the Jews in "the whole land" will be exterminated (Zechariah 13:8–9):

"In the whole land, says the LORD, two thirds shall be cut off and perish, and one third shall be left alive. And I will put this third into the fire, and refine them as one refines silver, and test them as gold is tested. They will call on my

[4] *E Supremi*, October 4, 1903.

name, and I will answer them. I will say, 'They are my people'; and they will say, 'The LORD is my God.'"

In fact, during the Holocaust almost exactly two-thirds of Europe's Jews perished (estimates vary between 60% and 72%).[5]

— The Jewish nation will be reborn in a single day (Isaiah 66:5–8):

> "Hear the word of the LORD.... Hark, an uproar from the city! A voice from the temple! The voice of the LORD, rendering recompense to his enemies! Before she was in labor she gave birth; before her pain came upon her she was delivered of a son. Who has heard such a thing? Who has seen such things? Shall a land be born in one day? Shall a nation be brought forth in one moment? For as soon as Zion was in labor she brought forth her sons."

This was quite literally fulfilled when on May 14, 1948, the modern State of Israel was born in a single day following the passage of UN Resolution 181 partitioning "Palestine" into the Arab State of Jordan and the Jewish State of Israel.

— Jews will be regathered to Israel from around the entire world. One such prophecy is Ezekiel 36:22–28. Although often taken in a spiritual sense as fulfilled at the first coming of Christ,[6] it might well also refer to the Second Coming, for biblical prophecies frequently refer to different events taking place in different epochs:

---

[5] For instance, the American Jewish Congress' 1955 estimate of 72% (*Yad Vashem Bulletin*, no. 10 [April 1961]) or that of the *Encyclopedia of the Holocaust* of 60% (p. 1799, Table 1).

[6] For example, St. Cyprian in his *Epistle LXIX*, no. 1; *Ante-Nicene Fathers* 5:376.

"Thus says the Lord God ... I will take you from the nations, and gather you from all the countries, and bring you into your own land.... You shall dwell in the land which I gave to your fathers; and you shall be my people, and I will be your God."

Similarly, Jeremiah 16:14–15 is typically seen as referring to the Jews' return from exile in Babylon. Yet since Moscow lies precisely[7] due north of Jerusalem, some see in it a reference to the current immigration to Israel of Jews from Russia:

"Therefore, behold, the days are coming," says the LORD, "when it shall no longer be said, 'As the LORD lives who brought up the people of Israel out of the land of Egypt,' but 'As the LORD lives who brought up the people of Israel out of the north country and out of all the countries where he had driven them.' For I will bring them back to their own land which I gave to their fathers."

The current return of the Jews to Israel apparently even includes Jews from the ten lost tribes. Over the past decade about 600 "B'nei Manashe", a tribe from the Indian-Burmese border, have immigrated to Israel. These people believe themselves to be the lost tribe of Manassah, exiled from Israel by the Assyrians in 723 B.C. Their oral tradition speaks of the Patriarchs Abraham, Isaac, and Jacob; they circumcise male children on the eighth day, as required by Jewish law; use prayer shawls with fringes, as do Jews; practice ritual purification as described in the Old Testament; and follow many other ancient Jewish religious customs. Their priests use the Hebrew name of God as it appears in the Torah ("*Yahweh*")

---

[7] A line drawn directly due north from Jerusalem passes within 100 miles of Moscow.

and invoke Mount Sinai, Mount Moriah, and Mount Zion. The Israeli government is allowing them to immigrate on the presumption that they are in fact the lost tribe of Manassah, while continuing to investigate their claim.[8]

— The new Jewish state shall be extremely prosperous (Isaiah 66:9–14):

> "Shall I bring to the birth and not cause to bring forth?" says the LORD; "shall I, who cause to bring forth, shut the womb?" says your God. "Rejoice with Jerusalem, and be glad for her, all you who love her; rejoice with her in joy, all you who mourn over her. . . . Behold, I will extend prosperity to her like a river, and the wealth of the nations like an overflowing stream . . . ; you shall be comforted in Jerusalem. You shall see, and your heart shall rejoice; your bones shall flourish like the grass; and it shall be known that the hand of the LORD is with his servants, and his indignation is against his enemies."

— The fight over the city of Jerusalem will cause a world war (Zechariah 12:1–3; also Joel 3:2 and Revelation 16:16):

> "Thus says the LORD . . . Lo, I am about to make Jerusalem a cup of reeling to all the peoples round about; it will be against Judah also in the siege against Jerusalem. On that day I will make Jerusalem a heavy stone for all the peoples; all who lift it shall grievously hurt themselves. And all the nations of the earth will come together against it."

Most would agree that Jerusalem, as the focal point of tensions in the Middle East, has become a "heavy stone for all

---

[8] *Jerusalem Post Magazine*, March 27, 2002.

the peoples", and certainly all who have "come together against it" since 1948 have "grievously hurt themselves".

—But Israel will be miraculously militarily strong and able to successfully defend itself (Zechariah 12:6–9):

> "On that day I will make the clans of Judah like a blazing pot in the midst of wood, like a flaming torch among sheaves; and they shall devour to the right and to the left all the peoples round about, while Jerusalem shall still be inhabited in its place, in Jerusalem. And the LORD will give victory to the tents of Judah.... On that day the LORD will put a shield about the inhabitants of Jerusalem so that the feeblest among them on that day shall be like David, and the house of David shall be like God, like the angel of the LORD, at their head. And on that day I will seek to destroy all the nations that come against Jerusalem."

—There will be a widespread conversion of the Jews. As the *Catechism of the Catholic Church* puts it: "The glorious Messiah's coming is suspended at every moment of history until his recognition by 'all Israel,' for 'a hardening has come upon part of Israel' in their 'unbelief' toward Jesus" (Rom 11:20–26; cf. Mt 23:39).[9] This has been the understanding ever since the Church Fathers, for instance, St. Augustine: "In connection with the last judgment, therefore, we who believe can be sure of the following truths ... the Jews will believe".[10] One of the scriptural sources for this belief is Hosea 3:5: "Afterward the children of Israel shall return and seek the LORD their God, and David their king; and they shall come in fear to the LORD and to his goodness in the

---

[9] *Catechism of the Catholic Church*, no. 674.

[10] St. Augustine, *City of God*, bk. 20, chap. 30 (Garden City, N.Y.: Doubleday Image, 1958), p. 492.

latter days." Blessed Pope Pius IX explicitly cited this passage as referring to the conversion of the Jews in the end times.[11]

St. Paul's Letter to the Romans contains an extensive discussion of the conversion of the Jews in the end times that will be explored at length in the next chapter (Romans 11:25–26):

> "Lest you be wise in your own conceits, I want you to understand this mystery, brethren: a hardening has come upon part of Israel, until the full number of the Gentiles come in, and so all Israel will be saved."

Jesus Himself prophesied the conversion of the Jews prior to the Second Coming when He said (Matthew 23:37–39):

> "O Jerusalem, Jerusalem. . . . Behold, your house is forsaken and desolate. For I tell you, you will not see me again, until you say, 'Blessed is he who comes in the name of the Lord.'"

Here Jesus is saying that he will not be seen again (i.e., the Second Coming will not occur) until "you" (the Jews) say, "Blessed is he who comes in the name of the Lord" (i.e., acknowledge Jesus as the Messiah).

Zechariah, too, foretold the conversion of the Jews when he said that they would weep bitterly over one "they have pierced" (Zechariah 12:10):

> "And I will pour out on the house of David and the inhabitants of Jerusalem a spirit of compassion and

[11] Letter written by Blessed Pope Pius IX to the Lemann brothers, February 14, 1877. Lemann brothers, *Histoire Complete de l'Idee Messianique*, translated in Rev. Denis Fahey, *The Kingship of Christ and the Conversion of the Jewish Nation* (Palmdale, Calif.: Christian Book Club of America, 1993), p. 102.

supplication, so that, when they look on him whom they have pierced, they shall mourn for him, as one mourns for an only child, and weep bitterly over him, as one weeps over a first-born."

— The Antichrist, also known as the Son of Perdition, will make his appearance (2 Thessalonians 2:3–4):

"Let no one deceive you in any way; for that day will not come, unless the rebellion comes first, and the man of lawlessness is revealed, the son of perdition, who opposes and exalts himself against every so-called god or object of worship, so that he takes his seat in the temple of God, proclaiming himself to be God."

— This is further explained in the *Catechism of the Catholic Church*:

Before Christ's second coming the Church must pass though a final trial that will shake the faith of many believers (Cf. Lk 18:8; Mt 24:12) . . . in the form of a religious deception offering men an apparent solution to their problems at the price of apostasy from the truth. The supreme religious deception is that of the Antichrist (Cf. 2 Thess 2:4–12; 1 Thess 5:2–3; 2 Jn 7; 1 Jn 2:18, 22).[12]

— The Antichrist's appearance will be followed by the war to end all wars, centered in the Holy Land. Just when it appears that evil has been victorious, Christ will come in glory and bring victory. This is suggested in a number of passages in both the Old and the New Testaments; most are mysterious in nature and subject to multiple interpretations. A few of the most commonly cited are:

---

[12] *Catechism of the Catholic Church*, no. 675.

Revelation 20:7–13: Satan will be loosed from his prison and will come out to deceive the nations which are at the four corners of the earth, that is, Gog and Magog, to gather them for battle; their number is like the sand of the sea. And they marched up over the broad earth and surrounded the camp of the saints and the beloved city; but fire came down from heaven and consumed them, and the devil who had deceived them was thrown into the lake of fire and sulphur where the beast and the false prophet were, and they will be tormented day and night for ever and ever. Then I saw a great white throne and him who sat upon it; from his presence earth and sky fled away, and no place was found for them. And I saw the dead, great and small, standing before the throne, and books were opened. Also another book was opened, which is the book of life. And the dead were judged by what was written in the books, by what they had done. And the sea gave up the dead in it, Death and Hades gave up the dead in them, and all were judged by what they had done.

This is one of Scripture's classic descriptions of Armageddon, the final battle between good and evil, and the Second Coming. The Antichrist (the "false prophet") will deceive the nations of the earth and will launch war against Jerusalem ("the beloved city"), appearing victorious until God directly intervenes, throwing the enemy into hell ("the lake of fire and sulphur"), at which point Christ will come in glory ("the white throne and him who sat upon it") to judge the living and the dead.

Zechariah 14:1–9: "Behold, a day of the LORD is coming, when . . . I will gather all the nations against Jerusalem to battle, and the city shall be taken and the houses plundered. . . . Then the LORD will go forth and fight against those nations as when he fights on a day of battle. On that day his feet shall stand on the Mount of Olives which lies before Jerusalem on the east; and the Mount of Olives shall be split in two from east to west by a very wide valley; so that one half of the Mount shall withdraw northward, and the other half southward ... and you shall flee as you fled from the earthquake in the days of Uzziah king of Judah. Then the LORD your God will come, and all the holy ones with him. On that day there shall be neither cold nor frost. And there shall be continuous day (it is known to the LORD), not day and not night, for at evening time there shall be light. On that day living waters shall flow out from Jerusalem.... And the LORD will become king over all the earth; on that day the LORD will be one and his name one."

This is another depiction of the final battle, in which all of the nations gather against and make war on Jerusalem and will be victorious until Christ appears, directly intervening and bringing victory. That will then be the end of the world as we know it (day and night shall end), and all will be ruled by Christ.[13]

Related to the prophecies about the Antichrist and the final war is the belief that prior to the Second Coming, the Temple in Jerusalem will be rebuilt. This is based on an interpretation of Daniel 9–12, in which Daniel 9 refers to the Second Coming of Christ. Jesus Himself explicitly associates this prophecy with the Second Coming in Matthew 24:15–30(extracts):

When you see the desolating abomination spoken of through Daniel the prophet standing in the holy place then those in Judea must flee to the mountains ... for at that time there will be great tribulation, such as has not

---

[13] Other relevant passages appear in Isaiah 66 and Ezekiel 38–39.

been since the beginning of the world until now, nor ever will be. And if those days had not been shortened, no one would be saved, but for the sake of the elect they will be shortened. . . . False messiahs and false prophets will arise, and they will perform signs and wonders so great as to deceive, if that were possible, even the elect. . . . Immediately after the tribulation of those days, the sun will be darkened and the moon will not give its light . . . and the powers of the heavens will be shaken. And then the sign of the Son of Man will appear in heaven . . . and they will see the Son of Man coming upon the clouds of heaven with power and great glory.

Although the prophecies of Daniel are at times associated with other events,[14] too, since Jesus explicitly applies them to the Second Coming, that must be at least one of their intended fulfillments. The prophecies mention the sacrifice ceasing and the temple being profaned; the Church Fathers [interpret] this in a spiritual sense, to refer to a cessation of the Holy Sacrifice of the Mass. But, it is conceivable that it might also have a literal fulfillment, if the Temple in Jerusalem should be rebuilt. And this is now within the realm of possibility. In 1967, for the first time in almost two thousand years, Jews regained possession of the Temple Mount, and there are now organizations in Israel attempting to rebuild the Temple.[15] Should it be rebuilt on the Temple Mount, also claimed by Islam as a holy site, it is not hard to envision

[14] Typically with the reign of Antiochus IV and with the first coming of Christ. See for instance *The New American Bible* (New York: Catholic Book, 1986), footnote to Daniel 9, p. 1035, and *The Holy Bible*, Douay and Confraternity Version, note, p. 965.

[15] For instance, The Temple Institute, 36 Misgav Ladach St., Jerusalem (www.templeinstitute.org).

how that in itself could precipitate the global war known as "Armageddon".

As stated earlier, the purpose of this discussion is *not* to "prove" that the Second Coming is near. Many of the proposed interpretations of the prophecies are speculative. Yet cumulatively they suggest that the Second Coming takes place at a time when the Jewish people have returned to Israel and formed a Jewish nation. If this is, in fact, a precondition for the return of Christ, the concerted efforts of the past century to eliminate the Jews and, failing that, to destroy the nascent State of Israel, well might be part of a diabolical attempt to prevent the Second Coming.

CHAPTER NINE

The Return of the Jews

The "Ingrafting"

It might seem odd to refer to the entry of Jews into the Catholic Church as "the return of the Jews". It is, however, the natural image for one who sees the Catholic Church as simply the continuation (and fulfillment) of Judaism after the first coming of Jesus, the Jewish Messiah. In such a case, it is the Jews who accepted Him and became the first Christians who stayed within the core of Judaism, while those who rejected Him left the mainstream, the fullness of the truth of the religion. This concept is shared, and most beautifully expressed, by St. Paul in his image of the "ingrafting". This image appears in Chapter 11 of his Letter to the Romans; let us return to it at some length, for in many ways it serves as an eloquent summary of this book:

> ¹ I ask, then, has God rejected his people? By no means! I myself am an Israelite, a descendant of Abraham, a member of the tribe of Benjamin.

> ^{2a} God has not rejected his people whom he foreknew.

Here is the definitive statement in Sacred Scripture that when the Old Covenant, which had been restricted to the Jews, was opened up to all peoples[1] in the New Covenant, it did not mean that God removed His special election from the Jews—not even from those Jews who did not recognize Him.

[2b] Do you not know what the scripture says of Elijah, how he pleads with God against Israel?

[3] "Lord, they have killed thy prophets, they have demolished thy altars, and I alone am left, and they seek my life."

[4] But what is God's reply to him? "I have kept for myself seven thousand men who have not bowed the knee to Baal."

[5] So too at the present time there is a remnant, chosen by grace.

[6] But if it is by grace, it is no longer on the basis of works; otherwise grace would no longer be grace.

[7] What then? Israel failed to obtain what it sought. The elect obtained it, but the rest were hardened,

[8] as it is written, "God gave them a spirit of stupor, eyes that should not see and ears that should not hear, down to this very day."

[9] And David says, "Let their table become a snare and a trap, a pitfall and a retribution for them;

---

[1] Or "universalized", hence the word "Catholic", which means "universal". As Cardinal Lustiger put it: "The grace given to Israel is, in the Messiah, given to the pagans. The Church is 'catholic' ... because she reunites two categories which divide history: those who participate in the Election, Israel, and those who did not have the right to" — translation by author (Jean-Marie Lustiger, *La Promesse* [Paris: Parole et Silence, 2002], pp. 15–16).

¹⁰ let their eyes be darkened so that they cannot see, and bend their backs for ever."

Here St. Paul states that God Himself "darkened" the eyes of the Jews, that they might not recognize Jesus as the Messiah, even down to the present time. "God gave them a spirit of stupor, eyes that should not see and ears that should not hear, down to this very day." It was God who "hardened" them, "darkened" their eyes. There is a mystery here, part of the "mystery of iniquity", just as there is a mystery to God "hardening" Pharaoh's heart during the Exodus (Exodus 9:12; 10:1, 20, 27; 11:10; 14:8), yet Paul clearly states that in some mysterious way, it was part of God's Providence that some Jews should remain unable to recognize Jesus as the Messiah. He then goes on to intimate some of the purpose for which God did this:

¹¹ So I ask, have they stumbled so as to fall? By no means! But through their trespass salvation has come to the Gentiles, so as to make Israel jealous.

¹² Now if their trespass means riches for the world, and if their failure means riches for the Gentiles, how much more will their full inclusion mean!

Here St. Paul implies that the Jews' rejection of Jesus was in itself part of the process that enabled salvation to come to the Gentiles. And their rejection of Jesus was not the end of their own salvation, since their "stumbling" was not "so as to fall".

¹³ Now I am speaking to you Gentiles. Inasmuch then as I am an apostle to the Gentiles, I magnify my ministry

¹⁴ in order to make my fellow Jews jealous, and thus save some of them.

¹⁵ For if their rejection means the reconciliation of the world, what will their acceptance mean but life from the dead?

¹⁶ If the dough offered as first fruits is holy, so is the whole lump; and if the root is holy, so are the branches.

Once again in verse 15, St. Paul repeats that it was the Jews' rejection of Jesus that brought about the salvation of the Gentiles—"the reconciliation of the world"—and that if such a great blessing was the result of the Jews *rejecting* Jesus, how great must the blessing be that will come about as a result of their *accepting* Him! Verse 16 then confirms the special election of the Jews as a holy people, in fact, as *the* holy people through whom salvation came to all of humanity. They are "the dough offered as first fruits" that makes the whole batch holy, "the root" that makes the whole tree holy.

¹⁷ But if some of the branches were broken off, and you, a wild olive shoot, were grafted in their place to share the richness of the olive tree,

¹⁸ do not boast over the branches. If you do boast, remember it is not you that support the root, but the root that supports you.

¹⁹ You will say, "Branches were broken off so that I might be grafted in."

²⁰ That is true. They were broken off because of their unbelief, but you stand fast only through faith. So do not become proud, but stand in awe.

Here is the central image. Some branches were broken off of the cultivated tree and wild shoots grafted on in their place. But since the original branches "were broken off so that [the Gentiles] might be grafted in", the implication is that they

were intentionally broken off by God. These branches are of
course the Jews who reject Jesus, and who are now outside
the Church. So again in this verse Paul suggests that the failure of some, or most, of the Jews to accept Jesus was part of
God's plan.

> [21] For if God did not spare the natural branches, neither
> will he spare you.

> [22] Note then the kindness and the severity of God: sever-
> ity toward those who have fallen, but God's kindness to
> you, provided you continue in his kindness; otherwise you
> too will be cut off.

This is a warning to the Gentile Christians not to see their
faith as superiority over the Jews.

> [23] And even the others, if they do not persist in their un-
> belief, will be grafted in, for God has the power to graft
> them in again.

> [24] For if you have been cut from what is by nature a wild
> olive tree, and grafted, contrary to nature, into a culti-
> vated olive tree, how much more will these natural branches
> be grafted back into their own olive tree.

Here is the beautiful promise—that when the Jews return to
the fullness of their faith, that is, return to the Church, they
will thus be grafted back onto what has always been, after
all, their own native root, and the result will be doubly graced.

> [25] Lest you be wise in your own conceits, I want you to
> understand this mystery, brethren: a hardening has come
> upon part of Israel, until the full number of the Gentiles
> come in,

²⁶ and so all Israel will be saved; as it is written, "The Deliverer will come from Zion, he will banish ungodliness from Jacob;

²⁷ and this will be my covenant with them when I take away their sins."

Again, the statement that the unbelief of the Jews was an integral part of God's plan to enable the Gentiles to be saved, but that when the "full number" of the Gentiles has come in—presumably at the end of this age of salvation history, at the "end of time"—the "hardening" resulting in the Jews' unbelief will be removed and "all Israel will be saved".

²⁸ As regards the gospel they are enemies of God, for your sake; but as regards election they are beloved for the sake of their forefathers.

²⁹ For the gifts and the call of God are irrevocable.

Once again Paul repeats that the Jews' rejection of the Gospel—their refusal to believe in Christ—was for the sake of the Gentiles ("for your sake"); their election, the special love that God has for them, and their special gifts remain.

³⁰ Just as you were once disobedient to God but now have received mercy because of their disobedience,

³¹ so they have now been disobedient in order that by the mercy shown to you they also may receive mercy.

³² For God has consigned all men to disobedience, that he may have mercy upon all.

Here, one final time, St. Paul repeats the assertion that the Jews' "disobedience"—i.e., rejection of the Gospel—was somehow, mysteriously, part of God's plan so that the Gentiles might be saved. Then St. Paul concludes in the only possible way, given the unfathomable depth, mystery, and mercy revealed in God's plan of salvation:

[33] O the depth of the riches and wisdom and knowledge of God! How unsearchable are his judgments and how inscrutable his ways!

[34] "For who has known the mind of the Lord, or who has been his counselor?"

[35] "Or who has given a gift to him that he might be repaid?"

[36] For from him and through him and to him are all things. To him be glory for ever. Amen.

Almost every Jew who enters the Catholic Church feels deeply the sense of "return" that St. Paul captures in his image of the olive branch being grafted back on to its original, natural root—that they are in no way leaving Judaism but rather coming into its fullness. As Rosalind Moss, a well-known contemporary Jewish-Catholic evangelist, put it, becoming Catholic is "the most Jewish thing a person can do".[2] In the book-length interview cited earlier, Cardinal Lustiger expounded at some length, and with great beauty, on his own similar perception:[3]

I explained [to my father] that baptism would not make me abandon my Jewish condition—quite the contrary, it would lead me to find it, to receive the plenitude of its meaning. I did not have the feeling that I was betraying

[2] Rosalind Moss, "O Jerusalem, Jerusalem. . .", *The Hebrew Catholic*, no. 77 (Summer-Fall 2002), p. 23.

[3] This quote is rather lengthy; it is included in some fullness because Cardinal Lustiger, as the Cardinal Archbishop of Paris, speaks with substantial authority on some of the key themes of this book.

my heritage, or camouflaging myself or abandoning anything whatsoever. Just the opposite: I felt that I was going
to find the import, the meaning of what I had received at
birth.[4]

[My instruction prior to baptism] confirmed my keen in-
tuition that Christianity is the continuation of Judaism. . . . Christianity is the fruit of Judaism! To be specific:
I believed in Christ, the Messiah of Israel. Something that
I had carried within me for years, without having spoken
about it to anyone, crystallized. I knew that Judaism held
the hope of the Messiah. I knew that the response to the
scandal of suffering was the hope of man's redemption
and the fulfillment of God's promises to his people. And
I *knew* that Jesus is the Messiah, the Christ of God.[5]

There was never for one instant a question of disowning
my Jewish identity. Quite the contrary, I perceived Christ
as Israel's Messiah, and I was surrounded by Christians
who had deep esteem for Judaism.[6]

[When I discovered Christianity it] was as though I knew
about it already. Not customs, rites, practices, but its content. I seemed to have understood beforehand. I was even
surprised when other people did not understand what I
understood. . . . Even though I had not had a Jewish education, I knew enough to recognize the ritual of the
Passover in the Eucharist. It is the sacrifice of the Lamb,
of the suffering Messiah; it is deliverance and salvation,
the grace of God. . . . I felt it was obvious that Catholics
were sharing the inheritance that God had initially des-

---

[4] Jean-Louis Missika and Dominique Wolton, *Choosing God—Chosen by God*
(San Francisco: Ignatius Press, 1991), p. 42.
  [5] Ibid., pp. 42–43.
  [6] Ibid., p. 45.

tined for Israel, the elder son, the firstborn. . . . I saw more than continuity . . . the key to the enigma was given to me, in a new mystery: the mystery of Christ, the crucified Messiah . . . I was not in alien country. I was one of the older sons. I did nothing more than begin to enjoy the heritage that had been promised to me. Only much later was I able to express more precisely what I had immediately understood intuitively: the problem of God's relationship to pagans and Jews is at the heart of all Scripture, of both the Old and New Testaments.[7]

[T]he fact that the Messiah is the eternal Son of God made flesh is also a metonymy: he is Israel not by substitution, but by inclusion. He is the one in whom the filial condition of the holy nation is realized. Jesus observed and fulfilled the commandments given by God to Moses for his people, Israel. He faultlessly fulfilled what had been required of the Jew for living in holiness—a holiness required for the salvation of all nations, for the redemption of the sons of Adam, for bringing together and uniting all that divine generosity has spread and lavished on the world. Through him comes deliverance from sin and access to life.[8]

The novelty of this visit by God [the coming of the Messiah] does not annul the preceding divine interventions, it attests to them and reveals their universal, divine significance. God did not go back on his promise when he revealed in his own Son what had been hidden in his chosen people and what, in the Resurrection of his Christ, became the eternal *nouveauté* [i.e., novelty] promised to Israel and hoped for by all the sons of Adam. It is in this

---

[7] Ibid., pp. 62–63.
[8] Ibid., p. 65.

way that the New Covenant realizes the divine Testament whose promises it makes "old" as well as fulfilled.[9]

Until the Messiah's coming in glory, the Jew remains, and he remains a Jew, whether he is Christian or not.[10]

This same perception, that a Jew in becoming Catholic is not changing his religion at all but rather coming into the fullness of its truth, is shared by virtually all Jews who have entered the Church. It is in fact the fundamental reason for Jewish conversion. The Lemann brothers, whose conversion was discussed at some length earlier, expressed it in the following words:

You have heard it said that an honorable man should not change his religion.... But this maxim is as false as it is cruel, and, with respect to a Jew who wishes to become Catholic, doubly false. It is false a first time because for him as for all who stray and then return, there is honor rather than dishonor in abandoning error to return to the Truth. It is false a second time, shamefully false, because a Jew in becoming Catholic does not change his religion, but fulfils his religion, completes it, crowns it. The Jew become Catholic is the religious man *par excellence*, who has grown into his fullness, as the seed grows into the flower.... The religion was initially patriarchal, that is, identified with the family of the Patriarchs; then it was enlarged into a chosen people who were given the beautiful name *People of God*; and finally, in being universalized it became something even more beautiful, the *Kingdom of God*, the Catholic Church which is for all people. This is always the work of the Eternal, the progression from

[9] Ibid., p. 66.
[10] Ibid., p. 79.

the less perfect to the more perfect, from the particular to the general[11] (emphasis in original).

Extraordinary Grace in Jewish Conversion

It is true that some Jewish conversion to Christianity, especially in the past when active persecution was an issue, has been less than genuine, motivated by social or economic considerations, rather than true conviction. Genuine conversions, on the other hand, are always the result of the working of grace, of God operating in the human soul. Sometimes grace inspires an intellectual exploration with a willingness to follow the truth wherever it goes, ending with a conviction of the truth of the Catholic faith. In other cases, the grace operates more suddenly, unexpectedly, and miraculously. A brief examination of some instances of conversion will reveal quite a bit about how God works in bringing His "chosen people" to the fullness of the truth and promise of Judaism. It will also give us an opportunity to see how these recipients of extraordinary graces see the relationship between Judaism and the Catholic faith.

The conversion of Alphonse Ratisbonne

A particularly dramatic conversion was that of Alphonse Ratisbonne. Ratisbonne was the son and heir of a wealthy aristocratic family of Jewish bankers in Strasbourg, France. When Alphonse was still a child his older brother, Theodor, converted to the Catholic faith and became a priest. The family reacted with hostility and horror. Alphonse resolved never

---

[11] Father Theotime de St. Just, *Les Frères Lemann: Juifs Convertis* (Paris: Librarie St.-François, 1937), p. 372 (translation by author).

to communicate again with his older brother and developed
a violent antipathy to the Catholic faith and to all things
Catholic. Although Alphonse was entirely atheist in his beliefs and non-practicing as a Jew, he felt a great love and
loyalty for his fellow Jews and devoted much of his effort
and wealth to better their social condition. At the time of his
conversion, Alphonse was twenty-seven years old and en-
gaged to marry his uncle's beautiful daughter and to take his
place as a partner in his uncle's bank. During his engagement Ratisbonne noticed a subtle change in his religious
feelings; he wrote:

> I must note a certain change that came about in my re-
> ligious thinking during my engagement. As I said, I did
> not believe in anything; in this absolute nihilism, in my
> denial of any faith, I felt myself to be in harmony with
> my Catholic and Protestant friends; the sight of my fian-
> cée awakened in me a sentiment of human dignity. I be-
> gan to believe in the immortality of the soul; instinctively
> I began to pray to God; I thanked him for my good for-
> tune, but nevertheless I still remained unhappy. . . . I could
> not account for my sentiments; . . . I often told her [my
> fiancée] that, and truly, the thought of her raised my heart
> to the God, that I did not know, to whom I had not prayed,
> whom I had not invoked.[12]

Because his fiancée was only sixteen, it was thought appropriate to delay the wedding, and to pass the time, Alphonse
decided to take an extended prenuptial tourist trip. An early
stop was Naples; there he found himself alone on New Year's
Day, 1847. In Ratisbonne's own description:

---

[12] General Postulation of the Minimi, *The Madonna of the Miracle* (Rome:
Minimi Booklets, 1971), p. 13.

It was a sad day for me. I was alone in Naples, I was not greeted by anybody, I had nobody to embrace. . . . I wept and the joy of the Neapolitans increased my sadness. I went for a walk following mechanically the flow of the crowd. I reached the piazza di Palazzo and found myself, I do not know why, at the door of a church. I entered. The Mass, I believe, was being celebrated. How did it come about, I do not know, but I stopped for a moment leaning against a column, and my heart seemed to open and breathe a known atmosphere. I prayed in my own way, without analyzing what was happening to me. I prayed for my fiancée, my uncle, my dead father, my dear mother who left me as an orphan when I was young, all my close friends, and I asked God for inspiration that could guide me in my projects of improving the lot of the Jews—an idea which I had always cherished. My sadness left me, as a dark cloud that is blown away by the wind; in my whole interior, inundated with an ineffable calm, I experienced a consolation as if a voice had told me: "Your prayer has been granted." Oh yes, my prayer has been heard one hundred per cent and beyond all expectation, because on the last day of that same month, I solemnly received the sacrament of baptism in a church in Rome![13]

After Naples, Ratisbonne went on to Rome. While there, he called on the Baron de Bussieres, who was the brother of one of his best friends. The Baron was a devout Catholic and dared Ratisbonne to wear a Miraculous Medal and to recite a short daily prayer to Mary[14] as a way of proving that there was nothing to such "detestable superstitions". (The Miraculous Medal is a medal of Mary that was widely propagated following her apparition to a young nun, later

[13] Ibid., pp. 17–18.
[14] The *Memorare* of St. Bernard.

St. Catherine Laboure, in her convent chapel in Paris.) On January 20, the last day of his planned stay in Rome, Ratisbonne encountered the Baron, riding in his carriage, who invited him to join him in his carriage for a ride. When the Baron stopped at a nearby church to conduct some business with the priest, Ratisbonne went into the empty church to wait. Let us continue with the Baron's account of what he found when he went into the church to get his friend:

> I caught sight of him on his knees, in the chapel of St. Michael the Archangel.[15] I went up to him and touched him. I had to do this three or four times before he became aware of my presence. Finally he turned towards me, face bathed in tears . . . with an expression no words can describe . . . he took hold of his Miraculous Medal and kissed it with passionate emotion. He broke into tears at the thought of all the heretics and unbelievers. . . . Gradually this delirious emotion subsided and he grew calmer, and now his face was radiant, almost transfigured. He begged me to take him to a priest and asked when he could receive holy Baptism, for now he was sure he could not live without it. I took him at once to the Gesù[16] to see Father de Villefort, who invited him to explain what had happened. Ratisbonne drew out his medal, kissed it, and showed it to me, saying, "I saw her! I saw her!" and again emotion choked his words, but soon he grew calmer and spoke. I shall give his [Ratisbonne's] own words:

> "I had only been in the church a moment when I was suddenly seized with an indescribable agitation of mind. I looked up and found that the rest of the building had

---

[15] It may not be entirely without significance that St. Michael the Archangel is, according to the Hebrew Scriptures, the patron saint of the Jewish people!

[16] The principal Jesuit church in Rome.

disappeared. One single chapel seemed to have gathered all the light and concentrated it in itself. In the midst of this radiance I saw someone standing on the altar, a lofty shining figure, all majesty and sweetness, the Virgin Mary just as she looks on this medal. Some irresistible force drew me towards her. She motioned to me to kneel down and when I did so, she seemed to approve. Though she never said a word, I understood her perfectly."

... At first he [Ratisbonne] had been able to see the Queen of Heaven clearly, appearing in all the splendor of her immaculate beauty; but he had not been able to bear the radiance of that divine light for long. Three times he had tried to look up to her, and three times he had found himself unable to raise his eyes higher than her hands, from which blessings and graces seemed to be falling like so many shining rays.

"Oh God," he cried, "only half an hour before I was blaspheming, and felt a deadly hatred for the Catholic religion! All my acquaintances know that humanly speaking I had the strongest reasons for remaining a Jew. My family is Jewish, my bride to be is a Jewess, my uncle is a Jew. By becoming Catholic I am sacrificing all my earthly hopes and interests; and yet I am not mad." [17]

Soon after the experience Ratisbonne wrote:

How can I describe it? Human words cannot attempt to explain the unspeakable; every description, however sublime, will only be a profanation of the ineffable truth. I was there, on my knees, in tears.... I took the medal ... and kissed passionately the image of the Virgin radiant with grace. It was She!

[17] Bro. Francis Mary Kalvelage, F.I., *Marian Shrines of France* (New Bedford, Mass.: Academy of the Immaculate, 1998), pp. 38–40.

I did not know where I was. I experienced an almost total change.... I tried to find myself and could not.... The greatest joy burst from the depths of my soul; I could not speak.... I could not account for the faith and awareness that I had acquired. All that I could say is that in the moment of this phenomenon, the band fell from my eyes; and not one band, but a whole collection of them, and they disappeared rapidly, one after the other, as snow, mud and ice disappear under the influence of the burning sun.

I came out of a tomb, out of the abyss of darkness and I was alive, perfectly alive.... But I wept! I saw in the bottom of the abyss the extreme misery from which I was torn out by an infinite mercy. I trembled at the sight of all my iniquities, and I was stupefied, emotionally moved and shocked in admiration and gratitude.... Oh, how many descend calmly into this abyss with their eyes closed by pride and recklessness! ... They descend alive into the chasm of terrible darkness.... And my family, my fiancée, my poor sisters!!! For you I offered my first prayers. Will you not lift up your eyes to the Saviour of the world whose blood cancelled the original sin? Oh, how terrible is the imprint of that stain! It renders the creature made in the image of God unrecognizable.

I wondered how I came to know this truth, since it is sure that I had not opened a religious book, I had not read a single page of the Bible, and the doctrine on the original sin, that is totally forgotten and denied by modern Jews, had not occupied my mind even for an instant; I doubt if I have ever heard the term. How did I arrive at this knowledge? I do not know. I know this; that entering the church I knew nothing; leaving it, I saw everything clearly. I can only explain this change with the image of a man who awoke from a deep sleep, or with that of a man born blind, who sees the light in one blow; he sees but cannot define the light that is the source of his illumination, and in which he contemplates the objects of his admiration.

Figure 9-1: Alphonse Ratisbonne as a young man.

... I felt ready for everything and [immediately] insistently demanded baptism. They wanted to delay it. "But how!", I exclaimed, "the Jews who heard the preaching of the Apostles were baptized immediately, and you want to delay it, even though I heard the Queen of the Apostles!" [18]

---

[18] *The Madonna of the Miracle*, pp. 37–42.

SALVATION IS FROM THE JEWS

Eleven days later Alphonse received baptism, confirmation, and First Communion. Soon afterward, he began religious studies (having broken off his engagement), and in 1847 was ordained a priest. He spent the rest of his life working and praying for the conversion of his fellow Jews. He moved to the Holy Land and, with his brother Theodor, founded a congregation of nuns—the Congregation of Our Lady of Sion—to pray for the conversion of the Jews. He built a convent for them on the site of Pilate's palace, the very spot where Pilate showed the beaten and bloody Jesus to the crowd suggesting that he be released, to which the crowd of Jews cried back, "Crucify him! His blood be on us and on our children!" (Matthew 27:25). He died in 1884 at Ain Karem, John the Baptist's birthplace near Jerusalem. His heartfelt prayer that New Year's Day in Naples, that God lead him to fulfill his cherished goal to work to improve the lot of the Jews, had been granted, as he said, "beyond all expectation".

The conversion of Rabbi Zolli

One of the best known Jewish "conversions" [19] of modern times is that of Rabbi Zolli, the former Chief Rabbi of Rome. Israel Zolli was born in 1881 in Galacia, on the border between Poland and Austria. He was the youngest of five children in a wealthy, cultured Jewish family; his mother came from a line of over two centuries of learned Rabbis. Israel followed in those august footsteps, going three days a week to a Jewish religious school, in addition to attending the ordinary elementary school. He was friends with a Catholic boy with whom he would sometimes do his homework; they

---

[19] The term "conversion" is used reluctantly since all of the Jews under discussion viewed entry into the Church as the completion of their Judaism rather than a conversion from it; it is, however, the conventional term.

would work together in the one main room of the boy's house, at the dining table beneath a large crucifix. That experience, at about eight years of age, marked him deeply. As he wrote:

It seemed that in that white room, and in the presence of the crucifix, one could not help being serene, gentle, and good. Sometimes—I did not know why—I would raise my eyes to that crucifix and gaze for a long time at the figure hanging there. This contemplation, if I may call it that without exaggeration, was not done without a stirring of my spirit.

Why was this man crucified? I asked myself. . . . Why did so many people follow him if he was so wicked? Why are [the people] who follow this "crucified one" so good . . . and they adore this crucified one? Why do we boys become so different in the presence of this crucifix?

This crucified one, moreover, awakened in me a sense of great compassion. I had the same strong impression of his innocence as of his pain . . . he was in agony. . . .

He does not cry out in his pain, he does not lament, he does not curse. On his face is no expression of hatred or resentment. The olive branch above his head seems to whisper softly of peace.

No, He, Jesus, that man—now he was "He" for me, with a capital "H"—He was not bad; He could not have been in any way wicked. Perhaps He was, or perhaps He was not, the "Servant of God" whose canticles we read at school. Perhaps He was, or perhaps He was not, that sufferer of whom the master told us. . . . I did not know. But of one thing I was certain: He was good.

But then, why did they crucify Him? In the book of Isaiah there are four canticles—42:1–7, 49:1–5, 50:4–9, and 52:13—53:12—which present to us an innocent man, purer than any other in the world. He is stricken and humiliated, exhausted by so much suffering; he dies in silence as in silence he suffered. Then the crowd seems to recover from its fury: "Why have we tormented and put to death Him who bore our sins?" [20]

Zolli continued his studies both in secular universities and in Rabbinical College, becoming, at the unprecedentedly young age of thirty-seven, the Chief Rabbi of Trieste, one of the most important Jewish centers in Europe at the time. He was consumed with a love for his Jewish people and for God, but also filled with loving sympathy for "the crucified one". In his autobiography Zolli quotes words written by Henri Bergson, a famous Jewish philosopher who was also drawn to Catholicism, as similar to his own attitude toward Catholicism at the time of his appointment as Chief Rabbi of Trieste:

> My thinking has always brought me nearer to Catholicism, in which I saw the perfect complement of Judaism. I would have embraced it if I had not witnessed the frightful wave of anti-Semitism which for some years deluged the world. I preferred to remain with those who would be persecuted tomorrow. Nevertheless, I hope that a Catholic priest ... may come to recite the prayers at my funeral.... [If not] a Rabbi would have to be called but without hiding from him, or anyone else, my moral adhesion to Catholicism. [21]

Rabbi Zolli remained the Chief Rabbi of Trieste from 1918 to 1938. During this period, he also distinguished himself as an academic and a scholar, writing several important scholarly works and becoming professor of Semitic languages at the University of Padua, where many of his students were

---

[20] Eugenio Zolli, *Why I Became a Catholic* (republished, New York: Roman Catholic Books, n.d.; originally published 1953), pp. 24–25.

[21] Ibid., p. 71.

priests. Zolli notes in his autobiography, "Even at that time they were remembering me in their holy Masses, asking God (as they told me years later) for my conversion." One of the books he wrote during this period was a study of Jesus of Nazareth entitled *The Nazarene*, which although written from a Jewish perspective was entirely sympathetic to the person of Jesus and so consistent with Catholic doctrine that an Archbishop in Rome told Zolli, "Everyone is susceptible of errors, but so far as I can see, as a bishop, I could sign my name to this book." [22]

In 1939, Zolli left Trieste to become the Chief Rabbi and spiritual leader of the Jewish Community in Rome. When four years later the Nazis took control of Rome, Zolli did all he could to protect the Jewish community. At one point the Nazis demanded a ransom of fifty kilograms of gold within thirty-six hours to spare the Jews; despite Zolli's frantic efforts, with a few hours left they were still short fifteen kilos. At that point Zolli secretly paid a call on the Vatican. The Holy Father, Pope Pius XII, immediately offered to provide the needed gold. [23]

Zolli's final conversion experience took place in 1944, while he was celebrating the Yom Kippur services—the most solemn holiday of the Jewish liturgical year—as Chief Rabbi of Rome. In his words:

It was the Day of Atonement in the fall of 1944, and I was presiding over the religious service in the Temple. The day was nearing its end, and I was all alone in the midst of a great number of persons. I began to feel as though a fog

[22] Ibid., p. iv.
[23] Sister Margherita Marchione, *Yours Is a Precious Witness* (New York: Paulist Press, 1977), p. 33, and Judith Cabaud, *Eugenio Zolli* (Paris: F.-X. de Guibert, 2000), pp. 126–27.

were creeping into my soul; it became denser, and I wholly
lost touch with the men and things around me.... And
just then I saw with my mind's eye a meadow sweeping
upward, with bright grass.... In this meadow I saw Jesus
Christ clad in a white mantle, and beyond His head the
blue sky. I experienced the greatest interior peace. If I
were to give an image of the state of my soul at that moment I should say a crystal-clear lake amid high mountains. Within my heart I found the words: "You are here
for the last time." ... The reply of my heart was: So it is,
so it shall be, so it must be.

[L]ater my wife, my daughter, and I were at home for
supper after the fast.... Suddenly my wife said to me:
"Today while you were before the Ark of the Torah, it
seemed to me as if the white figure of Jesus put His hands
on your head as if He were blessing you." I was amazed
but still very calm.... At this very moment we heard ...
our younger daughter, Miriam [call] from afar, "Papaaa!"
I went to her room. "What is the matter?" I asked....
"You know, Papa, tonight I have been dreaming that I
saw a very tall, white Jesus, but I don't remember what
came next."

It was a few days later that I resigned my post in the
Israelite Community and went to a quite unknown priest
in order to receive instruction. An interval of some weeks
elapsed, until the 13th of February, when I received the
Sacrament of Baptism and was incorporated into the Catholic Church, the Mystical Body of Jesus Christ.[24]

In gratitude for all that Pope Pius XII had done to save Jews
during the war, Zolli took as his baptismal name the Pope's
given name, Eugenio.

[24] Ibid., pp. 182–84.

Figure 9-2: Rabbi Zolli, former Chief Rabbi of Rome

Like all of the other Jewish converts in this book, Zolli did not view entry into the Catholic Church as a conversion away from Judaism, but as its completion. The conversion itself is the result of grace working in the soul; God, not the recipient, is the author of the conversion. As Zolli wrote:

The convert, like someone who is miraculously healed, is the object and not the subject of the prodigy. It is false to say of someone that he himself converted, as if it were a matter of personal initiative. One does not say of someone who was miraculously healed that he healed himself, but that he *was* healed. One must say the same of the convert.[25]

Is conversion an infidelity, an infidelity towards the faith previously professed?... Faith is an adherence, not to a tradition or family or tribe, or even nation, it is an adherence of our life and our works to the Will of God as it is revealed to each in the intimacy of conscience....

But the Spirit of God breathes where it wills and how it wills.... Unconsciously, quite unconsciously, I was beginning to find in Christianity a springtime of the spirit, full of the expectation of new life made eternal; Christianity represented for me the object of a longing for a love which should temper my soul's winter, an incomparable beauty which should quench my desire for beauty.... In the words of the Canticle of Canticles: "Winter is now past, the rain is over and gone. The flowers have appeared in our land: the time of pruning is come; the voice of the turtle-dove is heard."

The slow preparation for spiritual rebirth is much like the preparation which takes place in nature: all is accomplished in silence, and no sign appears of the wondrous event to come. All of a sudden, it seems, the earth is covered with green and the trees are decked with red and white blossom. Like snow-crystals petals float in the air, and there is promise of fruit. One great biological process has reached completion, and a fresh cycle of life is taking on concrete reality, becoming crystallized. The dying we saw was only apparent; it meant the transformation of the life lived into a new life, a life to be lived.... What seemed

[25] Cabaud, *Eugenio Zolli*, p. 102.

to die in me had left in my soul the germs of a new life, the life of Jesus Christ.[26]

When asked why he had given up the Synagogue for the Church, Zolli replied:

> "But I have not given it up. Christianity is the integration, completion or crown of the Synagogue. For the Synagogue was a promise, and Christianity is the fulfillment of that promise. The Synagogue pointed to Christianity: Christianity presupposes the Synagogue. So you see, one cannot exist without the other. What I converted to was the living Christianity." [27]

It was not simply Christianity that Zolli saw as the completion of Judaism, but more specifically the Catholic Church. His response to why he did not become Protestant was:

> The Catholic Church was recognized by the whole Christian world as the true Church of God for fifteen consecutive centuries. No one can halt at the end of those 1500 years and say that the Catholic Church is not the Church of Christ without embarrassing himself seriously. I can accept only that Church which was preached to all creatures by my own forefathers, the Twelve Apostles, who, like me, issued from the Synagogue.[28]

Zolli, rather than repudiating his Jewishness, was on the contrary proud of having Jewish blood. In explanation he quoted the words of St. Ignatius of Loyola: "I would consider it a special thing to be united to Christ, our Lord, and to Our Lady, the glorious Virgin Mary, with ties of blood!" [29]

---

[26] Zolli, *Why I Became a Catholic*, pp. 108–12.
[27] Ibid., p. iii.
[28] Cabaud, *Eugenio Zolli*, p. 109.
[29] Ibid., p. 191.

The conversion of Charlie Rich

Charlie Rich was born in 1899 to a devout Hasidic family in a small village in Hungary. As a child, his schooling was entirely religious, and he had a prayerful, pious nature, spending many hours alone in the woods around his home in loving contemplation of God. However, after his family immigrated to the United States and settled in a Jewish ghetto in New York City, Charlie lost the faith of his childhood and became an atheist. He retained, however, an intense thirst for philosophical and religious truth, and during his twenties he spent hours a day, day after day and month after month, in the public library studying philosophy and religion. Let us continue in his own words:

> At the age of thirty-three I had read every important literary work held famous in the eyes of men.... And yet ... there was distress in my spiritual and intellectual make-up, so much so that I thought of suicide as a way out of the misery, spiritual and intellectual I was in ... faith failed me, and I felt that without supernatural faith I could not go on living and this in the same way as anyone would soon die if he was not given food to eat.... I actually went to the Bronx Park with the intention of hanging myself. I had picked out a tree and had a rope in my hand, when someone passed by and courage failed me.... Anyway, I one day passed a Catholic Church—it was a hot summer day, and I felt weary and exhausted. So I thought if I went inside I could cool off.... I went inside and found myself completely alone.[30]

---

[30] Charles Rich, *Autobiography* (Petersham, Mass.: St. Bede's Publications, 1990), p. 4.

There, seated in the shadows in the empty church, he looked up to a stained glass window depicting Jesus stilling the waters during the storm (Luke 8:22–25) and said to himself:

> If only I could believe with the same assurance as those who come to worship here believe! that the words in the Gospels are really true, that Christ really existed, and that these words are exactly those that came from His own mouth, were uttered from His own human lips, and that they are literally true. Oh, if this were only a fact, if I could only believe that this were a fact, how glorious and wonderful that would be, how consoled, happy and comforted I would be, to know that Christ was really divine, that He was God's own Son come down from another world to this earth to save us all! Could it be possible, I felt, that that which seemed too wonderful to be true actually was true, that it was no deception, no fraud, no lie? All of a sudden something flashed though my mind and I heard these words spoken in it. "Of course it is true, Christ is God, is God come down to make Himself visible in the flesh. The words in the Gospels are true, literally true."
>
> The next thing I remember was that I found myself on my knees in fervent prayer and thanksgiving. I felt a deep gratitude in my heart for something which made me feel very happy, but what it was I could not say. All that I know is that, from that day on the name of Our Lord Jesus Christ took on a significance which it never before had. There was an ineffable fragrance about the words "Jesus Christ," a sweetness with which nothing can be compared. The sound of these words to this day fills me with a strange inexpressible joy, a joy which I feel does not come from this world. . . .
>
> I have, since my Baptism and First Communion, acquired a happiness which I would not exchange for anything in all the world. It has given to me a peace of

mind and a serenity of outlook which I did not think was possible on this earth.... I suppose the Buddhist would characterize this sort of peace by the word "Nirvana," but I would much prefer to call it by the familiar language of Paul: "The peace of God that surpasses all understanding." [31]

Later Charlie Rich wrote:

It would in my case have been in vain to have been born had God not been good enough to extend me the grace to become a member of the Mystical Body of Christ the Church of Rome is. Without the Life Christ is, there is no life at all, and for him also the Life Christ is can only be had where he now so blessedly is.... It is for heaven we have been made and for no other earthly good thing. It is to heaven every good and beautiful experience points and has in view.

I became a Catholic so that I may in that way be happy, not just for a few years, but forever and ever. I became a Catholic that I may in that way get the grace to one day participate in the joys of the angels and saints in the life to come. It is to that life the grace of conversion is meant to lead. It is meant to lead to a happiness we cannot now imagine or conceive.

No, it is not for this life alone we are Catholics. We are Catholics that by being so we may get the grace to live the Life Christ Himself is and which can never have a limit to it.... It is not of the earth my holy Catholic faith speaks to me. It does so of the transcendent Good Jesus can alone be for a human being.

And so, one can write and write and write about the story of one's conversion and never come to an end. He can never

---

[31] Charles Rich, *Reflections* (Petersham, Mass.: St. Bede's Publications, 1986), p. x.

Figure 9-3: Charlie Rich

come to an end of enumerating the blessings conferred upon him by the grace of becoming a Catholic. "The favors of the Lord I will sing forever" (Hebrew: "mercy"; Psalm 89:2). What mercy of the Lord can exceed the mercy of God enabling me to be able to believe in all the Catholic Church teaches? Can the mercy of God be made more manifest [than] in the grace extended to us to become a member of the only true Church? It is becoming a Catholic that matters and not in any other thing the world has to offer be this good and beautiful as it may. The Church of Rome gives us God Himself. It does so in all His fullness—a greater gift than God is, a human being cannot hope to receive. We receive the gift God Himself is when we receive Holy Communion. Can Protestantism and Judaism endow the soul with such a sublime gift? It is to the Church we must go to have God in the fullness He may be experienced by us this side of heaven. To become more intimately united with God than the Church enables us to be by means of the Holy Sacraments, we must take leave of this life. It is Christ the Church gives us as he may be had under the conditions of the present life. To have God in all His fullness we have to have the grace of membership in His Mystical Body. It is the Voice of Christ the Church makes use of when He says "I came that they might have life and have it to the full" (John. 10:10).[32]

Charlie Rich recently passed away, in his late nineties, having lived out his life as a contemplative, much of it with a community of Jesuits in New York City.

The Nature of Jewish Conversion

We have seen how in the cases of the Lemann brothers, of Alphonse Ratisbonne, of Edith Stein, of Charlie Rich, of Cardinal Lustiger, none saw his entry into the Catholic Church as conversion at all. Rather, they all saw it as their completion as Jews, of their coming into the ultimate fullness of Judaism and of their identity as Jews. In fact, throughout this book the term "conversion" applied to the entry of Jews into the Church has been used with great reluctance. It has been used for the sake of convenience, and because it is the common term, but is fundamentally at odds with the experience of virtually ev-

<hr>

[32] Rich, *Autobiography*, pp. 93–95.

ery Jew who "converts". They experience it as no conversion at all. They do not perceive themselves as any less a Jew, but rather after their "conversion" they see themselves as more Jewish than ever, filled with a fire to spread their joy and fulfillment in having found the Messiah to their fellow Jews. We saw this with the Lemann brothers, who worked so hard to get the *postulatum* inviting the Jews into the Church approved at the First Vatican Council and founded a confraternity to pray for the conversion of the Jews. We saw it with the Ratisbonne brothers, who founded a religious community in the Holy Land in order to pray and work for the conversion of the Jews. And we saw it with Edith Stein, who gave her life "for the Jewish people, that the Lord may be received by his own and his Kingdom come in glory".[33]

This dedication to the welfare of their fellow Jews is not new among Jewish "converts". It goes all the way back to St. Paul, who wrote that he would willingly give up his *own* salvation if that could help his fellow Jews come into the fullness of the promise of their own religion (Romans 9:3–5):

> For I could wish that I myself were accursed and cut off from Christ for the sake of my brethren, my kinsmen by race. They are Israelites, and to them belong the sonship, the glory, the covenants, the giving of the law, the worship, and the promises; to them belong the patriarchs, and of their race, according to the flesh, is Christ, who is over all things, God blessed for ever. Amen.[34]

In fact, it goes even further back to St. Stephen, who was called before the Sanhedrin on a charge of blasphemy and

---

[33] Waltraud Herbstrith, *Edith Stein* (San Francisco: Ignatius Press, 1992), p. 169.

[34] The translation is RSV except for the ending, which is Douay-Rheims.

rather than defend himself took the opportunity to preach that Jesus was the Messiah, resulting in his death (Acts 7).

This zeal to convert their fellow Jews is a common pattern with Jewish "converts". During different eras this zeal took different forms. In the period following the invention of the printing press several Jewish converts dedicated themselves to making the New Testament available in the native language of their co-religionists—Johann Harzuge translated it into Hebrew and Yiddish in Cracow in the 1540s and Giovanni Baptista Jonas into Hebrew in Rome in the 1620s. Then the activity of Jewish converts turned to missionary activity. In 1808, Joseph Frey, a Jewish cantor, founded the London Society for Promoting Christianity among the Jews. In the 1820s Jewish "convert" Joseph Wolff of Prague learnt Arabic, Persian, Sanskrit, and other languages, to spend the rest of his life evangelizing Jews in the East. In 1824, Rabbi Michael Alexander became the Anglican Bishop of Jerusalem, where he established a training center for Jewish Christian missionaries as well as a hospital for indigent Jews. In 1893, in Britain, David Baron founded the missionary organization Hebrew Christian Testimony to Israel.

In the more recent past a number of Jewish converts started organizations to enable Jews who become Christian to maintain their Jewish identity. In 1913, Arthur Kuldell founded the Hebrew Christian Alliance of America, and twenty years later Leon Levison the International Hebrew Christian Alliance. In 1965, Jewish Carmelite Father Elias Friedman began working toward what would become the Association of Hebrew Catholics, dedicated to establishing a visible permanent Jewish presence within the Catholic Church, and in 1976, Jewish Redemptorist Father Arthur Klyber founded a community of Jewish Catholics called the Remnant of Israel.

Although of these Jewish "converts" only Elias Friedman was a Carmelite, they all shared the archetypically Jewish

charism of Elijah, the spiritual father of the Carmelites—
that zeal for God conveyed when he said, "I have been very
zealous for the LORD God of hosts"(1 Kings 19:10, NKJ) and
which David referred to when he said, "[z]eal for thy house
has consumed me" (Psalm 69:9). "Zeal for *thy house*"—"thy
house" the House of God, but also "thy house" the House
of Israel.

This zeal for the House of Israel was inflamed rather than
quenched when the "converts" came to the knowledge that
Jesus was the Messiah. Rather than diminishing their identification with and loyalty to the Jewish people, it intensified them:

Isaac da Costa, a Dutch Jew baptized in 1822 who became the country's leading poet: "In the midst of the contempt and dislike of the world for the name of Jew I have
ever glorified in it." [35]

Benjamin Disraeli, elected Prime Minister of Britain in
1868: "[T]he second Testament is avowedly only a sup-
plement. Jesus came to complete 'the law and the prophets.' Christianity is completed Judaism, or it is nothing." [36]

Isaac Lichtenstein (d.1909), forty years a rabbi in Hungary before his "conversion": "From every line in the New
Testament, from every word, the Jewish spirit streamed
forth light, life, power, endurance, faith, hope, love, charity, limitless and indestructible faith in God." [37]

Joseph Lansman, a Polish Talmud scholar: "Has God
opened our eyes and brought us out of bondage into liberty, out of darkness into His marvelous light in order

[35] Olasky, Marvin, "Timeline of Notable Jewish Christians of the Past Five
Centuries", *World Magazine*, March/April, 2002, pp. 33–57.
[36] Ibid.
[37] Ibid.

that we should leave our nation in its spiritual darkness, without knowledge of Messiah? ... If we do not care, who should?"[38]

Rabbi Israel Zolli, Chief Rabbi of Rome who "converted" in 1945, when asked why he had given up Judaism: "I have not given it up. Christianity is the completion of the synagogue, for the synagogue was a promise, and Christianity is the fulfillment of that promise. ... I am so firmly convinced of the truth of it that I can face the whole world and defend my faith with the certainty and solidity of the mountains."[39]

Current Jewish Entry into the Church

As mentioned, St. Paul suggested in his Letter to the Romans that the last days will see the widespread conversion of the Jews. This has led many to consider the current wave of Jewish conversion and ask whether it might be the beginning of the fulfillment of that prophecy.

It is probably impossible to determine whether the current wave of Jewish conversion is numerically greater than any previous one. For one thing, good statistics are lacking for both present and the past conversions. Further complicating matters is the fact that past conversions were often induced by external persecution, while the current ones are almost all genuine. But whether or not the largest in history, the current wave of conversions does have some distinctive characteristics that are suggestive.

One of these is the emergence of Jewish Christian communities in which Jews accept the principles of Christianity

[38] Ibid.
[39] Ibid.

while still maintaining their identity as Jews. The aforementioned associations, Remnant of Israel and the Association
of Hebrew Catholics, are examples of this in the Catholic
Church. Within Protestant Christianity, such communities
are represented by what is known as "Messianic Judaism".

The numbers associated with Messianic Judaism are impressive and almost certainly unprecedented since the first
decades of Christianity.[40] Before 1967, there were only a few
thousand Messianic Jews in the U.S., and at most four or five
Messianic Jewish synagogues.[41] By the mid 1970s, *Time* magazine placed the number of Messianic Jews in the U.S. at
over 50,000; by 1993 this number had grown to 160,000 in
the U.S.[42] and about 350,000 worldwide (1989 estimate[43]).
This compares to a total of 5.3 million Jews in the U.S. in
2001, of whom about 420,000 are orthodox (or strictly observant).[44] There are currently over 400 Messianic synagogues worldwide, with at least 150 in the U.S.

Of particular interest is the spread of Messianic Judaism in
Israel itself. Despite opposition by the Israel government,
there is now practically no town or city in Israel without a
"Messianic Jewish" congregation,[45] and the total number of

[40] All of the statistics that follow are open to question, but are the best
available.

[41] Dan Cohn-Sherbok, ed., *Voices of Messianic Judaism* (Baltimore, Md.: Lederer Books, 2001), pp. 12ff.

[42] Sheri Ross Gordon, "Inside Jews for Jesus", *Reform Judaism* 22 (Winter
1993), 24, cited in William Greene, PhD., *The Ascendance of Messianic Judaism
in the Context of Hebrew Christianity*, from the Internet.

[43] Susan Birnbaum, in *Jewish Echo*, Glascow, Scotland, April 14, 1989, cited
in Dr. Philip Moore, *Messiah Conspiracy* (Atlanta, Ga.: Ramshead Press, 1996),
p. 623.

[44] Statistics from the American Jewish Identity Survey, cited in *World* magazine, March 2, 2002.

[45] Source: author's interview with an Israeli Messianic Jew at Congregation
Ruach Israel, Needham, Mass., September 9, 1999.

Jewish converts to Christianity in Israel is over 5,000.[46] This cannot help but call to mind Jesus' prophecy, when he sent his apostles out on their mission to evangelize (Matthew 10:6–7, 23):

> [Go] to the lost sheep of the house of Israel. And preach as you go, saying, "The kingdom of heaven is at hand." ... When they persecute you in one town, flee to the next; for truly, I say to you, you will not have gone through all the towns of Israel, before the Son of man comes.

Many, perhaps most, in the Messianic Jewish community, both in Israel and around the world, see themselves as living within the biblical prophecies about the Second Coming. And they are not the only ones. For the Second Coming is inextricably linked with the mystery of the relationship between Israel (the "Old Covenant") and the Church (the "New Covenant"). This relationship has been the subject of much confusion, and not a few heresies, over the ages. We have seen how, at the very outset of Christianity, many held the mistaken belief that one must be a member of the Old Covenant (i.e., be a Jew) to be eligible for participation in the New. This error was quickly corrected, but was soon followed by another known as "supersessionism"—that the Old Covenant had been entirely replaced (or superseded, hence "supersessionism"), made null and void, by the New. This view dominated Christian theology for much of the past two thousand years. It has only recently been definitively rejected by the Church.[47] With its rejection, however, a new

---

[46] Jewish Community Relations Council of New York, www.jcrcny.org.

[47] Cf. Vatican II's *Nostra Aetate* and Pope John Paul II during remarks to Angelicum Colloquium on *Nostra Aetate* on April 19, 1985; at the Synagogue of Rome on April 13, 1986; and to the Jewish community in Mainz, Germany, on November 17, 1980 (reprinted in Pope John Paul II, *On Jews and Judaism, 1979–1986* [Washington, D.C.: U.S. Catholic Conference, 1987]).

and perhaps even more pernicious error has emerged—that the Old and New Covenants are two "separate but equal" parallel paths to salvation, the one intended for Jews, the other for Gentiles. This has been presented as though it were the only logical alternative to supersessionism, despite the fact that it is utterly irreconcilable with both the core beliefs of Christianity and with the words of Jesus Himself in the New Testament.

This book proposes a third alternative—that as the Old Covenant was brought to fruition by the New at the first coming, so will the New Covenant be brought to fruition by the Old, by the return of the Jews at the Second Coming. Thus, the current wave of Jewish entry into the Church may be among the most important things going on today, or indeed, in the history of the world.[48]

Conclusion

We have seen that God created the Jews with a very special and noble purpose, in fact, the noblest purpose conceivable for man, that of bringing salvation to all mankind. In so doing He imbued them with particular qualities and characteristics—some of these have always engendered admiration and respect, while others have at times been met with suspicion or distaste. Nonetheless, all were put there by God to serve His purposes.

One of the most notable attributes with which God has imbued the Jews is their passionate loyalty to their own identity as Jews. To the extent that it represents loyalty to the one true God, this is pure virtue. However, this virtue has stood

---

[48] This also means that the misguided attempt on the part of some in the Church to say that such entry is inappropriate plays directly into the hands of the enemy.

in the way of the recognition of Who Jesus was, both two thousand years ago and today. Two thousand years ago, because even during His life as a man Jesus posed a threat to the Jewish nation, both in His assertion of representing a higher authority than Mosaic law as represented by the Jewish authorities and in the perception that He was a danger to the status quo with the Romans. When Caiaphas "condemned" Jesus it was in precisely these terms, that it is better "that one man should die and that the whole nation should not perish" (John 11:50). And still today Jews perceive Jewish acceptance of Jesus as the destruction of the Jewish people. There is a tragic irony in this, because it is just their fierce loyalty to God that results in their rejection of that very same God when He comes to them as the Messiah. They are rejecting Him out of loyalty to Him.

This places Christians in a difficult situation. Evangelization efforts aimed at Jews are most frequently seen by Jews as a threat to their religion and their people and even compared to the Nazis' attempt to exterminate them. Yet the words of Jesus and the Scriptures themselves make it abundantly clear that God Himself, and certainly Jesus Himself, very much wish the Jews to come to Him. It was one of His greatest sorrows just before His crucifixion, when He exclaimed, "O Jerusalem, Jerusalem. . . . How often would I have gathered your children together as a hen gathers her brood under her wings, and you would not!" (Matthew 23:37).

Not only does God seem to very much want the conversion of the Jews, but His adversary seems to very much want to prevent it. We have seen evidence of this in the evolution of Jewish theology since biblical times away from the expectation of a personal Messiah, in the incitement to Jewish hostility to Christianity produced by repeated "Christian" persecution of Jews, and in past and present attempts to exterminate the Jews. It is precisely this seemingly diabolical fury against the Jews that provides the best evidence, outside of the Scriptures themselves, that the Jews have yet a crucial role to play in the salvation of all mankind.

In confronting Jewish hostility to Jewish conversion, it is most important, especially for Christians who are trying to work for the Lord and for the coming of His Kingdom, to be aware of the experiences and perceptions of Jews who *have* received the grace of conversion. For with one voice they all attest to the same thing—that in their perception they were far more Jewish after their conversion than before it, and that their deepest, archetypically Jewish thirst for God could never have been met outside Christianity.

Thus it is not only the eschatological implications, for the individual and for all humanity, of Jewish conversion that are at stake, but also the earthly happiness of the individuals themselves. Even if not every Jew needs to know the truth of Christianity and the intimacy with God that comes from the sacraments, to be happy, many do, and for those there is no true happiness or true purpose in life until they do.

Of course all disrespect for the freedom of the individual is entirely wrong, as is any disrespect for the religion of Judaism, all the more so since Christians know that Judaism was God's own religion, given to the Jews by Him and followed by Him during His life as a man. Yet at the same time fear of God—that is, the desire to do His will—must always take precedence over fear of human respect, and the greatest service that anyone can do for God, or for an individual, is to bring that individual into deeper knowledge of and fuller communion with God. Jesus Himself said that He will not come again "until you [the Jews] say, 'Blessed is he who comes in the name of the Lord!'"

(Matthew 23:39). It is incumbent on us, as His disciples and servants, to do everything we can to hurry that day, when both Jew and Gentile together say the words with which the "Christian" Scriptures close:

"Come Lord Jesus."
The grace of our Lord Jesus Christ be with you all. Amen.
—Revelation 22:20–21

Postscript

My own conversion

I grew up Jewish in a middle-class suburb of New York City, the son of Jewish refugees who had fled Germany in the early days of Hitler's reign. My parents were active in the local "conservative" congregation and, by American standards, I had a fairly religious Jewish upbringing. I went for after-school religious instruction twice a week all the way through from first grade until college, was Bar Mitzvah'd, and frequently (although not always) attended services on Sabbath, in addition to, of course, the Jewish holidays. I grew close to the extraordinary Rabbis whom God graced me with for my religious formation and even wrestled with the issue of a "religious vocation" for myself. The summer between high school and college, I spent traveling throughout Israel with a charismatic, "mystic" Hasidic Rabbi, Rabbi Shlomo Carlebach, who each night gave a "concert", which was, in reality, an ecstatic Hasidic worship and praise service. I briefly considered staying in Israel to study at one of the many ultra-orthodox yeshivas there (the closest thing which Judaism has to "religious life"), but returned to begin my studies at M.I.T. in mathematics and computer science. In college I initially tried to maintain my religious fervor and was active in a local counterculture neo-Hasidic congregation-cum-seminary, but soon fell into both the mores and the mindset more typical of M.I.T. There is a close relationship between the maintenance of purity, both in mind and in behavior, and intimacy with God; although He might initially relax

357

His rules as a sort of "loss-leader" to draw one into a relationship with Him, sooner or later one can no longer expect the consolation of experienced intimacy with God if one does not play by His rules. As I abandoned the rules I lost the intimacy. By the end of college, the joy of prayer had become an abstract memory, and I was almost entirely ensconced in the ways of the world. After a few years of working on the design of new computer systems, I went on to Harvard Business School for an M.B.A. and, as a result of an exceptional performance there, was invited to join the faculty to teach and pursue studies toward a doctorate, in preparation for a tenure-track career.

While all this was going on, there was, however, another and deeper dimension to my life. In losing touch with God, I also lost the sense of intrinsic purpose and direction to my life; at each juncture, I chose the path of least resistance, the path which, in the eyes of the world, constituted success (which being on the faculty of Harvard Business School at thirty most certainly did); yet as I achieved each milestone, I was met with an ever deeper sense of emptiness, of meaninglessness to the victory. By this time—about four years into my Harvard "tenure-track" career—I was inwardly overwhelmed with a sense of pointlessness bordering on despair. (This was by no means unique to me. A colleague on the faculty, a chaired professor and department head, once revealed to me that the day after he was finally granted tenure, the culmination of over a decade of effort, he almost quit, overwhelmed with the sense of emptiness and pointlessness in everything for which he had strived so hard.) Although I had long since left behind a conscious religious life or prayer, my primary solace during this period was found in long solitary walks in nature. It was on one of these that I received the most singular grace of my life.

It was early one morning in early June, during a midweek break I had given myself, two or three days on Cape Cod before the crowds arrived. I was walking in the dunes between Provincetown and Truro, alone with the singing birds before the world woke up, when I, for lack of better words, "fell into heaven". That is, I found myself most consciously and tangibly in the presence of God. I saw my life to date laid out before me, seeing it as though I were reviewing it in the presence of God after death. I saw everything that I would be pleased about and everything I would regret. I also knew, from one instant to the next, that the meaning and purpose of my life was to love and serve my Lord and God; I saw how His love enveloped and sustained me every moment of my existence; I saw how everything I did had a moral content, for good or for ill, and which mattered far more than I would ever know; I saw how everything that had ever happened in my life was the most perfect thing that could be arranged for my own good by an all-good, all-loving God, *especially* those things which caused me the most suffering at the time; I saw that my two greatest regrets at the moment of death would be all of the time and energy I had wasted worrying about not being loved, when every moment of my existence I was held in the sea of God's unimaginably great love, and every hour I had wasted not doing anything of value in the eyes of God. The answer to any question I mentally posed was instantly presented to me; in fact, I could not hold a question in my mind without already being shown the answer, with one, all-important exception—the name of this God Who was revealing Himself to me as the meaning and purpose of my life. I did not think of Him as the God of the Old Testament Whom I held in my imagination from my childhood. I prayed to know His name, to know what religion to follow to serve and worship Him properly. I remember praying, "Let me know your name—I don't mind if you are Buddha, and I have to become a Buddhist; I don't mind if you are Apollo, and I have to become a Roman pagan; I don't mind if you are Krishna, and I have to become a Hindu; as long as you are not Christ and I have to become a Christian!" This deep-seated resistance to Christianity was based on the sense I had of Christianity as the "enemy", the perversion of Judaism that had been the cause of two millennia of Jewish suffering. As a result, although this God Who revealed Himself to me on the beach had heard my prayer to know His name, He also heard, and respected, my refusal to know it, too, and so gave no answer at the time to the question.

I returned to my home in Cambridge and to my ordinary life, yet everything was changed. I spent all of my free time in seeking after this God, through quiet time in nature, reading, and asking people whom I thought might know more than I did about such "mystical" experiences. Since this was Cambridge in the 1980s, it inevitably led in some New Age directions, and I ended up reading primarily Hindu- and Buddhist-based spiritual writings. Yet one day, walking through Harvard Square, the cover illustration of a book in a store window caught my eye, and without knowing anything at all about the book or its author, I went in and bought St. Teresa of Avila's *The Interior Castle*. I devoured it, finding great spiritual nourishment within, but still gave no credence to the particular claims of Christianity.

I continued in this undiscriminating, eclectic path for exactly one year, until one year to the day after the experience on the beach, I received the second great extraordinary grace of my life. I frankly admit that, in all external aspects, what took place was a dream. Yet when I went to sleep I knew little about, and had no special sympathy for, Christianity or any of its aspects; when I awoke I was hopelessly in love with the Blessed Virgin Mary and wanted nothing more than to become as totally Christian as I could. In the "dream", I was taken to a room and granted an audience with the most beautiful young woman I could have ever imagined; without it being spoken, I knew that it was the Blessed Virgin Mary. She agreed to answer any questions I might ask her; I clearly remember standing there, weighing a number of possible questions in my mind, and asking her four or five of them. She answered them, then spoke to me for several more minutes, and then the audience was ended. My experience of the event, and my memory of it, are as of something which took place in full wakefulness. I remember all of the details, including of course the questions and the answers, but all pales beside by far the greatest aspect of the experience: the ecstasy of simply being in her presence, in the purity and intensity of her love.

When I awoke, as I said, I was hopelessly in love with the Blessed Virgin Mary and knew that the God Who had revealed Himself to me on the beach had been Christ. Yet I still knew almost nothing about Christianity, including having no idea of the difference between Protestants and Catholics. My initial foray into Christianity was into a Protestant church, but when I brought up the topic of Mary with the pastor, his thinly veiled contempt made me say to myself, "I'm outta here!" Meanwhile, my love for Mary inspired me to spend time at Marian shrines, especially those of Our Lady of La Salette (both the one in Ipswich, Massachusetts, and the one at the site of the original apparition, high in the

French Alps).[1] So I found myself, willy-nilly, frequently present at Masses, and although I still had no belief in the Catholic Church, I was filled with an intense desire to receive Communion. In fact, the first time I approached a priest and asked to be baptized, I still held no Catholic beliefs. When he asked me, "Why do you want to be baptized?" I angrily blurted out the truth, "Because I want to receive Communion and you guys won't let me unless I am baptized!" I thought he would throw me out on my ear; instead he nodded sagely and said, "A-hah. That's the Holy Spirit at work."

I still had to wait several years and mature in my faith before baptism, but throughout the process my love of Mary and my thirst for the Eucharist guided me, like a compass, toward the goal. I am infinitely grateful to God for my conversion; I am infinitely grateful to God for the people He gave me to lead me on my path, and I am particularly grateful to God for the opportunity to have written this book, and to you, dear reader, for having read it.[2]

---

[1] The Blessed Virgin Mary appeared to two young shepherd children high in the French Alps in 1846, giving them a message of prayer and repentence; this apparition, named after the nearest village, is known as "Our Lady of La Salette". For a description, see for instance Jean Jouen, M.S., *A Grace Called La Salette* (Attleboro, Mass.: La Salette Publications, 1991), or Bro. Francis Mary Kalvelage, F.I., *Marian Shrines of France* (New Bedford, Mass.: Academy of the Immaculate, 1998).

[2] The author can be contacted by email at schoeman@catholic.org, or via his website www.salvationisfromthejews.com.

BIBLIOGRAPHY

Books, Documents, etc.

al-Sadr, Ayatollah Muhammad Baqer. *The Source of Power in the Islamic Government/State*. Tehran, 1980.

American Birth Control League. *Proceedings: First American Birth Control Conference, 1921*.

_____. *Proceedings: Sixth International Neo-Malthus and Birth Control Conference, 1926*.

The Arab Higher Committee, Its Origins, Personnel and Purposes, The Documentary Record Submitted to The United Nations. Nations Associates of N.Y., May 1947.

Augustine. *City of God*. Garden City, N.Y.: Doubleday Image Books, 1958.

The Babylonian Talmud. Edited by Rabbi Dr. I. Epstein. London: Soncino Press, 1935–1938.

Biblia Hebraica Stuttgartensia BHS (Masoretic Text of Hebrew Old Testament). K. Elliger and W. Rudoph, eds. Stuttgart: Deutsche Bibelgesellschaft, Fourth Corrected Edition, 1990.

Blavatsky, Helena. *The Secret Doctrine*. Theosophical University Press electronic version ISBN 1-55700-124-3. Originally published 1888.

Bleuel, Hans Peter. *Strength through Joy: Sex and Society in Nazi Germany*. London: Secker and Warburg, 1973.

Bluher, Hans. *Die Rede des Aristophanes*. Hamburg: Kala-Verlag, 1966.

Bodansky, Yossef. *Islamic Anti-Semitism As a Political Instrument*. Houston, Tx.: Freeman Center For Strategic Studies, 1999.

Brewer, E. C. *Dictionary of Phrase and Fable*. London: Cassell, 1900.

Brown, R. M. *Elie Wiesel: Messenger to All Humanity*. Notre Dame, Ind.: Notre Dame Press, 1983.

Cabaud, Judith. *Eugenio Zolli*. Paris: F.-X. de Guibert, 2000.

Cargas, Harry James. *Harry James Cargas in Conversation with Elie Wiesel*. New York: Paulist, 1976.

Carr, Joseph. *The Twisted Cross*. Shreveport, La.: Huntington House, 1985.

Catechism of the Catholic Church. Second ed. Vatican City: Libreria Editrice Vaticana, 1994, 1997.

Chamberlain, Houston Stewart. *Foundations of the Nine-teenth Century*. Translated by John Lees. London: John Lane Co., 1910.

Chase, Allan. *The Legacy of Malthus: The Social Costs of the New Scientific Racism*. New York: Alfred A. Knopf, 1975.

Chief of Counsel for Prosecution of Axis Criminality. *Nazi Conspiracy and Aggression—A Collection of Documentary Evidence Prepared by the American and British Prosecuting Staffs for Presentation before the International Military Tribunal at Nurnberg*. Washington, D.C.: U.S. Government Printing Office, 1946.

Christian Prayer: The Liturgy of the Hours. Boston: St. Paul Editions, 1976.

Cohn-Sherbok, Dan, ed. *Voices of Messianic Judaism*. Baltimore, Md.: Lederer Books, 2001.

Davis, Leonard J. and Moshe Decter, eds. *Myths and Facts 1982: A Concise Record of the Arab Israeli Conflict*. Washington, D.C.: Near East Report, 1982.

De Marchi, John. *Fatima: The Full Story*. Washington, N.J.: AMI Press, 1986.

dos Santos, Sister Lucia. *Fatima in Lucia's Own Words*. Fatima, Portugal: Postulation Center, 1976.

Edersheim, Alfred. *The Life and Times of Jesus the Messiah*. Grand Rapids, Mich.: Eerdmans, 1953.

Editors of Time-Life Books. *The SS*, The Third Reich Series. Alexandria, Va.: Time-Life Books, 1988.

Ellwood, Robert S. and Partin, Harry B. *Religious and Spiritual Groups in Modern America*. Englewood Cliffs, N.J.: Prentice Hall, 1988.

Emmerich, Venerable Anne Catherine. *The Life of the Blessed Virgin Mary*. Rockford, Ill.: TAN Books, 1970.

Fahey, Dennis. *The Kingship of Christ and the Conversion of the Jewish Nation*. Palmdale, Calif.: Christian Book Club of America, 1993.

Faligot, Roger and Remi Kauffer. *Le Croissant et la Croix Gammee*. Paris: Albin Michel, 1990.

Friedman, Elias. *Jewish Identity*. New York: Miriam Press, 1987.

González, Servando. *The Riddle of the Swastika: A Study in Symbolism*. Oakland, Calif.: Servando González, 1998.

Goodrich-Clarke, Nicholas. *The Occult Roots of Nazism*. New York: New York University Press, 1985, 1992.

Greek New Testament (GNT) Münster/Westphalia. Fourth ed. United Bible Societies (UBS) 1975. Stuttgart: Deutsche Bibelgesellschaft, 1994.

Green, D. F., ed. *Arab Theologians on Jews and Israel: Extracts from the Proceedings of the Fourth Conference of the Academy of Islamic Research*. Third ed. Geneva: Éditions de l'avenir, 1976.

Guillaume, Alfred. *The Life of Muhammad: A Translation of Ibn Ishaq's Sirat Rasul Allah*. London: Oxford University Press, 1968.

Gutman, Israel, ed. *The Encyclopedia of the Holocaust*. New York: Macmillan, 1990.

Hafner, Georg and Schapira, Esther. *Die Akte Alois Brunner*. Frankfurt and New York: Campus Verlag, 2000.

Hardon, John, S.J. *A Treasury of Catholic Wisdom*. San Francisco: Ignatius, 1995.

Hart, Alan. *Arafat*. London: Sidgewick and Jackson, 1994.

Hartshorne, E. Y. *German Youth and the Nazi Dream of Victory*. New York: Farrar and Reinhart, 1941.

Herbstrith, Waltraud. *Edith Stein*. San Francisco: Ignatius Press, 1992.

————, ed. *Never Forget: Christian and Jewish Perspectives on Edith Stein*. Washington, D.C.: ICS Publications, 1998.

Herford, R. Travers. *Christianity in Talmud and Midrash*. London: Williams and Norgate, 1903.

Hertzberg, Rabbi Arthur. *A Jew in America*. San Francisco: Harper, 2002.

————. *Judaism*. New York: Braziller, 1961.

————, ed. *The Zionist Idea*. Garden City, N.Y.: Doubleday, 1959.

Hess, Moses. *Rome and Jerusalem*. New York: Philosophical Library, 1958.

Hippolytus. *Treatise on Christ and Antichrist*, in *Ante-Nicene Fathers*. Vol. 5. Edited by Roberts and Donaldson. Peabody, Mass.: Hendricksen, 1995.

Hitler, Adolf. *Mein Kampf*. New York: Reynal and Hitchcock, 1940.

Holy Bible, American Standard Version. Oklahoma City, Okla.: Ellis Enterprises, 1988.

Holy Bible, Douay/Confraternity Version. New York: P. J. Kenedy and Sons, 1961.

Holy Bible, Douay-Rheims Version. Baltimore, Md.: John Murphy Co., 1899. Reprint TAN Books and Publishers, Inc.: Rockford, Ill., n.d.

Holy Bible, King James Authorized Version. Online Bible Foundation and Woodside Fellowship of Ontario, Canada, 1997.

Holy Bible, New King James Version. Nashville, Tenn.: Thomas Nelson, 1982.

Holy Bible, Revised Standard Version, Catholic Edition. San Francisco: Ignatius Press, 1966.

Holy Bible, Revised Standard Version. Division of Christian Education of the National Council of Churches of Christ in the U.S., 1973.

Hughes, Philip. *A Popular History of the Catholic Church*. New York: Doubleday, 1954.

Igra, Samuel. *Germany's National Vice*. London: Quality Press, 1945.

The Imam Versus Zionism. Tehran: Ministry of Islamic Guidance, 1984.

Irenaeus. *Irenaeus against Heresies*, in *Ante-Nicene Fathers*. Vol. 1. Edited by Roberts and Donaldson. Peabody, Mass.: Hendricksen, 1995.

Jacobs, Steven, ed. *Contemporary Christian Responses to the Shoah*. Lanham, Md.: University Press of America, 1993.

Jame Tirmizi. Karachi, Pakistan: Muhammad Ali, n.d.

Jameelah, Maryam. *Islam versus Ahl al-Kitab*. Delhi: Taj, 1989.

Johnson, Philip E. *Darwin on Trial*. Downers Grove, Ill.: InterVarsity Press, 1993.

Jouen, Jean, M.S. *A Grace Called La Salette*. Attleboro, Mass.: La Salette Publications, 1991.

Kaiser, Walter C., Jr. *The Messiah in the Old Testament*. Grand Rapids, Mich.: Zondervan, 1995.

Kalvelage, Brother Francis Mary, F.I. *Marian Shrines of France*. New Bedford, Mass.: Academy of the Immaculate, 1998.

Kersten, Felix. *The Kersten Memoirs 1940–1945*. London: Hutchinson, 1956.

Khalidi, Dr. Salah. *The Jewish Mentality Based on the Qu'ran*. Damascus, 1987.

Klausner, Joseph. *The Messianic Idea in Israel*. New York: MacMillan, 1955.

Klotz, Helmut. *The Berlin Diaries: May 30, 1932–January 30, 1933*. New York: William Morrow, 1934.

Knickerbocker, H. R. *Is Tomorrow Hitler's?* New York: Reynal and Hitchcock, 1941.

Koran. Translated by N. J. Dawood. London: Penguin, 1999. (Also made use of translations by Yusufali, M.M. Pickthall, and M.H. Shakir.)

Kowalska, Sister M. Faustina. *Divine Mercy in My Soul: The Diary of Sister M. Faustina Kowalska*. Stockbridge, Mass.: Marian Press, 1987.

Kuhl, Stefan. *The Nazi Connection: Eugenics, American Racism, and German National Socialism*. New York: Oxford University Press, 1994.

Langer, William L. *The Mind of Adolf Hitler: The Secret Wartime Report*. New York: Basic Books, 1972.

Lanz-Lieberfels, J. *Theozoologie oder die Kunde von den Sodoms-Afflingen und dem Gotter-Elektron*. Vienna, 1905.

Lemann, Augustin and Joseph Lemann. *La Cause des Restes d'Israel Introduite au Concile Oecumenique du Vatican*. Paris: Librarie Lecoffrre, 1912.

———. *Valeur de l'Assemblee qui Prononca la Peine de la Mort contre Jesus-Christ*. Villegenon, France: Editions Ste. Jeanne d'Arc, 1997 (reprint).

Levin, Nora. *The Holocaust*. New York: Schocken Books, 1973.

Lifton, Robert J. *The Nazi Doctors: Medical Killing and the Psychology of Genocide*. London: Papermac, 1986.

Lively, Scott and Kevin Abrams. *The Pink Swastika: Homosexuality and The Nazi Party*. Keizer, Ore.: Founders Publishing Corp., 1995.

Lively, Scott. *The Poisoned Stream*. Salem, Ore.: Lively Communications, 1997.

Lustiger, Cardinal Jean-Marie. *La Promesse*. Paris: Parole et Silence, 2002.

LXX Septuaginta (LXT) (Old Greek Jewish Scriptures). Edited by Alfred Rahlfs. Stuttgart: Württembergische Bibelanstalt/ Deutsche Bibelgesellschaft, 1935.

Machtan, Lothar. *The Hidden Hitler*. New York: Basic Books, 2001.

MacLean, French. *The Cruel Hunters*. Atglen, Pa.: Schiffer, 1998.

Madonna of the Miracle. Rome: Minimi Booklets, 1971.

Mahmud, Shaykh Abd-al-Halim. *Jihad and Victory*. Cairo, 1979.

Maimonides, *The Code of Maimonides (Mishneh Torah)*. Translated by Abraham Hershman. New Haven: Yale Univ. Press, 1949.

Maimonides, *Mishneh Torah: The Book of Knowledge*. Translated by Moses Hyamson. New York: Bloch, 1938.

Marchione, Sister Margherita. *Yours Is a Precious Witness*. New York: Paulist Press, 1977.

Marshall, Robert and Charles Donovan. *Blessed Are the Barren: The Social Policy of Planned Parenthood*. San Francisco: Ignatius, 1991.

Melton, J. Gordon, Jerome Clark, and Aidan A. Kelly, eds. *New Age Almanac*. Detroit, Mich.: Gale Research Inc., 1991.

Mermelstein, Mel. *By Bread Alone: The Story of A-4685*. Los Angeles, Calif.: Crescent Publications, 1979.

Mishka Sharif. Lahore, Pakistan: Farid, n.d.

Missale Romanum. Editio Typica Tertia. Vatican: Typus Vaticanis, 2002.

Missika, Jean-Louis and Dominique Wolton. *Choosing God— Chosen by God*. San Francisco: Ignatius, 1991.

Moore, Dr. Philip N. *Messiah Conspiracy*. Atlanta, Ga.: Ramshead Press, 1996.

Morse, Arthur. *While 6 Million Died*. New York: Ace Books, 1968.

Neher, Andre. *The Exile of the Word*. Philadelphia, Pa.: Jewish Publication Society, 1981.

Neusner, Jacob. *Introduction to Rabbinic Literature*. New York: Doubleday, 1994.

New American Bible. New York: Catholic Book Publishing Co., 1986.

Newton, P. and M. Rafiqul-Haqq. *Allah, Is He God?* Rowley Regis, U.K.: T.M.F.M.T., 1993.

Nugent, Dr. Christopher. *Masks of Satan*. London: Sheed and Ward, 1983; Westminster, Md.: Christian Classics, 1989.

Osterhuis, Harry and Hubert Kennedy, eds. *Homosexuality and Male Bonding in Pre-Nazi Germany: Original transcripts from Der Eigene*. New York: Harrington Park Press, 1991.

Ott, Dr. Ludwig. *Fundamentals of Catholic Dogma*. Rockford, Ill.: TAN Books, 1960.

Parkes, James William. *A History of Palestine from 135 A.D. to Modern Times*. New York: Oxford University Press, 1949.

Persecution of the Catholic Church in the Third Reich (anonymous 1941). Republished: Fort Collins, Colo.: Roger McCaffrey Publishing, n.d.

Peters, Joan. *From Time Immemorial*. Chicago: JKAP Publications, 2002.

Pope Eugenius IV. *Cantata Domino*. 1442.

Pope John Paul II. *On Jews and Judaism, 1979–1986*. Washington, D.C.: U.S. Catholic Conference, 1987.

_____. *On the Christian Meaning of Human Suffering (Salvifici Doloris)*. 1984.

Pope Paul VI. *Dignitatis Humanae*. 1965.

_____. *Gaudium et Spes*. 1965.

_____. *Nostra Aetate*. 1965.

Pope Pius X. *E Supremi*. 1903.

Pope Pius XI. *Casti Connubii*. 1930.

Pope Pius XII. *Humani Generis*. 1950.

Proceedings of the First National Conference on Race Betterment 1941. Battle Creek, Mich.: Race Betterment Association, 1941.

Program for St. Edith Stein's Canonization. Vatican, Oct. 11, 1998.

Ratzinger, Cardinal Joseph. *God and the World*. San Francisco: Ignatius Press, 2002.

Rector, Frank. *The Nazi Extermination of Homosexuals*. New York: Stein and Day, 1981.

Rhodes, James M. *The Hitler Movement: A Modern Millenarian Revolution*. Stanford, Calif.: Hoover Institution Press, 1980.

Rhodes, Richard. *Masters of Death*. New York: Knopf, 2002.

Rich, Charles. *Autobiography*. Petersham, Mass.: St. Bede's Publications, 1990.

———. *Reflections*. Petersham, Mass.: St. Bede's Publications, 1986.

Rosenbaum, Irving. *The Holocaust and Halacha*. New York: KTAV Publ., 1976.

Rosenberg, Alfred. *Myth of the Twentieth Century*. Torrance, Calif.: Noontide Press, 1982.

Rossman, Parker. *Sexual Experience between Men and Boys*. New York: Association Press, 1976.

Roszak, Theodore. *The Unfinished Animal: The Aquarian Frontier and the Evolution of Consciousness*. New York: Harper and Row, 1975.

Rottenberg, Isaac C. *Jewish Christians in an Age of Christian-Jewish Dialogue*. Published by family and friends of the author, 1995.

Rubenstein, Richard. *After Auschwitz*. Indianapolis: Bobbs-Merrill, 1966.

Ruter, Dr. C. F. and Dr. D. W. de Mildt. *Nazi Crimes on Trial: German Trials concerning National Socialist Homicidal Crimes*. Amsterdam: University of Amsterdam Institute of Criminal Law, 2002.

Sachar, Howard Morley. *A History of Israel*. New York: Knopf, 1976.

Sahih al-Bukhari: The Translation of the Meanings of Sahih al-Bukhari in Arabic-English. Translated by Dr. Muhammad Muhsin Khan. Ankara, Turkey: Hilal Yayinlari, n.d.

Sanger, Margaret. *The Pivot of Civilization*. New York: Brentano's Press, 1922.

Scholder, Klaus. *A Requiem for Hitler*. Philadelphia: Trinity Press International, 1989.

Sebottendorf, Rudolf. *Bevor Hitler Kam*. Munich: Deufula-Verlag Grassinger, 1933.

Sereny, Gitta. *Into That Darkness: From Mercy Killing to Mass Murder*. London: Andre Deutsch, 1974.

Seward, Desmond. *Napoleon and Hitler*. London: Harrap, 1988.

Shaikh, Anwar. *Islam: Sex and Violence*. Cardiff, U. K.: Principality Publishers, 1999.

Shirer, William L. *Berlin Diary: The Journal of a Foreign Correspondent*. New York: Alfred Knopf, 1941.

———. *The Rise and Fall of The Third Reich*. New York: Ballantine Books, 1992.

Singer, I., ed. *The Jewish Encyclopedia*. New York: KTAV Publ., 1901.

Sklar, Dusty. *The Nazis and the Occult*. New York: Dorset Press, 1977.

Snyder, Dr. Louis. *Encyclopedia of the Third Reich*. New York: Paragon House, 1989.

St. Just, Father Theotime de, O.M.C. *Les Frères Lemann: Juifs Convertis*. Paris: Librarie St. François, 1937.

Steiner, Jean-François. *Treblinka*. New York: Signet, 1968.

Stoddard. Lothrop. *Into The Darkness: Nazi Germany Today*. New York: Duell, Sloan, and Pierce, 1940.

Telushkin, Rabbi Joseph. *Jewish Literacy*. New York: William Morrow and Co., 1991.

Tucker, William H. *The Science and Politics of Racial Research*. Urbana, Ill.: University of Illinois Press, 1994.

Twersky, Isadore, ed. *A Maimonides Reader*. New York: Behrman House, 1972.

Walker, Graham B., Jr. *Elie Wiesel: A Challenge to Theology*. Jefferson, N.C.: McFarland, 1988.

Walsh, William. *Our Lady of Fatima*. New York: Doubleday, 1990.

Wasserstein, Bernard. *Britain and the Jews of Europe 1939–1945*. New York: Oxford University Press, 1979.

Wiesel, Elie. *A Beggar in Jerusalem*. New York: Random House, 1970.

_____. *A Jew Today*. New York: Random House, 1978.

_____. *Messengers of God: Biblical Portraits and Legends*. New York: Random House, 1976.

_____. *Night*. New York: Hill and Wang, 1960.

_____. *Souls on Fire: Portraits and Legends of Hasidic Masters*. New York: Random House, 1972.

_____. *The Accident*. New York: Avon, 1970.

_____. *The Gates of the Forest*. New York: Holt, Rinehart and Winston, 1966.

_____. *The Town beyond the Wall*. New York: Holt, Rinehart and Winston, 1964.

_____. *Trial of God*. New York: Schocken Books, 1995.

Willenberg, Samuel. *Revolt in Treblinka*. Warsaw: Jewish Historical Institute, 2000.

Wurmbrand, Richard. *Marx and Satan*. Bartlesville, Okla.: Living Sacrifice, 1986.

The Zohar. Translated by Maurice Simon and Dr. Paul P. Levertoff. London: Soncino Press, 1949.

Zolli, Eugenio. *Why I Became a Catholic.* New York: Roman Catholic Books, n.d. Originally published 1953.

Articles, etc.

ABC News biography of Saddam Hussein. www.abcnews.go.com/reference/bios/shussein.html/.

Ajami, Fouad. "Two Faces, One Terror." *Wall Street Journal,* November 11, 2002.

Bonfils Studio: Beirut, 1875. Photographs of the Temple Mount, Joseph Regenstein Library, University of Chicago. Viewable at www.lib.uchicago.edu/e/su/mideast/photo/Jerusalem.html/.

Brooks, David. "Saddam's Brain." *The Weekly Standard,* November 11, 2002.

Cyprian. *Epistle LXIX,* in *Ante-Nicene Fathers.* Vol. 5. Roberts and Donaldson, eds. Peabody, Mass.: Hendricksen, 1995.

Ehrlich, Ernst Ludwig. "The Jews Did Not Want to Bring Burnt Offerings." *Christ in der Gegenwart,* 1988.

Ellis, Havelock. "The World's Racial Problems." *Birth Control Review,* October 1920.

Gamble, Clarence M.D. "Suggestions for a Negro Project." November 1939. Sophie Smith Collection, Smith College.

Gordon, Sheri Ross. "Inside Jews for Jesus." *Reform Judaism* 22, Winter 1993.

Greenberg, Gershon. "Orthodox Theological Responses to Kristallnacht." 18th Annual Scholar's Conference on the Church Struggle and the Holocaust. Washington, D.C., 1988.

Henneberger, Melinda. "A Priest Not Intimidated by Satan." *The New York Times*, January 1, 2001.

Hoess, Rudolf. Affidavit of April 5, 1946, at War Crimes Tribunal, Nürnberg, Germany. www.nizkor.org/ftp.cgi/imt/nca/nca-06/nca-06-3868-ps/.

Honig, Sarah. "Fiendish Hypocrisy." *Jerusalem Post*, March 29, and April 6, 2001.

Knopf, S. Adolphus, M.D. "The Survival of the Unfit." *Proceedings—Sixth International Neo-Malthus and Birth Control Conference*, American Birth Control League, 1926.

Kuiper, Gerard P. "German Astronomy during the War." *Popular Astronomy*, vol. 54, no. 6, June 1946. Northfield, Minn.: The Goodsell Observatory of Carleton College.

Laughlin, Harry H. "Eugenical Aspects of Legal Sterilization." *Birth Control Review*, vol. 17, no. 4, April 1933.

———. "Legal Status of Eugenical Sterilization." *Birth Control Review*, vol. 12, no. 3, March 1928.

———. Testimony from U.S. House of Representatives Immigration Hearings. *Birth Control Review*, November 1926.

———. "Calculations on the Working out of a Proposed Program of Sterilization." *Proceedings of the First National Conference on Race Betterment*. January 8–12, 1914.

Lefkovits, Etgar. "1930 Moslem Council: Jewish Temple Mount Ties 'Beyond Dispute.'" *Jerusalem Post*, January 26, 2001.

Lehmann, Dr. Manfred R. "The Moslem Claim to Jerusalem is False." *Algemeiner Journal*, August 19, 1994.

Lenski, Mordecai. "Who Inspired Hitler to Destroy the Jews?" *Yad Vashem Bulletin*, no. 14, March 3, 1964.

Lustiger, Cardinal Jean-Marie. Address to the European Jewish Congress, Paris, January 28–29, 2002. *L'Osservatore Romano*, English edition, March 13, 2002.

Maimonides, *Mishneh. Torah*, in *A Maimonides Reader.* Isadore Twersky, ed. New York: Behrman House, 1972.

Marcus, Itamar. *Report No. P-01-03: The Palestinian Authority School Books.* Center for Monitoring the Impact of Peace, www.edume.org/reports/1/6.htm/.

Moss, David. "Canonization of Theresa Benedicta of the Cross." *The Hebrew Catholic*, no. 70, May–June and September–October 1998.

Moss, Rosalind. "O Jerusalem, Jerusalem . . ." *The Hebrew Catholic*, Summer–Fall 2002.

Nazis: The Occult Conspiracy, video no. 621631. Produced by the Discovery Channel.

New Jersey Jewish Standard, June 8, 2001. Article quoting Rabbi Arthur Hertzberg.

Olasky, Marvin. "Timeline of Notable Jewish Christians of the Past Five Centuries." *World* magazine, March–April, 2002, pp. 33–57.

Palestinian National Charter. Permanent Observer Mission of Palestine to the U.N. www.palestine-un.org/.

Pope John Paul II. Address to the Pontifical Academy of Sciences, October 22, 1996. *L'Osservatore Romano*, October 23, 1996.

———. Homily, February 1, 2003. *L'Osservatore Romano* (English ed.), February 5, 2003.

Roberts, Walter Adolphe. "Birth Control and the Revolution." *Birth Control Review*, vol. I, no. 6, June 1917.

Rudolph, David. "Jesus and the Food Laws: A Reassessment of Mark 7:19b." *The Evangelical Quarterly*, October 2002, pp. 291–311.

Saetz, Stephen B. "Eugenics and the Third Reich." *The Eugenics Bulletin*, Winter 1985.

Sanger, Margaret. Letter to Gamble, December 10, 1939. Sophie Smith Collection, Smith College.

Skobac, Rabbi Michael (Toronto Jews for Judaism Education Director). *Counter-Missionary Audiotape on Zechariah 12.* Baltimore, Md.: Jews for Judaism.

United States Conference of Catholic Bishops Committee on Ecumenical and Interreligious Affairs. *Reflections on Covenant and Mission,* 2002.

Wiesel, Elie. "Jewish Values in the Post-Holocaust Future", *Judaism* 16, 1967.

_____. Interview in Sun Valley, Idaho. American Academy of Achievement, June 29, 1996. www.achievement.org.

_____. "To Remain Human in Face of Inhumanity." *The Jewish Digest,* September 1972.

Wolf, Arnold J., "Maimonides on Immortality and the Principles of Judaism" (Helek: Sanhedrin, Ch. 10), *Judaism,* vol. 15, 1966.